Fifty years ago

I am pleased that it is all over, though it has taken all of my adult life to persuade the public that I had been nothing other than a young and innocent teenage girl trying to make an honest living for myself in London.

There have been too many disreputable and self-righteous people only too eager to get paid for lying about me and putting me down in order to make themselves appear better.

Macmillan's daughter Sarah once told me that her father had regretted calling me a tart. So Lord Denning and other people of influence set about blackening my character. That was to cover for the spies I knew about and what they did, and so the stitch up of Keeler started, making a fortune for many. Some honestly believed that they were acting out of loyalty to the Crown and doing the right thing, and others of course liked the money and got used to it. So it went on and on and on, but in the end the truth, which I told in my book Secrets and Lies (written with Douglas Thompson), and the extraordinary events in which I became entangled, proved more interesting than the stories that were told about me.

That was yesterday, and today is a fine new day. I can hold my head up. I warned Denning of the spies that were working against the country's interests, and years later I was proved right. I feel vindicated.

Christine Keeler

Author:
Dan Sharp

Designers:
Libby Fincham, Justin Blackamore

Reprographics:
Jonathan Schofield, Simon Duncan

Group production editor:
Tim Hartley

Production manager:
Craig Lamb

Marketing manager:
Charlotte Park

Publisher:
Dan Savage

Commercial director:
Nigel Hole

Managing director:
Brian Hill

Published by:
Mortons Media Group Ltd,
Media Centre,
Morton Way, Horncastle,
Lincolnshire LN9 6JR
Tel: 01507 529529

Printed by:
William Gibbons and Sons, Wolverhampton

Credits:
All photographs courtesy PA Images unless otherwise stated.
Foreword © C M Sloane 2013.
Main cover photograph by Lewis Morley.

ISBN 978-1-909128-07-1

All material copyright Mortons Media Limited, 2013. All rights reserved.

© Mortons Media Group Ltd. All rights reserved. No part of this publication may be produced or transmitted in any form or by any means, electronic or mechanical, including photocopying, recording, or any information storage retrieval system without prior permission in writing from the publisher.

MORTONS
MEDIA GROUP LTD

The Great Game
1963: an introduction

British secret agent James Bond has failed. He sits silent, frozen with bitter defeat at the Casino Royale's baccarat table, having played sinister Soviet agent Le Chiffre 'The Number' and lost. He knew every trick of the game, took every precaution and weighed the odds carefully but in the end he ran out of money and out of luck. Now he knows he must fly back to Britain and face M's forced sympathy and 'better luck next time', but he also knows that there won't be a next time. It's over. Then he's handed an envelope and a note from CIA operative Felix Leiter. The envelope is stuffed with cash and the note says: "Marshall Aid. Thirty-two million francs. With the compliments of the USA." Bond is back in the game.

This scene from author Ian Fleming's first James Bond novel, Casino Royale, published in 1953, was a perfect metaphor for Britain's position at the end of the 1940s. Britain had been bankrupted by the Second World War but just when it seemed as though the nation would have to abandon what remained of its empire and cancel its defence projects, America stepped in with a blank cheque and catapulted Britain back into the fray and the top table of world politics.

The Yanks needed a strong ally in Europe to help stave off the growing Soviet menace and Britain was happy to oblige. Despite handing over billions of dollars though, the one thing the US refused to do was hand over its atomic secrets – so Britain simply used American cash to fund its own nuclear programme, plus a host of other military developments including the world-beating V-force bombers, the powerful English Electric Lightning jet fighter and the Royal Navy's first nuclear submarine HMS Dreadnought. The American money helped to pay for costly adventures abroad too, such as Britain's ill-judged intervention in Egypt during the Suez Crisis. Work began on Concorde and other expensive 'prestige' projects while British industry grew lazy on its successes and the nation's roads and railways crumbled through lack of investment.

No one minded too much though because unemployment had almost disappeared and growth was high, prompting Prime Minister Harold Macmillan to tell the public "you've never had it so good", in 1957.

During the 1950s though, Russia rapidly developed a terrifying nuclear capability. Had it launched an attack, Britain would have been first in the firing line and there would have been just four minutes between the missiles first being detected and British cities disappearing beneath nuclear mushroom clouds. The explosive force unleashed would have been equivalent to 20,000 Hiroshimas with London alone taking eight direct missile hits. Destruction would have been total.

Fear of nuclear annihilation soared in 1962 with the Cuban Missile Crisis. Britain was just a single wrong move away from oblivion but with Macmillan running the Government it seemed any storm could be weathered. The former First World War army captain who had fought on the Somme, a protégé of Sir Winston Churchill, wasn't nicknamed 'Supermac' for nothing. His coolness under pressure, his irresistible powers of persuasion, his dry wit and his problem-solving prowess made him a formidable champion of the British stiff upper lip on the world stage.

By 1963 though, the American money had run out. Britain was running on fumes and this time there would be no handouts, no Felix Leiter sending Bond a wad of bills to put him back on top. Macmillan was left juggling Britain's worldwide responsibilities, a series of expensive and unfinished defence projects and a growing sense of public dissatisfaction. Trouble was brewing and the stiff upper lip began to quiver.

Little did the nation know that 1963 would see its seemingly invincible prime minister brought low by a scandalous love triangle involving one of his closest cabinet colleagues, a glamorous young dancer and a Soviet spy. The year saw Beatlemania taking hold, the Vietnam War escalating wildly, the Great Train Robbers playing Monopoly with real money, Beeching axing the railways, a top British intelligence officer revealed as a Soviet agent, Sean Connery in From Russia With Love and the assassination of the US president. The nuclear holocaust was close at hand yet it seemed that the fresh-faced youth of Britain, with their pop music, their peace protests and their optimism might just save the day. This is the story of Britain at the height of the Cold War: a snapshot of the sex, the spies and the nuclear missiles of 1963.

Contents

Cold War: Sex, Spies and Nuclear Missiles

6 Chapter 1 — Reds under the bed — the Cold War from 1945 to 1963

The Soviet Union was Britain's greatest enemy in 1963 but it had been one of the nation's greatest allies – so what went wrong?

16 Chapter 2 — The spy who loved me — the Profumo Affair

A love triangle involving a beautiful young dancer, a Russian spy and the man responsible for Britain's defence proved to be political dynamite.

24 Chapter 3 — To catch a spy (or not) — the Third Man

The most dangerous spy ever to operate in Britain was unmasked in 1963 but he wasn't a Russian with an impeccable English accent – his father knew Sir Winston Churchill and Lawrence of Arabia.

30 Chapter 4 — Two tribes go to war — the Vietnam War

America fought communism wherever it threatened to rear its ugly head but in Vietnam it bit off more than it could chew. It wasn't long before the Yanks were asking Britain for help.

38 Chapter 5 — Behind the Iron Curtain — the Soviet threat

Vast tank armies waited in the cold behind the Iron Curtain, nuclear missiles were aimed at Britain and bombers idled on their runways. The Soviets commanded a huge arsenal of terrifying weaponry.

50 Chapter 6 — Follow the Bear — the Tupolev Tu-95

It flew slowly but it could carry a devastating payload of nuclear cruise missiles. The Tu-95 Bear was frequently intercepted by British fighters and has become a potent symbol of the Cold War.

52 Chapter 7 — Playing catch-up — Britain's nuclear weapons

Denied atomic weapons by the Americans, Britain used US dollars to bankroll its own A-bombs. When the US finally relented a new wave of nuclear weapons gave the British military a powerful deterrent.

60 Chapter 8 — Ruling the waves — Britain's first nuclear submarines

Britain's first nuclear sub entered service in 1963 with a little help from the US Navy. Polaris missiles were the future of the nation's atomic defence but advanced new submarines were needed to carry them.

68 Chapter 9 — V-bombers and Centurions — Britain's conventional armed forces

As the strongest power in Western Europe after the Second World War, Britain spent vast sums on maintaining its military might. Weapons such as the V-bombers and the Lightning jet were the result.

80 Chapter 10 — The Flaming Pencil — and Britain's other expensive experimental aircraft

For every dazzling success story of British design innovation and engineering achievement there was a costly white elephant left lurking in the shadows. The Bristol Type 188 was just such a beast.

84 Chapter 11 — Duck and cover — preparations for a nuclear attack

A nuclear strike on Britain in 1963 would have caused devastation beyond the wildest dreams of most people. Bunkers were built, evacuation plans were laid, but the chances of survival were slim.

92 Chapter 12 — The teenage dream — rise of youth culture

The baby boomers were coming of age in 1963. They had sexual freedom, the power of protest and some of the best pop music the world had ever seen… but could they end the Cold War?

100 Chapter 13 — Swinging 1963 — from the headless man to The Great Escape

The cultural impact of 1963 is still being felt today. Horrifying crimes were committed, classic films were screened, sex scandals shocked the nation, iconic cars were launched and… the lava lamp was invented.

112 Chapter 14 — The assassination of JFK — paranoia seizes America

Three bullets were enough to kill the American dream. The death of President John F Kennedy plunged the US into a nightmare of fear, recrimination and indecision that would last for decades.

120 Chapter 15 — What happened next? — The Cold War after 1963

Britain's role in the Cold War diminished after 1963 but it still had one eye on a return to greatness and a seat at the top table of world politics.

Man of steel. A rare candid image of Joseph Stalin's ice cold stare. The dictator's ruthlessness and paranoia ensured that the Cold War got off to a frosty start immediately after the Second World War.

CHAPTER 1

REDS UNDER THE BED

The Cold War from 1945 to 1963

Ioseb Besarionis dze Jughashvili was the most ruthless man in the world. He was also one of the most paranoid and one of the most powerful. Ioseb, better known as Joseph Stalin, trusted no one and his regime in Soviet Russia was built on fear. He had been systematically executing millions of Soviet citizens since the early 1930s and encouraging the survivors to spy on one another to avoid being next on his list. So during the Second World War, Stalin naturally spied on his allies – Britain and the US – and was astonished that they did not seem to be returning the favour.

Britain was shattered and bankrupted by the war, suffering 357,000 casualties and untold damage from bombing, but as one of the victorious Big Three it was forced to maintain its military and continue its peacekeeping duties all over the world. America had suffered up to 300,000 casualties but it had barely been touched by the war at home.

The Soviet Union, on the other hand, had suffered an estimated 27 million casualties and utter devastation of its western reaches. It also had the only leader to survive the war in office. America's Franklin D Roosevelt died before the war's end, on April 12, 1945, and Sir Winston Churchill was unceremoniously dumped by the British public when he lost the General Election on July 5 of the same year. Their replacements, Harry S Truman and Clement Attlee respectively, could scarcely hold a candle to Stalin's leadership CV. As his British and American opposite numbers did their best to pick up the reins of leadership, Stalin set about getting what he wanted out of the war's aftermath.

He greedily eyed an opportunity to expand the USSR over Poland, Finland, Romania and all of the Baltic nations – plus all of Germany if he could get it. The British and Americans were more or less willing to let him have the others but not Germany. It was split four ways, with the French getting the fourth quarter. The capital, Berlin, mirrored the four way split in microcosm even though it was deep inside the Soviet zone. The West, particularly America, felt certain that Stalin – a name which meant 'man of steel' – would never go further because of the atomic weapon the US possessed. Russia though had learned of the programme to develop it, the

Britain was being forced to walk a perilous tightrope in 1963. One wrong move could result in a nuclear apocalypse being unleashed upon the nation by the Soviet Union. But just 15 years earlier the Russians were among our closest friends — so how did the biggest falling out in history happen?

The Soviet army was the largest military fighting force the world had ever seen in the wake of the Second World War. It posed a very real threat to Western Europe.

Manhattan Project, through its covert intelligence networks at an early stage, and had spies embedded in it, feeding data back to Stalin's intelligence staff.

Stalin knew about the atom bomb before Truman did – the latter only being informed of its existence when he was sworn in as president in 1945. When Truman gave the order to use the atom bomb on Japan, Hiroshima was razed by a 16 kiloton device – the equivalent of 16,000 tonnes of dynamite – called Little Boy on August 6, 1945. Nagasaki was hit by a second bomb, the 21 kiloton Fat Man, three days later, and Stalin ordered his scientists to redouble their efforts to create a duplicate weapon for the USSR.

The Marshall Plan

Secure in the knowledge that the Soviets would take years to develop their own atomic bomb, the Americans busied themselves with the European Recovery Program, otherwise known as the Marshall Plan. The idea was to pump money into European nations for a period of four years starting in April 1948. The participating states were Britain, France, West Germany, Italy, Ireland, the Netherlands, Belgium, Austria, Denmark, Greece, Iceland, Luxembourg, Norway, Sweden, Switzerland and Turkey.

By January 1947, Britain had run out of money. It had two million men serving in its armed forces around the world for starters. Then there was the welfare state, which Attlee's new Labour government was determined to bring into existence. Funding Britain's role as a top flight military power and setting up the NHS meant there was little cash left for industrial modernisation – one of the key areas where Marshall Plan money was meant to be spent by its recipients. Britain's potholed roads, run-down railways and worn out industrial base suffered as a result.

The Marshall Plan offered fresh hope – injecting a total of $3 billion into Britain between 1948 and 1951, of which $586 million was in loans. Britain also received, separately, around $3.75 billion in credit from the US – the final repayment of which was made in May 2006.

In setting out what Britain would do with the money though, rather than a detailed business plan of industrial modernisation, the Americans were given what Sir Stafford Cripps, Labour Chancellor of the Exchequer at the time, described as a "general statement" outlining Britain's economic needs. Then a series of

The big three: Stalin (left) and Harry S Truman (centre) with British Prime Minister Clement Attlee at the Potsdam Conference in 1945 after the defeat of Germany. Stalin was determined to gain dominance over Eastern Europe in the war's aftermath.

8 THE COLD WAR SEX, SPIES AND NUCLEAR MISSILES

RIGHT: An atomic mushroom cloud rises over Nagasaki, Japan, in 1945. The blast killed 70,000 people and thousands died later from radiation poisoning. America believed the USSR would be kept at bay by this devastating weapon.

BELOW: Britain was revitalised during the 1950s thanks to a huge injection of American cash.

US Secretary of State George C Marshall who became the US spokesman for the European Recovery Program. The billions of dollars it pumped into Britain's economy kept the nation going.

financial mishaps and missteps meant that very little of the money ever found its way into industrial modernisation or infrastructure at a time when Germany was investing heavily in both by using Marshall Plan money in the way it was intended. German industry was rebuilt and the French and Italians used their money to create modern railway networks which were the envy of the world.

The Berlin Airlift

While Britain wrestled with its finances and struggled to retain its place at the top table of world affairs, the Cold War kept on getting colder. On April 1, 1948, the Soviets began restricting traffic from the western German zones to Berlin in the eastern zone. Planes flying in and out of Berlin were also subjected to harassment by Soviet military aircraft. Restrictions were partially lifted 10 days later but disruption continued on and off until June 19, the day after a new German currency, the Deutsche mark, had been announced. The British and Americans had proposed the replacement of the old Reichsmark in February but the Soviets rejected the idea. The Western powers went ahead with it anyway and when it became clear that the mark was about to be launched, the Soviets declared that it would not be legal tender in their zone, including Berlin in its entirety.

Soviet soldiers effectively blocked all traffic to Berlin from the west on June 19 – whether by road, rail or waterway – and on June 22 it was announced that the Soviet zone would start using its own new currency, the Ostmark. Food and electricity supplies from the east to civilians living in the western sectors of Berlin were then cut off. The only way to reach the German capital from the west was now by air. With barely enough coal to keep homes heated for 45 days and food for just 36 days, the West Berliners were now in a desperate situation. Although the Americans had the ultimate weapon if the worst came to the worst – 35 B-29 Superfortress bombers capable of dropping the 50 or so atomic bombs that had been built up to that point – none of them were in Europe and the Soviet armed forces in the area outnumbered the combined British, American and French forces 10 to one.

There was no agreement in place between the Western allies and the Soviets regarding ground routes to Berlin from the west. It simply hadn't been considered necessary because the Soviets were allies too. Until suddenly they weren't and now there was no way of appealing the decision to cut off all ground access to Berlin. However, it had previously been agreed that there would be three air corridors into Berlin and this, fortunately, had been put in writing. The British had already begun airlifting supplies into their beleaguered troops in Berlin and after some discussions with the Americans it was decided that this process would be dramatically expanded to provide everyone in the city's western sectors – more than two million people – with an airborne supply lifeline. Earlier in the year, RAF Air Commodore Reginald White had worked out that this would mean dropping off more than 5000 tons of food, coal and fuel every day and the allies now decided to use this figure as a target.

Readily available aircraft could transport about 700 tons a day but numbers rapidly increased as cargo carrying planes from all over Britain, France, Canada and the US joined in. Operation Plainfare, or Operation Vittles to the Americans, began on June 25, 1948. The Australians, who joined in September, dubbed the airlift Operation Pelican. By the second week, more than 1000 tons were being airlifted in every day. A month after the airlift began, the allies began to realise that they could be in for the long haul and wartime specialist in large-scale military airlift operations Major General William H 'Tonnage' Tunner of the US Air Force was brought in to oversee proceedings.

He set about devising a new set of safety rules for the operation. He also replaced smaller C-47 aircraft with larger C-54s, which were quicker to unload, banned flight crews from leaving their planes in Berlin to get snacks, tightened up the flight schedule to squeeze in more drops and centralised control of the operation rather than having individual air forces controlling their own units. Berliners pitched in to get aircraft unloaded more swiftly and by the end of August more than 4500 tons of cargo were being dropped off every day – just barely enough to keep the city going. This rose to the magic 5000 tons by the end of September as all smaller aircraft were replaced with larger ones.

The Soviets started offering free food to anyone who entered East Berlin and registered with the authorities. They also harassed allied aircraft by flying close to them and shining searchlights on to them at night to dazzle the pilots. Other tricks were tried, up to and including an attempt to take over the whole city

RAISIN BOMBERS

Pilot Gail Halvorsen ties small cloth parachutes to chocolate bars ready for another drop over Berlin. AP

One airlift pilot, Gail Halvorsen, who had befriended some Berlin children, began dropping chocolate bars to them attached to improvised parachutes as he flew over, wiggling the wings of his plane to signal that the sweets were about to descend. Tunner heard about this and soon other pilots were doing it too, as part of 'Operation Little Vittles'. These chocolate dropping aircraft were known as 'raisin bombers' to the German youngsters.

A Douglas C-54 Skymaster flies into Berlin loaded with essential supplies during the airlift while children watch from the ground. Pilots were frequently harassed by Soviet military aircraft on the way into the city.

by preventing the city's ruling parliament from meeting – its meeting place being in the eastern sector – on September 6. A crowd of 500,000 concerned people gathered at the Brandenburg Gate, fearful that the airlift might be ended and that they might be handed over to the Soviets. As they milled around, city councillor Ernst Reuter spoke out over the public address system, saying: "You people of the world, you people of America, of England, of France, look on this city, and recognise that this city, this people, must not be abandoned, cannot be abandoned."

During the winter of 1948/49 an extra 6000 tons of fuel were needed on top of the 5000 tons already being airlifted in to keep homes warm. An extra runway was added to one airport, two auxiliary runways were upgraded and still more large aircraft were brought in, including RAF Handley Page Hastings transports, and the French built an entirely new airport in their sector in less than 90 days. Poor weather, though, meant there were still days when no aircraft could land in Berlin. When spring arrived, the airlift got back into gear and supplies arrived smoothly again and on May 12, 1949, the Soviet blockade was ended, although drops still continued until September 30 to build up a surplus – just in case.

The Soviet atom bomb

Having put an end to the debacle of the Berlin blockade, Stalin was almost ready to play his next card. The first atom bomb built by Soviet scientists, codenamed First Lightning, was detonated on August 29, 1949, in the Kazakhstan desert. American air sampling planes soon began to detect radioactive fallout from the blast and the West woke up to the fact that the Soviets had developed an A-bomb much sooner than anyone outside the Iron Curtain had thought possible. This changed everything. The Americans, now concerned that they had entered a new arms race, began to increase their own atomic bomb production and to consider an even more devastating weapon – the hydrogen bomb. The West, which had by now formed an organised military alliance, NATO, was stunned when on October 1, just a week after Truman had revealed word of the Soviet bomb to the world, Mao Zedong announced the formation of the People's Republic of China. This ended a long running civil war in China and established a second huge communist state. Not long after this, in January 1950, President Harry S Truman authorised work on this new 'H-bomb'.

At this point it became clear how the Soviets had managed to develop their A-bomb. Former US State Department official Alger Hiss was convicted of perjury for denying under oath that he had been a Soviet spy during the late 1930s and early 1940s. Then the British government revealed that Klaus Fuchs, a scientist who had worked as part of its delegation to Los Alamos during the Manhattan Project to develop the first atomic weapon, was also a Soviet agent. Everyone suddenly began to wonder whether there were still more 'reds under the bed'. US Senator Joseph McCarthy wondered the loudest and so began a series of communist witch hunts in the US which would rumble on for four years.

March saw the US sending 60 B-29 Superfortress bombers, famous for their role in delivering the atomic devices which devastated Hiroshima and Nagasaki, to the UK for service with the RAF. It wasn't revealed at the time, but they did not come equipped with A-bombs.

Mao Zedong in 1950 – a year after announcing the formation of the People's Republic of China. NATO was stunned to find itself facing two huge communist states.

Scientist Dr Klaus Fuchs, the spy responsible for the single most significant act of espionage in British history. He betrayed secrets which helped the USSR to develop its own atom bomb.

US Senator Joe McCarthy led efforts to find the 'reds under the bed'. His efforts were applauded at first but within four years his popularity had faded.

The Korean War

North Korean forces launched an invasion of the South on June 25, 1950, at 4am. The nation had been jointly occupied by Soviet and American forces at the end of the Second World War and they had agreed that it would be divided at the 38th Parallel until a single Korean government could be established – a move ratified by the United Nations. Both superpowers had withdrawn their forces during 1948-49 but with a unifying government still absent. The US-backed Republic of Korea ran the south and the USSR-backed Democratic Republic of Korea the north. Each side claimed to be the rightful ruler of the whole country and was hostile to the other.

Part of the reason the US had pulled out was because it feared the unpredictable South Korean leader Syngman Rhee might suddenly invade the north and commit it to a war it had no desire to fight. The North Korean leader Kim Il-sung was of a similarly volatile character but after the Soviets had pulled out he had continued to petition for support to launch an attack on the south. These requests were ignored by Stalin until, following events in Europe, he decided that the time was right to direct American attention elsewhere. Kim Il-sung could scarcely believe it when Stalin gave the proposed invasion his blessing. Mao Zedong also came on board with an offer to give the North Koreans practical Chinese support during their struggle.

The invasion began and Truman went to South Korea's aid. This was an attack on the UN's authority in international affairs as much as it was on South Korea itself in his view. An international force was assembled under the UN banner including troops from Britain, Canada, France, Turkey, the Netherlands, Colombia and others and combat was joined. Unfortunately, the North held the initiative and during the summer almost succeeded in booting the UN forces right off the tip of the peninsula. Fortunately, the American commander General Douglas MacArthur was a tactical genius. He made an amphibious landing way behind the front line on September 15 and attacked the North Koreans from the rear. They were trapped between the two forces and because the entire North Korean army was deployed in the South, MacArthur was also able to advance unopposed into the North.

It seemed that the war was over but then China decided to weigh in with 300,000 of its own troops advancing in support of the North. The Republic of Korea and UN forces were pushed back south and by January 1951 the fighting was 60 miles south of the 38th Parallel, loosely marked by the Imjin river. At this point, the British involvement amounted to some 12,000 troops. By March, the situation had reversed again, with the Chinese and North Koreans shoved back beyond the river.

In this way, the war ground on for two more years and involved some of the most brutal close quarters trench fighting seen since the First World War. Dwight D Eisenhower became the new US president on November 29, 1952, and began looking for a way to end the war.

An armistice was eventually signed on July 27, 1953, with the conflict reduced to a stalemate and both sides exhausted.

Total British casualties were 1078 dead, 2674 wounded and a further 1060 either missing or held prisoner. The Americans suffered 36,568 deaths, the Chinese 150,000 and an estimated one million Koreans lost their lives, including many civilians.

Desperate days: British troops march through Suwon, South Korea, on January 5, 1951. The city fell to the communists two days later.

The first US hydrogen bomb test on November 1, 1952, in the Pacific at Eniwetok Atoll, Marshall Islands.

President Eisenhower in 1956.

EISENHOWER'S CHILLING VISION

When President Eisenhower was told in 1956 that a Soviet attack on the United States could annihilate the government and kill 65% of the population outright, he said it would "literally be a business of digging ourselves out of the ashes, starting again". In 1959 he was quoted as saying that if a nuclear war began "you might as well go out and shoot everyone you see and then shoot yourself".

The H-bomb

Joseph Stalin died aged 74 on March 5, 1953, not long before the end of the Korean War. His body was embalmed four days later and put on public display next to the body of Lenin inside his mausoleum in Red Square for the next eight years. A bitter power struggle followed his death, with Nikita Khrushchev finally emerging as the new Soviet premier three years later in 1956.

In the meantime, a trio of Russian politicians – Vyacheslav Molotov, Georgi Malenkov and Khrushchev himself – did their best to fill the power vacuum and operate the apparatus of state.

With the Russians busy fighting their internal battles and the Americans recovering from the Korean War, the Cold War simmered on into 1954 without major incident before the status quo was once again rattled – this time by a hydrogen bomb test.

The first experimental thermonuclear or hydrogen explosion, known as 'Ivy Mike', had taken place on November 1, 1952, but 'Mike' itself was a huge 62 ton instrument rather than a bomb in the conventional sense. On March 1, 1954, the Americans conducted the first test of an actual H-bomb as part of Operation Castle, codenamed Castle Bravo, at Bikini Atoll in the Pacific. Unfortunately, the bomb, known as 'The Shrimp', turned out to be three times more powerful than anyone had expected it to be – 15 megatons instead of five.

The resulting cloud of radioactive debris spread rapidly, immediately contaminating a nearby Japanese fishing vessel, the Lucky Dragon No. 5, killing one of its crew before entering the global weather system and setting off radiation detectors all over the world. At the Kremlin in Moscow, just 12 days after the blast, Malenkov declared publicly that a war fought with H-bombs would result in "the end of world civilisation". He had received a report from Soviet scientists which estimated that 100 hydrogen bomb detonations would create global conditions "impossible for life". The Soviets had created their own thermonuclear explosion on August 12, 1953, but this had had a very low yield and is not considered to have been a 'true' hydrogen bomb.

Two weeks after Malenkov's speech, the Americans detonated a second H-bomb. This time the test was called Castle Romeo and the weapon was 'The Runt' but the effect was the same and the blast was again significantly more powerful than expected.

While all this was going on, the French were being roundly defeated by the Soviet and Chinese-backed Viet Minh during the Battle of Dien Bien Phu in north-western Vietnam. They had been battling communist forces in the region for nine years but this time their defeat was so crushing that the French were forced to withdraw their forces altogether and Vietnam was temporarily divided along the 17th parallel – a move which was to have serious repercussions a decade later. The first US Army advisers were sent to Vietnam by Eisenhower in February 1955, shortly after he'd announced plans to develop the first intercontinental ballistic missiles, and the Vietnam War proper began in November between forces of the North and South.

The same year saw West Germany inducted into NATO and the Warsaw Treaty Organisation of Friendship, Co-operation and Mutual Assistance, better known as the Warsaw Pact, was formed in response by eight communist states in Eastern Europe.

The Soviets also managed to detonate their own hydrogen bomb for the first time on November 22, 1955, although they claimed to have had the H-bomb since the thermonuclear explosion of August 1953.

OPERATION HURRICANE BRITAIN'S 'FAT MAN'

Britain joined the nuclear club on October 3, 1952, while the Korean War still raged. It detonated a bomb similar to the one the Americans had dropped on Nagasaki at the end of the Second World War inside a frigate, HMS Plym, anchored off Trimouille Island, Western Australia.

Plutonium for the weapon came from Royal Ordnance Factory Sellafield in Cumbria which had been renamed 'Windscale' after the war and converted to produce nuclear materials.

The blast carved a crater 20ft deep and nearly 1000ft across into the seabed.

Soviet premier Nikita Khrushchev took up the reins of power after Joseph Stalin's death on March 5, 1953, aged 74. He initially faced a power struggle with Stalin's closest advisors, foremost among them being secret police chief Lavrentiy Beria – who was swiftly executed.

America sent 60 B-29 Superfortress bombers – famous for delivering the bombs which destroyed the Japanese cities of Hiroshima and Nagasaki during the war – to be stationed in Britain.

The Suez Crisis

When Gamal Abdel Nasser decided to nationalise the Suez Canal on July 26, 1956, it was the latest round in a series of tit for tat blows between the country he ruled as president, Egypt, and its erstwhile allies Britain and the US. Colonel Nasser had led a successful military coup d'etat against the former ruler King Farouk in 1952 and had then begun to form alliances with both the Soviets and the Chinese in opposition primarily to the British, who still occupied the country. He had tried negotiating with the British to abandon the canal – an economic lifeline for transporting goods between Europe and Asia without having to sail all the way around Africa – but subsequently set himself up as an Arab nationalist in opposition to the West. This irked Britain and the US and they withdrew a previous offer of funding for the Aswan High Dam project, which was regarded as vital to Egypt.

Spotting an opportunity, Khrushchev, who had by now assumed full control over the USSR, offered to lend Egypt £700 million for the dam at just 2% interest. Nasser then took control of the Suez Canal. Britain, which had been controlling it up to this point, was stunned and quickly opted to use military force in taking it back. The French and their allies the Israelis also decided to intervene and offered to make common cause with the British. The Americans persuaded British Prime Minister Anthony Eden to gather together all the countries that used the canal for a conference in London but meanwhile, large quantities of Soviet military hardware were arriving in Egypt. The conflict began with Israeli air strikes at 3pm on October 29. Then Israeli paratroopers dropped in near the Suez Canal, ground forces entered Egypt and French made Dassault Mystere IV fighters provided air cover.

Britain and France issued an ultimatum to Nasser and the Israelis – withdraw from the canal within 12 hours. The Israelis did so, the Egyptians did not. Instead, Nasser sank all 40 vessels which were using the canal at the time, blocking it to all further traffic. Operation Musketeer was therefore launched by the British on October 31 to recapture the canal.

Royal Navy vessels reduced one Egyptian frigate to a burning hulk before sinking it and by November 1, Israeli forces were in the Gaza Strip. Meanwhile British carrier based fighter bombers rapidly annihilated the Egyptian air force. British and French paratroopers landed on November 5 and Royal Marines using Second World War landing craft made an amphibious assault. A ceasefire was then called.

During the six days that fighting had been going on, MPs in the House of Commons were comparing Anthony Eden to Hitler; the Americans had condemned the invasion and set out a resolution at the United Nations, calling for an end to hostilities; the opportunistic Soviets had invaded Hungary and the value of the pound had fallen by 15% with the Americans threatening to devalue it still further by selling Sterling. US Treasury Secretary George Humphrey also blocked an application by Britain for emergency funding from the International Monetary Fund.

Downing Street also received a phone call from the White House: "Is that you, Anthony? Well, this is President Eisenhower and I can only presume you have gone out of your mind."

Eden quickly agreed to the ceasefire and troop withdrawals began on November 6. Eden resigned on January 9, 1957, to be succeeded by Harold Macmillan. Egypt reopened the Suez Canal to all traffic three months later on April 9.

Soldiers waiting to go ashore and Westland Whirlwind helicopters of 845 Naval Air Squadron share the flight deck of HMS Theseus, a Colossus Class light carrier, as it waits outside Port Said, Egypt, during the Suez Crisis. In the background, smoke billows up from burning oil tanks.

LITTLE CURLY GOES WHERE NO DOG HAS GONE BEFORE

The second Soviet space vehicle, Sputnik 2, was launched on November 3, 1957. It consisted of a 13ft high cone shaped capsule with a pressurised cabin inside. Its passenger was a dog originally called Kudryavka 'Little Curly' but later renamed Laika 'Barker'. She had oxygen supplies, could lie down or stand and had some padding to cushion her journey. Food and water were available in the form of jelly and there was a bag to collect her waste.

She was held in place with a harness and had electrodes attached to monitor her vital signs. Shortly after entering orbit, the capsule transmitted data showing that Laika was agitated but was eating her food. After a few hours though, she was dead from overheating and stress. Had she lived any longer, the Russians had planned to put her down with poisoned food to prevent her from suffering when the capsule burned up on re-entry.

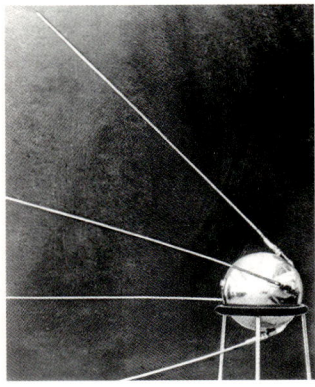

Laika in her compartment prior to launch aboard Sputnik 2.

The first official image of Sputnik released on October 9, 1957, by the Soviet Union. It is seen here resting on a stand prior to launch. While it may have been a simple device, its successful launch stunned the Americans who had not yet developed satellite technology.

Sputnik and the space race

Much soul searching followed Britain's withdrawal from Egypt. The 'special relationship' between Britain and America was called into question and the possibility of closer ties with the rest of Europe was given serious thought. Macmillan had served alongside Eisenhower in North Africa during the Second World War and believed that this relationship would go some way towards repairing the two nations' damaged relations but the Americans could no longer be trusted to stand by Britain no matter what.

Eisenhower met Macmillan at Bermuda in March 1957 and agreed to station 60 Thor nuclear missiles in Britain. Their deployment had not yet begun however when the Soviets upped the ante once again. On October 4, a two-stage R-7 Semyorka missile was used as a vehicle to launch the world's first satellite into space – Sputnik. The small sphere measured just 23in in diameter and was designed to emit a series of electronic beeps which relayed information on the ionosphere's electron density and the temperature both inside and outside the satellite.

The launch went without a hitch and Sputnik began orbiting the earth 139 miles up every 90 minutes. The distinctive beep-beep-beep signals began and anyone with a shortwave radio receiver anywhere in the world could pick them up. Its shiny surface could be easily seen shooting through the sky too and the broadcasts continued until January 4, 1958, when it burned up upon re-entering the atmosphere.

The Americans were shocked. Their own satellite wouldn't be ready for months. Not only that, the Sputnik launch demonstrated that the Soviets had missiles capable of tremendous feats of technical accuracy and control.

The first American attempt to launch a satellite failed on December 6 with the rocket exploding on the launch pad but on January 31, 1958, Explorer 1 successfully entered orbit and the 'space race' was well and truly under way. Not long afterwards, the US launched the first satellite capable of taking surveillance photos – Corona. The first Soviet spy satellite, the Zenit, was not launched until 1961. Meanwhile, on January 1, 1959, revolutionaries under Fidel Castro finally succeeded in ousting dictator Fulgencio Batista from power in Cuba.

US Army tanks in the foreground at Checkpoint Charlie opposite Soviet Army T-62 tanks on October 28, 1961. The armour remained in position for more than 16 hours before both sides gradually withdrew.

The U-2 incident

Before Corona, the Americans had the Lockheed U-2 spy plane. It took its first flight on August 1, 1955, and the first of its many missions over Soviet territory took place on July 4, 1956. It flew so high, above 70,000ft, there was nothing the Russian air force could do to stop it and U-2s took thousands of photographs showing airfields, factories, research facilities, shipyards, military bases, uranium mines and more.

Khrushchev, appalled, made regular protests to Eisenhower but the flights continued. The Russians therefore began to develop anti-aircraft missile systems. By 1957 they had the SA-2 Guideline surface-to-air missile. On May 1, 1960, Captain Francis Gary Powers flew a U-2 on a mission to photograph ICBM sites within the Soviet Union. Several fighters tried to fly high enough to attack him but then his aircraft and one of the MiG-19s following him were hit by a salvo of SA-2s. The Russian pilot was killed but Powers bailed out and was captured.

Khrushchev revealed that Powers was alive and in custody and Eisenhower was humiliated but refused to apologise. The pilot returned to the US as part of a prisoner exchange in 1962. Overflights of the USSR were stopped but the Corona spy satellite programme was stepped up.

The Berlin Wall

A successor to Dwight D Eisenhower emerged in November 1960 when 43-year-old John F Kennedy defeated Republican rival Richard Nixon in presidential elections. Kennedy's term as the 35th President of the US began in January 1961 and he was immediately forced to deal with a nasty hangover of Eisenhower's last year in office. With the communists of Fidel Castro now in power in Cuba, thousands opposed to his rule fled to nearby Florida. Many dreamed of overthrowing the revolutionary and Eisenhower had started the ball rolling on a plan to do it with $13 million of funding to the CIA. This paid for the training of a 1400 strong Cuban exile paramilitary group known as Brigade 2506,

US pilot Gary Powers in front of a Lockheed U-2 reconnaissance aircraft. He is pictured in the pressure suit U-2 pilots had to wear for missions lasting up to 12 hours. They usually lost about 4lb per flight through perspiration. Powers was shot down by a Soviet surface-to-air missile.

The Cuban Missile Crisis

Two days after the Berlin Crisis, on October 30, the Soviet Union exploded the most powerful nuclear device in history – the Tsar Bomba or 'Emperor Bomb'. It was capable of a 100 megaton yield but safety concerns saw this reduced to 50.

Two months later Cuba and the Soviet Union signed a trade pact and a month after that, in February 1962, the US announced a trade embargo against the tiny communist state. In May, Khrushchev devised a plan that would take the world to the brink of nuclear annihilation – although he only intended it to give the US a taste of its own medicine.

The Americans were stockpiling nuclear weapons because they believed there was a 'missile gap' between their own arsenal and what they feared that the Russians possessed but the Soviets, knowing that they had fewer than 50 ICBMs capable of hitting the US, were terrified of a pre-emptive strike. The Soviet Union was already surrounded by US nuclear bases – in Britain, France, Germany, Italy, South Korea, Japan and Turkey.

In July the CIA learned that a fleet of 65 Soviet ships was heading for Cuba, at least 10 of them carrying military hardware.

On September 2, the Soviet Union formally agreed to extend its trade agreement to include weapons and between September 8 and September 15 two shipments of medium range SS-4 Sandal nuclear missiles arrived in Havana. Bases were also prepared for more advanced SS-5 Skean missiles. From Cuba, the former would be able to hit around 40% of US strategic bomber bases. The latter would be able to strike almost anywhere in the US. A total of 40 launchers and 80 warheads were destined for Cuban bases and it was estimated that this would be enough to leave just 15% of US nuclear forces in a position to retaliate if the Soviets struck first.

An American U-2 flying over Cuba on October 14 photographed the first Sandals and preparations for further bases. The president was informed on October 16. Kennedy announced the situation in a TV broadcast on October 22. During those six days, four options had been discussed. The first was to attack the missile bases but CIA reports suggested that four were already operational by October 19 and ready to fire. An attack could result in a nuclear strike on the US. An appeal to the United Nations would take too long. An invasion of Cuba was dismissed for the same reason as option one. The final idea, a naval blockade, seemed to be the only solution.

Kennedy's advisers pointed out that new intelligence from Corona satellites and U-2 photographs showed that if it came to a fight, the US would suffer far less than the Soviet Union due to the Soviets' lack of ICBMs but this was of little comfort to Britain and the rest of Europe since the Russians did have plenty of nuclear missiles capable of hitting them.

By October 27, Soviet ships were approaching the perimeter of the blockade. Then one vessel, the Grozny, began to approach the line. FBI reports suggested the Soviet diplomats in Washington had begun to destroy sensitive documents. The US bomber fleet was put on standby. Then a message was received from the Russians suggesting that a pledge to leave Cuba unmolested and a dismantling of the US missile bases in Turkey would be enough to warrant the withdrawal of nuclear weapons from Cuba. Kennedy publicly accepted the first part of the deal and made arrangements to accept the second part. The crisis was over but now the world knew just how close it was possible to get to the point of no return. As 1963 began, the true ramifications of what a nuclear war might mean were still sinking in.

which, with a green light from Kennedy, launched an invasion of Cuba on April 13.

The invasion force landed at the Bay of Pigs on April 17 with air support from US bombers. Unfortunately, it was mopped up in short order by the communists who had Soviet tanks. This embarrassment to the fledgling Kennedy administration was forgotten when years of simmering tension began to boil over in Berlin.

At a summit in Vienna on June 4, Khrushchev threatened to end British, French and American access to West Berlin. He gave a six month deadline for US forces to leave West Berlin. As this loomed, more and more of the Berliners began emigrating to the west. On August 13, 1961, the border between East and West Berlin was closed by units of the East German army. Then construction of a wall between the two halves was rapidly begun.

Two months later, in October 1961, American diplomat Albert Hemsing was stopped by East German police at Checkpoint Charlie. US military police then escorted him over the border. He did the same again a few days later, this time with tanks to back him up. Again he was allowed through but this time 33 Soviet tanks rumbled forwards on the eastern side of the wall. Ten of these came within 100m of it. Hemsing's US tanks stopped an equal distance from the western side, creating a stand-off.

This went on until 11am the next day when Khrushchev and Kennedy agreed to withdraw the tanks. The Soviets made the first move – a T-62 retreating by 5m – before the Americans did the same and the armoured vehicles retreated.

A Soviet ship carrying eight canvas-covered missiles and transporters, visible on deck, sails away from Cuba on November 7, 1962. Kennedy's uncompromising stance during the crisis cemented his legacy as one of America's greatest presidents.

President Kennedy makes an address during the Cuban Missile Crisis in 1962. His refusal to back down brought the world to the brink of war. Khrushchev's capitulation was the death knell for his premiership.

The luxurious outdoor pool at Cliveden House in Berkshire as it is today. This is the spot where dancer Christine Keeler and top government minister John Profumo first met. It is also where Soviet spy Yevgeny 'Eugene' Ivanov became involved with her. Cliveden House is now a five star hotel. Cliveden

CHAPTER 2

THE SPY who loved me

John Profumo, then Minister of State for Foreign Affairs, and his wife Valerie Robson arrive at a dinner party in London, on May 13, 1959, the year that Christine Keeler met Dr Stephen Ward.

The Profumo Affair

The idea of a minister getting caught with his pants down was deeply shocking in 1963 but the idea of the man responsible for Britain's defence having an affair with a woman who was also sleeping with a Russian intelligence officer was political dynamite. The explosive repercussions were enough to shake the nation...

Major John Profumo landed in Normandy on D-Day with the Royal Armoured Corps and took part in the ferocious battles which followed to liberate France from the Nazis. He had been elected to the House of Commons as its youngest MP, representing Kettering for the Conservatives four years earlier while still serving in the Army, and when the war ended his rise to the corridors of power began. A succession of ministerial appointments led, eventually, to his appointment as Secretary of State for War in July 1960. He was part of Prime Minister Harold Macmillan's inner circle and was involved in every aspect of Britain's defence during the Berlin Crisis and the Cuban Missile Crisis. The stress of the job was enormous and Profumo needed to blow off steam.

At the time of Profumo's appointment, Christine Keeler, who had been just two years old and living in Middlesex when he led his forces against the German defences in western France, was working as a topless dancer at Murray's Cabaret Club in Beak Street, Soho, London.

Murray's was a members-only nightspot frequented by the rich and, occasionally, the famous including the Kray twins, Jean Harlow and even Princess Margaret. Girls danced on stage while hostesses moved between the tables persuading customers to buy bottles of expensive champagne and it was here that Keeler, aged 17, met 47-year-old osteopath Dr Stephen Ward in 1959.

Ward, by his own admission, liked "pretty girls" and had become involved in setting up London's brightest young things with the rich, powerful and frustrated men who ran the British establishment. At their first meeting, he took down Keeler's phone number and rang her incessantly thereafter. It wasn't long before he was inviting her to his country cottage. It was here, in the grounds of Cliveden, a grand stately home in Buckinghamshire on the banks of the Thames, that Ward charmed Keeler with his affluent lifestyle, his famous friends and his interest in her. The pair then began living together at Ward's flat in Orme Court, Bayswater, near Hyde Park, London, although

CRISIS AND SCANDAL THE COLD WAR 17

Keeler has always insisted that their relationship was strictly platonic.

Ward not only used his osteopathic skills to treat the aches and pains of the wealthy and powerful, including Sir Winston Churchill and Elizabeth Taylor, he drew them too, being a talented sketch artist. Among his portraiture subjects were the Duke of Edinburgh and the Duke and Duchess of Kent. Among his friends were MI5 chief Roger Hollis, Daily Telegraph editor Colin Coote, whom he treated for lumbago, and surveyor of the Queen's pictures Anthony Blunt. Coote even sent him to Israel to sketch Nazi Adolf Eichmann, one of the main organisers of the Holocaust, during his trial in April 1961.

The Cliveden cottage was given to Ward for a token rent of just £1 a year by Bill Astor, 3rd Viscount Astor, who owned the estate. Ward had treated him after a hunting accident in 1950. His nearest neighbour at the cottage and another friend was actor Jon Pertwee who later became the third Doctor Who.

Ward introduced Keeler to a kinky world of sex behind the closed doors of the highest levels of British society and told her stories about the hang-ups and preferences of the apparently well-to-do circles he moved in. He told her about the Thursday Club, essentially a regular drinking session where influential men would play risqué games with young women; black magic parties where women would pretend to worship a phallic totem pole; parties where men and women whipped one another and wore bondage gear and about London's secret homosexual scene – secret because homosexuality was illegal until 1967.

After months of talking about sex games and introducing Keeler to characters such as bondage queen Mariella Novotny, Ward tried to get her involved in an orgy but she wasn't interested. The pair eventually fell out over one of Keeler's boyfriends and she moved out of Orme Court, met up with 16-year-old good time girl Marilyn 'Mandy' Rice-Davies and ended up moving in with her.

After a while, Keeler ended up back in Ward's good books and in 1961 she moved back in with him at his new flat in Wimpole Mews, Marylebone, London. Earlier, Ward had become friends with Captain Yevgeny 'Eugene' Ivanov, a naval attaché at the Russian embassy. He would come round while Keeler was there and talk politics with Ward. Another interest of Ward's around this time was London's black community and it was through this interest that Keeler met blues singer Aloysius 'Lucky' Gordon.

The cottage on the Cliveden estate that Stephen Ward rented from Lord Astor for £1 a year. It was the weekend retreat where he often brought Christine Keeler.

Relaxing by the Cliveden pool are Stephen Ward and Christine Keeler, right, with two of Stephen's girlfriends. The photo was taken by John Profumo on July 9, 1961, the day after he met Keeler.

Swimming naked

Ward, Keeler, another girl and Keeler's friend Leon Norell went to the Cliveden cottage for the weekend on Saturday, July 8, 1961. When they arrived, there was a party going on at the big house – Lord and Lady Astor were entertaining guests. It was a warm summer's evening and the party of four from the cottage decided to use the Astors' large outdoor pool surrounded by a high brick wall. Keeler was swimming around in the nude when Lord Astor and his friend John Profumo walked into the pool enclosure.

Keeler tried to get out of the water and put some clothes on but ended up being chased around the poolside by Astor and Profumo, who had both been drinking. Profumo's wife, the actress Valerie Hobson, then arrived with a number of other guests and the frivolity came to an abrupt end. The four from the cottage were invited up to the house and after Keeler had got dried off and dressed, the party continued in the grand surroundings of Cliveden House proper. Profumo offered to show Keeler around and the two of them quickly hit it off.

The following day, Ward and Keeler returned to the pool at Astor's invitation and this time Ward had invited Eugene Ivanov along too. Profumo had also returned and they all fooled around playing bawdy games in the swimming pool together with Keeler riding around on Profumo's shoulders during a race.

This time Keeler left with Ivanov, who drove her home to Wimpole Mews. Keeler says Ivanov asked if he could come in with her and she agreed. The two of them drank vodka and ended up having sex on the floor. The following day, Ward gave Keeler's phone number to Profumo and he rang her on July 12, suggesting that they go for a drive together. Later that day they drove along Downing Street, the metal barriers in place today only having been installed in 1973, and over

ABOVE: The swimming pool at Cliveden as it was on July 11, 1963, after the Profumo Affair became a public scandal.

Lord Astor, owner of Cliveden, the estate where the liaison between Profumo and Keeler began.

The 'Darling' letter

This love letter was sent to Christine Keeler by John Profumo, dated August 9, 1961. It was subsequently printed in newspapers around the world and was quoted in the Denning Report on the Profumo Affair.

> Darling,
>
> In great haste and because I can get no reply from your phone. Alas something's blown up tomorrow night and I can't therefore make it. I'm terribly sorry especially as I have to leave the next day for various trips and then on holiday so won't be able to see you again until sometime in September. Blast it! Please take great care of yourself and don't run away.
>
> Love, J.
>
> PS
> I am writing this 'cos I know you're off for the day tomorrow and I want to know before you go if I still can't reach you by phone.

the next few days began a sexual relationship. Profumo sent Keeler several love letters and showed her around his home in Regent's Park including his office.

Keeler says that during this time Ward asked her to subtly question Profumo about when American nuclear weapons would be deployed in West Germany. The affair continued until October when Profumo broke it off. Keeler moved out of Wimpole Mews and went to live with Mandy Rice-Davies again at her Pimlico flat.

In December 1961, Keeler and Rice-Davies went to a flat in Bayswater between Paddington station and Kensington Gardens in the City of Westminster, where Mariella Novotny was holding one of her sex parties, known as the Feast of Peacocks. Mariella, who jokingly called herself the 'Chief Whip' because so many MPs attended her gatherings, was extremely well connected. According to Keeler in her autobiography Secrets and Lies, the Feast of

Yevgeny Ivanov, Soviet assistant naval attache in London and secret agent. He slept with Christine Keeler after spending a day at the pool with her, Ward, Profumo and their friends.

Labour MP Barbara Castle's probing questions in the House of Commons prompted War Minister John Profumo to deny "any impropriety" in his relationship with Christine Keeler.

MP George Wigg, whose friend John Lewis, a former MP, had a vendetta against Stephen Ward. Wigg voiced rumours of his involvement with Keeler and Profumo in the Commons.

Peacocks was "a lavish dinner in which this man wearing only a black mask with slits for eyes and laces up the back and a tiny apron – one like the waitresses wore in 1950s tearooms – asked to be whipped if people were not happy with his services".

In her own autobiography, entitled Mandy, Rice-Davies said: "The door was opened by Stephen – naked except for his socks. All the men were naked, the women naked except for wisps of clothing like suspender belts and stockings. I recognised our host and hostess, Mariella Novotny and her husband Horace Dibbins, and unfortunately I recognised too a fair number of other faces as belonging to people so famous you could not fail to recognise them: a Harley Street gynaecologist, several politicians, including a cabinet minister of the day, now dead, who, Stephen told us with great glee, had served dinner of roast peacock wearing nothing but a mask and a bow tie instead of a fig leaf." Lucky Gordon appeared on the scene again around this time, but Keeler was afraid of him. She travelled to New York with Mandy for a break and on her return she met a West Indian man called Johnny Edgecombe who she hoped would help her to get away from Gordon. For added protection, she also bought herself a black market Luger semi-automatic pistol with 13 bullets.

By October 1962, Keeler had moved in with Edgecombe at a hotel in Kensington but on the 27th they were involved in an incident at the Flamingo Club in Wardour Street where Edgecombe confronted Gordon and cut his face open with a knife – a wound which needed 17 stitches. After this, Keeler left Edgecombe and moved into a new flat in Great Cumberland Place with the financial aid of Stephen Ward. Meanwhile, Rice-Davies had moved in with Ward and on December 14 Keeler went over to go Christmas shopping with her. Johnny Edgecombe rang up while she was there and they argued on the phone. Ten minutes later the doorbell rang and, looking out of the window, Rice-Davies reported that he had turned up on the doorstep. Edgecombe said he was going to come in but the women kept the door locked. While they were dialling 999 he took out Keeler's Luger and began firing at the flat. He emptied a whole magazine – seven bullets – into the door trying to shoot out the lock before retreating.

Unravelling the affair

The police arrived and began to investigate the shooting – which in the London of 1963 was an uncommon event. The press arrived too and soon it was hitting the national news. It didn't take long for the police to arrest Edgecombe and his trial date was set for January. Keeler, terrified at the thought of having to appear in court, consulted her

LEFT: Mandy Rice-Davies, 18, in 1963. She was with Christine Keeler at Stephen Ward's flat when Johnny Edgecombe fired Keeler's gun at the door lock while trying to get in.

RIGHT: At the beginning of 1963, Christine Keeler went to the national newspapers with her story but had no idea just how explosive it would become.

Christine Keeler arrives at London's Old Bailey on April 1, 1963. Inside, a judge declared her bail forfeited because she failed to show up as a court witness for Johnny Edgecombe's trial two weeks earlier.

friend Michael Eddowes, a lawyer. He asked her why she'd had a gun and she told him about Gordon, Edgecombe and Ward. At one point in the long conversation she said Ward had asked her to ask Profumo about nuclear weapons in Germany.

When he heard about Ward, Profumo and nuclear weapons Eddowes was fascinated. After he'd finished interviewing Keeler he approached Ward with her information and the osteopath said Keeler had got it wrong: it had been Eugene Ivanov who had done the asking.

At a Christmas Eve party not long after, Keeler happened to meet former Labour MP John Lewis who, unbeknown to her, held a deep grudge against Stephen Ward. During the 1950s Ward had introduced one of Lewis's girlfriends to another of his contacts, a lesbian, and the girlfriend had run off with her.

Lewis convinced Keeler that he had the experience and the connections to help her. He invited her over to his house and when she turned up he told her she could end up in jail for her role in the saga and she told him everything she had told Eddowes plus details of her liaisons with Profumo. Realising he had uncovered a potent political weapon, Lewis told his friend George Wigg, who was a sitting Labour MP, what he had learned.

Keeler quickly fell out with Lewis and on January 22, 1963, through a contact of Mandy Rice-Davies, she met up with a journalist from the Sunday Pictorial, which became the Sunday Mirror later that year, and he suggested that her story could be worth more than £1000. She went with him to the newspaper's offices and discussed the story further before handing the journalist one of the love letters she had received from Profumo – the 'Darling' letter.

A police officer later called round to Keeler's Great Cumberland Place flat to take her statement about the shooting. During the interview, Detective Sergeant John Burrows asked her how she had come to know Profumo. She told him some of the story including mentions of Ivanov, and also that she had left the 'Darling' letter with the Sunday Pictorial.

On January 29, Yevgeny Ivanov left London, never to return. Edgecombe's trial was then postponed until March 14 and Keeler, fearful of what was happening, decided to flee the country.

Another of Keeler's friends, Paul Mann, drove her first to Paris and then through France and on into south-east Spain. The pair of them stayed in a village near Alicante. Back in Britain, Johnny Edgecombe's trial began at the Old Bailey but Keeler, called as a witness, failed to show up to give evidence. The case having already hit the national headlines, this caused further scandal.

Profumo denies 'impropriety'

MP George Wigg made a lengthy speech to the House of Commons on March 21, 1963, about freedom of the press relating to reports of spies and at the end he raised the issue of rumours about Christine Keeler, the shooting, and "the minister concerned" and challenged Home Secretary Henry Brooke to make a statement

Witness statement

Detective Sergeant John Burrows filed the following witness statement after interviewing Christine Keeler in January 1963.

She said that Doctor Ward was a procurer of young women for gentlemen in high places and was sexually perverted; that he had a country cottage at Cliveden to which some of these women were taken to meet important men – the cottage was on the estate of Lord Astor; that he had introduced her to Mr John Profumo and that she had an association with him; that Mr Profumo had written a number of letters to her on War Office notepaper and that she was still in possession of one of these letters which was being considered for publication in the Sunday Pictorial to whom she had sold her life story for £1000. She also said that on one occasion when she was going to meet Mr Profumo, Ward had asked her to discover from him the date on which certain atomic secrets were to be handed over to West Germany by the Americans, and that this was at the time of the Cuban missile crisis; and that she had been introduced by Ward to the naval attaché of the Soviet embassy and had met him on a number of occasions.

Bodyguard Robin Drury escorts Christine Keeler from her London home on June 7. She was leaving for the Old Bailey hearing at which Aloysius 'Lucky' Gordon was sentenced to three years for beating her.

Lord Alfred Denning, Master of the Rolls, who compiled a 55,000 word report on the security aspects of the Profumo Affair.

Stephen Ward attending his Old Bailey trial to face vice charges.

Profumo and his wife en route to the House of Commons on March 22, 1963, to make his 'personal statement'.

about them. A discussion followed where several MPs including Labour's Barbara Castle mentioned Keeler's disappearance and the keenness with which the press were pursuing her story. The next day, as parliament began, John Profumo stood up in the House and said he wanted to make a personal statement on his relationship with Christine Keeler.

He said: "I last saw Miss Keeler in December 1961, and I have not seen her since. I have no idea where she is now. Any suggestion that I was in any way connected with or responsible for her absence from the trial at the Old Bailey is wholly and completely untrue. My wife and I first met Miss Keeler at a house party in July 1961 at Cliveden. Among a number of people there was Dr Stephen Ward, whom we already knew slightly, and a Mr Ivanov, who was an attaché at the Russian embassy. The only other occasion that my wife or I met Mr Ivanov was for a moment at the official reception for Major Gagarin at the Soviet embassy. My wife and I had a standing invitation to visit Dr Ward.

"Between July and December 1961, I met Miss Keeler on about half a dozen occasions at Dr Ward's flat, when I called to see him and his friends. Miss Keeler and I were on friendly terms. There was no impropriety whatsoever in my acquaintanceship with Miss Keeler."

The grave misdemeanour

The national newspapers printed Profumo's denials and Keeler flew home from Spain with a team from the Daily Express. She made contact with Stephen Ward again and he persuaded her to sign away the film rights to her story.

An Old Bailey hearing was convened regarding Keeler's non-attendance of the Edgecombe trial and she was interviewed again by Detective Sergeant Burrows, this time at Marylebone Police Station and with Chief Inspector Samuel Herbert also present. An interview with MI5 followed. It was announced that an investigation into the affair would begin on May 30 and Profumo wrote to the Prime Minister Harold Macmillan on June 4 to offer his resignation.

He wrote of his relationship with Keeler: "In my statement I said there had been no impropriety in this association. To my very deep regret I have to admit that this was not true, and that I misled you and my colleagues and the House. I ask you to understand that I did this to protect, as I thought, my wife and family, who were equally misled, as were my professional advisors. I have come to realise that by this deception I have been guilty of a grave misdemeanour."

Macmillan wrote back: "Dear Profumo, this is a great tragedy for you, your family and your friends. Nevertheless, I am sure you will understand that in the circumstances, I have no alternative but to advise the Queen to accept your resignation."

Profumo's resignation was made public the following day and the media circus continued throughout another court case, Lucky Gordon's trial for causing actual bodily harm to Keeler. He was found guilty and sentenced to three years in jail but he appealed. Meanwhile, Stephen Ward was arrested on June 8 and charged with five criminal offences: three counts of living on the earnings of prostitution, one of inciting Christine Keeler to procure a girl then under 21 years of age to have unlawful sexual intercourse with a third person, and one of attempting to procure a girl then under 21 years of age to have sexual intercourse with a third person. His trial began on June 13 and lasted until July 31.

Macmillan called in Lord Alfred Denning, a high ranking judge, to investigate the Profumo Affair on June 21 and he started hearing evidence on June 24. Among the witnesses he interviewed were Keeler twice, Profumo also twice and Stephen Ward three times. He also took statements from newspaper editors, various friends of Ward and even the prime minister. During Ward's trial, the jury was told Keeler had

Christine Keeler in 1965, two years after the Profumo Affair made her a household name in Britain.

Mariella Novotny, 19, with her night club owner husband, Horace Dibben, 55, in 1961 after her return to London.

Mariella Novotny and JFK

US Defence Secretary Robert McNamara was concerned about Christine Keeler's possible involvement with American servicemen but he'd also been forced to deal with concerns about President John F Kennedy's alleged involvement with another British girl – the 'Chief Whip' herself, Mariella Novotny. She had travelled to New York in 1960 for modelling work, it was suggested, at the behest of Stephen Ward who was a friend of her husband. She went with TV producer Harry Towers and through him met Peter Lawford, Kennedy's brother-in-law. In this way she is said to have met Kennedy before his swearing in as president, and started sleeping with him. On one occasion, it is claimed, she dressed up as a nurse with another girl and Kennedy was their only patient. She was deported back to London in 1961, after being charged with loitering for the purposes of prostitution, and then started hosting her sex parties. The FBI had been watching Novotny and had drawn links between her and Ward.

paid for telephone calls she had made while using his flat with money she was given by her rich male acquaintances. On June 28, Mandy Rice-Davies, then 19, gave evidence. A defence barrister put it to her that one of the men she claimed to have slept with, Lord Astor, had denied any involvement with her. She replied: "Well, he would, wouldn't he." The court burst out laughing.

On the last day of the trial Ward took an overdose of Nembutal sleeping tablets. He was found guilty even though he was in a coma at St Stephen's Hospital in Fulham Road, Chelsea, and died on August 3. He left a suicide note which said: "It's really more than I can stand. The horror day after day at court and in the streets. It's not only fear. It's a wish not to let them get me. I'd rather get myself."

The aftermath

Less than two months later, on September 25, Denning's report was published. It featured chapter headings such as "the Cliveden weekend and its sequel", "Stephen Ward helping the Russians", "the slashing and shooting" and "the disappearance of Christine Keeler". It concluded that Profumo's affair with Keeler had not endangered national security but Denning later described Ward as "the most evil man I have ever met". In October, Macmillan was diagnosed, wrongly as it turned out, with inoperable prostate cancer and he resigned on October 18.

Christine Keeler published her first autobiography, Nothing But… Christine Keeler, in 1983 while she worked in telephone sales in Fulham. She later worked for a dry-cleaning business in Battersea. The most recent edition of her autobiography, Secrets and Lies, written with Douglas Thompson, was published in 2012.

John Profumo, having resigned from the Government, went to work as a volunteer cleaning toilets at a charity aimed at tackling poverty, Toynbee Hall, based in London's East End. He was aided by his wife and eventually became the charity's top fundraiser, being made a Commander of the Order of the British Empire – CBE – in 1975. He died in 2006 aged 91.

Yevgeny 'Eugene' Ivanov's work in Britain did not meet with the approval of the Soviet authorities. His wife left him after details of his involvement with Keeler were published and by 1993, aged 67, he was suffering from the effects of a lifetime of alcohol abuse. He died on January 17, 1994.

Harold 'Kim' Philby gave Britain's secrets to the Russians.

CHAPTER 3

TO CATCH A SPY (OR NOT)

The Third Man revealed

FOR YOUR EYES ONLY

It had been a long time coming but 1963 finally saw the unmasking of the most dangerous spy ever to infiltrate the British establishment. The notorious 'third man' was not a Russian though — he had been the chief of British secret intelligence in the US, he had an OBE and his dad knew Lawrence of Arabia...

Dozens of British secret agents – the real life James Bonds – were captured, tortured and killed by the Soviets using information supplied by Harold Adrian Russell 'Kim' Philby, an upper class renegade who despised the British establishment as much as he was a product of it.

Born in 1912, his schooling was typical of the ruling elite. He attended the Aldro preparatory school at Meads in Eastbourne, Sussex, then Westminster School, then Trinity College at Cambridge. His upbringing, however, was anything but typical. His early years were spent in the Punjab province of India under British rule since his father, Harry St John Bridger Philby, worked for the Indian Civil Service.

St John Philby, also known as Jack Philby and later Sheikh Abdullah, was a fervent socialist. He too studied at Westminster School where one of his friends was Jawaharlal Nehru, who later became Prime Minister of India. He married his first wife Dora Johnston in Lahore in 1910 with his cousin Bernard Law Montgomery, later to become the Second World War Field Marshal 'Monty' Montgomery, as best man.

St John nicknamed his son 'Kim' after the poverty stricken hero of the 1901 Rudyard Kipling novel of the same name. In 1915 he joined the British administration in Baghdad and was sent on a mission to meet with Ibn Saud, later the first king of Saudi Arabia, in 1917. In 1921 he was named head of the Secret Service for the British Mandate of Palestine and in 1922 returned to Britain for talks with Sir Winston Churchill, King George V and the Prince of Wales regarding the Palestine question. While he was in the Middle East he studied both the archaeology and the wildlife of the region and sent numerous specimens back to the British Museum.

As the 1920s wore on, he was deeply involved with the foundation of the Saudi state and the brokering of oil deals which netted both the Saudis and himself a fortune. He had always been contemptuous of the British establishment but now he turned his back on it completely, converted to Islam and took a second wife – a slave girl given to him by King Ibn. Back at home it was said that he had 'gone native'. St John was Kim Philby's role model and his mentor. He was taught from an early age to hate the class system which dominated British society even as he took advantage of it.

Cambridge spy Guy Burgess.

Trinity College at Cambridge University where Kim Philby met Guy Burgess, Donald Maclean and Anthony Blunt.

The first man – Guy Burgess

Three of Kim Philby's fellow spies have been definitively identified – Guy Burgess, Donald Maclean and Anthony Blunt. It is strongly suspected that there was in fact a 'fifth man' but his identity has never been conclusively proven. Some suggest that he was John Cairncross though other names have also been put forward.

Guy Burgess, born in April 1911 in Devonport, Plymouth, was a flamboyant drunk who was as openly homosexual as it was possible to be at a time when it was still illegal to be gay. He worked as a radio producer for the BBC after leaving Cambridge University. He was recruited as a propaganda specialist during the Second World War by SIS. He joined the Foreign Office news department in 1944. When Hector McNeil became Secretary of State for the Foreign Office in 1946, Burgess became his secretary and was able to let an NKVD operative take photographs of top secret Government documents. He later went on to work in the Far East before being posted to the British embassy in Washington DC with Kim Philby.

After his defection, he struggled to adjust to life in the USSR and in 1959 he tried to return to Britain to visit his dying mother. This request was denied and he died himself in 1963 after years of alcohol abuse, his body being repatriated to West Meon in Hampshire where he is buried in the St John the Evangelist Churchyard.

Forging the Cambridge spy ring

Joining Trinity College in 1929, aged 17, he read history and economics and became treasurer of the Cambridge University Socialist Society. He had a stutter and was not regarded as gifted academically, but contemporaries noted that he had a quick and analytical mind.

The following year he met fellow student Guy Burgess, a big personality, loud mouthed and funny but also a gifted scholar and a Marxist. Donald Maclean joined the university in 1931. He was a year younger than Philby and the son of a Scottish Labour politician. These three knew and socialised with Anthony Blunt, who was five years older than Philby and became a don specialising in the history of art in 1932.

The early 1930s saw the Great Depression. By the end of 1930 unemployment was spiralling out of control as demand for British products dried up all over the world. More than 20% of the workforce – 2.5 million people – were out of a job. There were hunger marches to London in 1929, 1930, and the largest, the National Hunger March, was in 1932. Labour Ramsay MacDonald formed a coalition government with Stanley Baldwin's Conservatives and in the process was seen as betraying his left wing values.

The young intellectuals of Cambridge University perceived that capitalism had failed. As Hitler's fascists took power in Germany, Philby, Burgess, Maclean, Blunt and others came around to the idea that communism was the only way forward. After Philby graduated with a 2:1 in economics, he travelled to Vienna to help refugees already fleeing the Nazis. Here he met Litzi Friedmann, an Austrian communist. They were married in February 1934. Friedmann then introduced Philby to her friend Edith Tudor Hart who persuaded him to help fight the fascists by working for Soviet intelligence.

She in turn arranged for him to meet a man named Otto. They first met on a bench in Regent's Park in June 1934. His first job for Otto was to draw up a list of well-connected left-wingers like himself who might be open to working for the Russians. There were seven names on Philby's list including Guy Burgess and Donald Maclean who were now both openly communist. Both were approached first by Philby and then by Otto – whose real name was Arnold Deutsch. Blunt was recruited in 1937. Otto made it clear that they had to convince the authorities that they had turned aside from their earlier left-wing leanings.

Burgess got a respectable job and joined a right wing organisation, the Anglo-German Fellowship, Maclean joined the civil service and Blunt furthered his career in the art world. Philby signed up to learn Russian and then worked for the *World Review of Reviews*, a right wing magazine. Philby and Friedmann separated but remained friends and then he too joined the Anglo-German Fellowship before making trips to Berlin to meet with prominent Nazis. His right-wing credentials were starting to look impressive.

In 1937, during the Spanish Civil War, Philby worked as a foreign correspondent for the *Times*. He reported from the fascist forces of General Francisco Franco. At the same time, he supplied reports to both the Russian NKVD and the British Secret Intelligence Service (SIS), now known as MI6. Otto was replaced as Philby's controller by a Hungarian Soviet citizen Theodore Maly, then Latvian Ozolin-Haskins, then Lithuanian Boris Shpak. Each of these were sent, one after the next, back to Moscow and executed by Stalin during his purges.

Among the intelligence gathered by Philby were details of German Messerschmitt Bf 109 fighter aircraft and Panzer tanks, Franco's personal security arrangements and the potential for a German attack on Gibraltar. In December 1937, Philby was travelling in a car when it was hit by a shell. The others were killed but Philby survived with a head wound and was given a medal by Franco himself on March 2, 1938.

British double agent Guy Burgess as a young man.

Donald Maclean at Cambridge University on November 14, 1931.

Prime Minister Ramsay MacDonald, Britain's first ever Labour Party leader, shortly before he stepped down in 1935. He was believed to have betrayed his left wing supporters.

King Ibn Saud of Saudi Arabia pictured on February 2, 1930. Harry St John Bridger Philby, Kim Philby's father, was one of his closest advisers.

Changing the world

Philby returned to England in July 1939, still working for the Times, and when Britain declared war on Germany in September he lost contact with his surviving Soviet controllers. He travelled to France with the British expeditionary forces and filed newspaper reports from the military headquarters in Boulogne until he was evacuated on May 21, 1940. He returned briefly to report for both the Times and the Daily Telegraph on the French military forces still resisting in Cherbourg and Brest before returning home again shortly before the Germans defeated them.

His next position was at the War Office where he met up again with Burgess. By July he was working for the Special Operations Executive in Hampshire training newly recruited sabotage agents in the art of writing clandestine propaganda. At this point the Russian managed to re-establish contact with him and asked how many of the agents were being trained to enter the USSR. Philby replied: none.

Thanks to his position in SIS, Philby was then able to supply the Russians with German communications decrypted by the British codebreakers working at Bletchley Park. In this way, Stalin received advance warning about German plans to invade the Soviet Union and about Japanese plans to attack Singapore instead of the USSR. The latter enabled Stalin to redeploy forces which had been earmarked for the defence of the Soviet Union in the east to Moscow, giving Red Army general Marshal Zhukov the forces he needed to prevent the Germans from capturing the Russian capital city.

With his British bosses still completely in the dark about his extracurricular activities, Philby was next moved on to command the Spain and Portugal branch of SIS's Section V – the department responsible for counter-intelligence. He was now running a whole network of spies operating across the region. His perceived success in this led to his being given even greater responsibility. He was made the deputy head of Section V and given overall command of agents operating across Italy and North Africa in addition to his other charges. He became the head of Section V in late 1944, aged 32.

At this stage Philby was supplying documents to the Russians in huge quantities but his position was endangered in August 1945 when an undercover NKVD agent posing as a diplomat at the Soviet embassy in Istanbul, Konstantin Volkov, approached SIS and offered to hand over the names of three Soviet agents operating inside Britain, two of whom worked in the Foreign Office and another who worked for SIS itself – in counter-intelligence. In return, he wanted asylum in Cyprus for himself and his wife.

Details of this deal were relayed to Section V where Philby read them, informed his Soviet controllers and persuaded his colleagues that he should fly out personally to meet Volkov. He went as slowly as he could, finally arriving there three weeks after Volkov's approach, by which time Volkov had already been captured, taken to Moscow, tortured and shot.

Philby was then made head of SIS in Turkey. Ironically, his position was similar to that of Volkov – he posed as a diplomat at the British Consulate in Istanbul with his second wife Aileen and their children at his side. Neither Philby nor his wife particularly enjoyed the posting and both smoked and drank heavily.

Two years later, Philby was promoted again, this time to become the head of British intelligence in Washington DC under a similar covert arrangement to that with which he had become familiar in Turkey. In this role he was even more valuable to the Soviets since he was able to see and pass on top secret communications between high ranking intelligence officials of both nations. He was also the chief liaison between SIS and the CIA.

The second man — Donald Maclean

Born on May 25, 1913, in Marylebone, London, Donald Maclean joined the civil service after leaving Cambridge with a first class degree in modern languages. He joined the Foreign Office in London and fell in love with the Soviet agent sent to control him – Kitty Harris. He was then posted to Paris in 1940 where he met his future wife Melinda Marling who was a liberal idealist. They were married in June that year, even as French resistance to the German invasion collapsed, and escaped back to Britain on a warship.

Back in London, Maclean continued his work for the Foreign Office where he sent the Russians details of the British Tube Alloys project which would lead to the creation of the first atomic bomb. In 1944 he was posted to Washington DC as first secretary where he was Stalin's primary source of information about Anglo-American relations. He was appointed head of chancery at the British embassy in Cairo in 1948 before suffering a nervous breakdown and being sent back to London.

In Moscow after his defection he fitted in well and became a model Soviet citizen. Melinda and their children joined him and he became a specialist on British home and foreign policy and relations between the Soviet Union and NATO.

Melinda left him in 1979 and returned to the West with their children. She died aged 93 in 2010 in New York. Maclean died of a heart attack in 1983 and his ashes were returned to Britain.

Donald Maclean fitted in well in Moscow.

The missing diplomats affair

Donald Maclean, Philby's fellow spy, had been working at the British embassy in Washington since 1944. During that time he had been able to tell the Russians about progress on American atomic weapons and pass on communications between prime ministers and presidents.

In 1948 he was given a new posting – to Cairo in Egypt – and it was here that the pressures of living a double life under constant scrutiny caught up with him. He suffered a breakdown and was send back to London to recuperate.

Shortly before this, in 1949, the FBI had begun the Venona Project, a secret operation to decode messages sent between the Soviet consulate in New York and Moscow. They discovered that between 1944 and 1945 a British embassy official codenamed Homer had been sending classified information to the Russians. They rapidly whittled down the possible suspects to four names including Donald Maclean. It wasn't too much of a leap to narrow this down further to just one name since it was well known that during that period Maclean's wife had been living in New York and that he regularly travelled from Washington DC to visit her.

As head of British intelligence in the US, details of the Venona Project were available to Kim Philby and he quickly realised that Maclean was close to being unmasked. In July 1950, Guy Burgess became second secretary to Philby's first secretary in the US but was barely able to conceal his hatred for the American way of life and like Maclean his ability to mask his true political views was close to being entirely eroded away. He was becoming a liability.

Philby decided to send Burgess back to London to warn Maclean in person that he needed to get out of the country. Philby specifically warned Burgess against fleeing himself because that would put Philby himself under direct suspicion. Burgess agreed to the plan and managed to get himself recalled to London in a way that would not raise suspicion – by getting three parking tickets in a single day and then trying to use diplomatic immunity to avoid paying them.

Once he was back in London, Burgess met up with Maclean. A few days later, Philby went to the embassy in the morning and went into the office of Geoffrey Paterson. Philby wrote: "He looked grey. 'Kim,' he said in a half whisper, 'the bird has flown'. I registered dawning horror (I hope). 'What bird? Not Maclean?' 'Yes,' he answered. 'But there's worse than that… Guy Burgess has gone with him'. At that, my consternation was no pretence."

Burgess had gone round to Maclean's house in Tatsfield, Surrey, on May 25 and at 10.15pm the pair of them had driven to Southampton and boarded the Falaise, which was just about to leave. Burgess abandoned their car in a way that suggested he did not intend to come back for it and the pair of them then travelled to France before continuing rapidly on to Moscow. They never came back.

The fall and rise of Kim Philby

Philby's close association with Burgess immediately brought him under suspicion. SIS was sure that someone, a 'third man', had tipped off Maclean that he was about to be brought in, and the fact that Burgess had gone too set alarm bells ringing at last. Just over a month after their disappearance, in July 1951, Philby resigned from SIS. He underwent a series of interrogations but was able to convincingly deny that he was in any way involved in the spying activities of his former colleagues. Even so, he had great difficulty in finding a new job and suspicions about him lingered – although he didn't lack for money since his father had by now become immensely wealthy through his dealings with the Saudis. He fell out of contact with his Soviet controllers and took a position with a

Thousands of hunger marchers assemble in Trafalgar Square on October 30, 1932, during the Great Depression. Scenes like this convinced the young students at Cambridge that capitalism had failed.

Bernard Law Montgomery, pictured here in later years as Field Marshal Sir Bernard 'Monty' Montgomery, was best man at Kim Philby's parents' wedding.

The third man unmasked

Philby was successfully rebuilding his career but the end was in sight. KGB operative Major Anatoliy Golitsyn defected to the US in 1961 and offered the CIA information about Soviet agents working in both the US and Britain. He claimed that Philby had been the 'third man' all along. In January 1963, SIS sent one of its operatives to interrogate him. Faced with Golitsyn's evidence, Philby offered a partial confession, saying that he had worked for the Soviets until 1946 and although he had tipped off Maclean in 1951 he had done so only as a friend.

Then Philby disappeared from Beirut. He had boarded a Soviet freighter, the *Dolmatova*, and on July 30 Soviet officials confirmed that he had been granted Soviet citizenship. Far from receiving a hero's welcome, Philby was treated with suspicion by the Russians. He was placed under guard in Moscow. It was feared that he would return to London and divulge everything to SIS. While he was kept under lock and key, Philby kept himself busy by writing his autobiography, My Silent War, which was published in Britain in 1968. He read the Times, listened to the BBC World Service and kept up with the cricket scores. In 1967, Sunday Times journalist Murray Sayle interviewed him. The spy denied being a traitor, saying: "To betray, you must first belong. I never belonged."

Four years after his interview with Sayle, Philby married his fourth wife, Rufina Ivanova Pukhova, a woman 20 years his junior. She would later describe his alcoholism in her book The Private Life of Kim Philby: The Moscow Years: "He used to begin his day with wine and then it went on and on, eternally, until it became a nightmare." The late Seventies saw him given a minor post teaching KGB officers how to pass unnoticed in British polite society. He died from heart failure in 1988 and was posthumously made a Hero of the Soviet Union.

diplomatic newspaper called the Fleet Street Letter in 1954. Philby's reputation was rescued the following year thanks to Labour MP Marcus Lipton who brought up his involvement in the missing diplomats affair during a discussion in the House of Commons on October 25, 1955.

On November 7, 1955, Foreign Minister Harold Macmillan gave a lengthy statement in the Commons addressing the issue, during which he said: "I have no reason to conclude that Mr Philby has at any time betrayed the interests of this country, or to identify him with the so-called 'third man', if, indeed, there was one."

Shortly after this statement, Philby called a press conference at the luxurious London flat of his mother, Dora, in Drayton Gardens, South Kensington, at which he proclaimed: "I have never been a communist." In the House of Commons, Lipton had withdrawn his earlier statement and said he was satisfied that his allegations about Philby were unjustified. Philby told his press conference: "I think Lipton has done the right thing. So far as I am concerned, the incident is now closed."

His name cleared, Philby was able to get work as a journalist once again and this time he was hired by the Observer and the Economist to report on developments in the Middle East from Beirut. He initially lived with his father in a village on the outskirts but when St John departed to continue his work in Saudi Arabia, he got a flat of his own in the city where he had an affair with the American wife of a correspondent for the New York Times, Eleanor Brewer. Aileen Philby died in 1957, leaving the way clear for Eleanor to divorce her husband and become Philby's third wife in 1959. Philby's father died in 1960.

The last man — Anthony Blunt

The youngest son of a vicar, Anthony Blunt was born on September 26, 1907, in Bournemouth, Dorset. He was a third cousin of Elizabeth Bowes-Lyon, the Queen Mother. As a 26-year-old, in 1933, he visited the Soviet Union. When the Second World War began, he joined the British Army and served as an intelligence officer before being rescued by the Royal Navy from Dunkirk in 1940. Later that year he was recruited by MI5 and during the war rose to the rank of major while passing sensitive intelligence documents to the Russians.

In 1945 he was given the position of Surveyor of the King's Paintings and Surveyor of the Queen's Paintings following the death of King George VI in 1952. He lost contact with his Soviet controllers and began to move in high society circles. He was friends with the head of MI5 and later MI6 Sir Dick White – he often spent Christmas at his home.

Following the defection of Burgess and Maclean in 1951, he came under suspicion and was interviewed 11 times by MI5's top interrogator Jim Skardon between 1952 and 1964 when he was finally presented with damning evidence of his spying activities – the confession of an American he had recruited for the Soviets called Michael Straight. Blunt confessed in April 1964 and the Queen was informed. In return for his full and frank confession in which he revealed the identities of four other Soviet spies operating in Britain, the Government agreed to keep his spying activities a secret for 15 years.

Margaret Thatcher finally revealed details of his activities to the House of Commons on November 15, 1979. He was stripped of his knighthood and numerous other honours before dying of heart failure at his London home in 1983 aged 75.

Queen Elizabeth II discusses some of the exhibits with Sir Anthony Blunt during her visit to the Courtauld Institute of Art, London University.

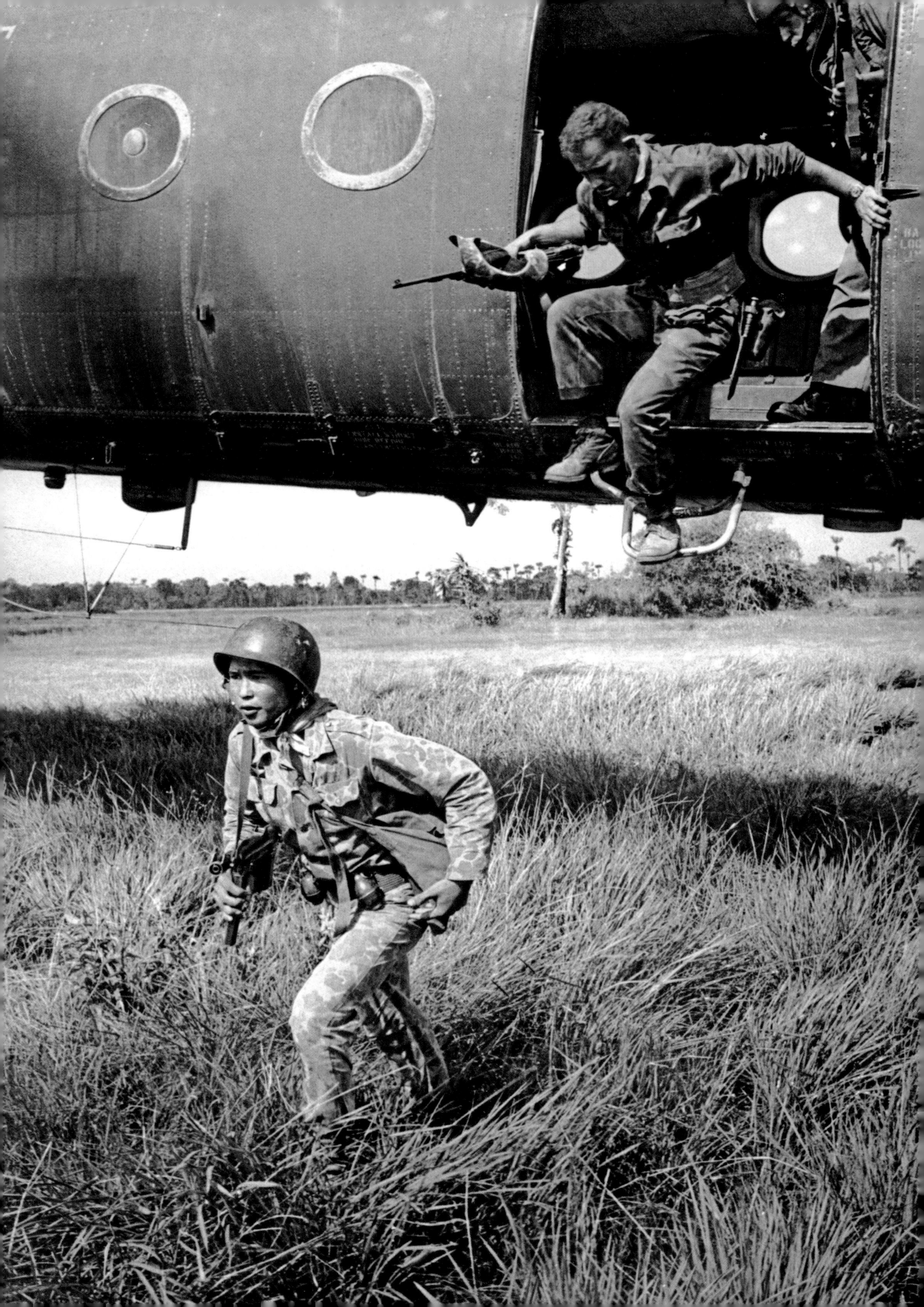

CHAPTER 4

TWO TRIBES GO TO WAR

America and the escalating war in Vietnam

A storm was gathering in Southeast Asia in 1963 that would drive a wedge between Britain and the United States. The US had been involved in Vietnam since 1950 but now it found itself propping up a dangerously weak dictator and being drawn ever deeper into a nightmarish war...

Battling the communist threat wherever it reared its ugly head was central to American foreign policy after the Second World War and in Korea this had meant engaging in front line combat with both Russian and Chinese conventional forces fighting under the banner of a much smaller state. It proved to be a horrifying experience, always one step away from escalating into full blown nuclear war, that both the Americans and the British were determined to avoid repeating. Yet the same situation was rapidly developing in Vietnam by 1963.

Before the Second World War it had been a French colony but the war had seen the French ruling merely as puppets of the Germans and their main ally in the region, the Japanese. The defeat of both Germany and Japan in 1945 left a power vacuum in Vietnam which was rapidly filled by the Viet Minh, a communist organisation formed to oppose French rule, and its charismatic leader Ho Chi Minh. Unfortunately for Minh, the Americans, British and Russians all agreed that Vietnam still belonged to the French but since the devastated French nation was in no position to reclaim it, British troops moved into the south and rearmed the surviving French forces who had been held prisoner there while the Nationalist Chinese moved into the north.

Minh tried to negotiate with the French and then won elections across the north and arranged for the French to replace the Chinese in the north on condition that they recognise the Democratic Republic of Vietnam as a semi-autonomous state within the French Union. The British and Chinese departed in March 1946, leaving the French back in charge. They immediately kicked the Viet Minh out of Hanoi and the embittered communists formed a guerrilla force to take back control of their nation.

A bloody eight-year conflict followed which left 75,581 French and several hundred thousand Viet Minh dead. US President Harry S Truman approved the formation of the Military Assistance and Advisory Group (MAAG) in 1950 which saw US military advisors working alongside the French in an effort to contain and defeat the communist forces. The war came to an abrupt end on May 7, 1954, after the Battle of Dien Bien Phu.

The battle, which lasted 57 days, saw the Viet Minh besiege a French position on a series of fortified hills. The dug-in French defenders fought off wave after wave of Viet Minh attackers on the ground from a network of trenches and emplacements while receiving supplies and reinforcements from the air. For a time it seemed as though this strategy might work but the Viet Minh were able to bring up anti-aircraft weapons to disrupt supply drops and position artillery pieces on the mountain range surrounding the base. The French perimeter defences gradually broke down and the garrison was overrun. Just a handful of French soldiers escaped into nearby Laos while the rest – 10,863 men – were captured. Four months later only 3290 survived to be repatriated, the rest having succumbed to disease or their wounds in captivity.

The garrison and the reinforcements fed into it through the course of the battle represented more than a 10th of the total French forces in the region and the crushing defeat fatally weakened the French grip on power in Vietnam.

Peace talks, which had been scheduled before the siege, began at Geneva on May 8, 1954. The resulting Geneva Accord saw Vietnam divided into two zones – the communist Democratic Republic of Vietnam in the north and the French-backed State of Vietnam in the south – with the eventual aim being national elections and unification under the winning party in 1956. France realised that it could no longer sustain its presence in the country and its combat units were steadily withdrawn. The US under President Eisenhower, fearful that the whole country could fall into communist hands and spark off a worldwide shift towards communism in developing nations – what it called the 'domino effect' – began giving substantial financial support to the south.

Earthquake McGoon and Wally – the first American casualties

Fighter pilot James McGovern and his co-pilot Wallace 'Wally' Buford were the first Americans to die in combat in Vietnam.

McGovern was a veteran who had claimed two kills, both Japanese Nakajima Ki-43 Oscars, while flying a P-51C Mustang over Shanghai during the war in occupied China in January 1945. He was nicknamed 'Earthquake McGoon' by one of his fellow pilots after a cartoon character that appeared in the American Li'l Abner comic strip.

After the war he went to work for a commercial airline called Civil Air Transport (CAT). The firm was acquired by the CIA as a front for its clandestine operations in Southeast Asia in 1949. Four years later, CAT began flying supply missions to French forces in Vietnam with French insignia painted over the company logo.

Buford was studying for an engineering degree in 1953, having flown B-24 bombers during the Second World War and C-119 Flying Boxcar transports during the Korean War. He saw a notice that the US government was looking for experienced C-119 pilots and signed up to earn $3000 a month fly missions for CAT in Vietnam.

McGovern and Buford were among two dozen American pilots assigned to fly supplies to the French garrison at Dien Bien Phu between March and May 1954.

Their C-119 was among six that took off in the direction of the siege on May 6. C-119 number 149 was carrying a howitzer artillery piece destined for Camp Isabelle, the southernmost French fire base, when it was hit twice on approach by 37mm anti-aircraft fire. The left engine and stabilizer were critically damaged. McGovern's French 'kickers' in the back of the aircraft – the men who 'kicked' out the cargo over the drop zone – immediately dumped the howitzer as McGovern shut down the burning engine.

The crippled aircraft carried on for another 75 miles on one engine, losing height all the while, before clipping a tree and cartwheeling into a wooded hillside in Laos. The crash killed McGovern, Buford and two of the four French crew. The survivors were captured by the Viet Minh and one died shortly afterwards. McGovern's remains were discovered in an unmarked grave in 2002, positively identified by forensic scientists in 2006 and finally buried in Arlington National Cemetery in Virginia, USA, in 2007.

ABOVE: Inhabitants of a newly built strategic hamlet pictured on April 16, 1963. Sometimes even the most basic American firearms were unavailable and the villagers were forced to defend themselves against Vietcong soldiers armed with automatic weapons using only long-handled machetes.

RIGHT: Captured French soldiers are marched away after their surrender at Dien Bien Phu in May 1954. More than 10,000 French troops were captured after a 55 day siege. Fewer than 3300 made it home.

James McGovern poses on the wing of his P-51 Mustang. He was one of the first two Americans to die in combat in Vietnam.

Stepping into the breach

The first shipment of American military supplies to the Republic of Vietnam arrived in January 1955, courtesy of Civil Air Transport (CAT) – a front for the CIA – and with Eisenhower's backing the Vietnamese Emperor Bao Dai appointed former civil servant, fervent Catholic and anti-communist Ngo Dinh Diem as prime minister. In July, Diem cancelled the elections which had been scheduled to unite Vietnam in 1956. He argued that no-one had been at the Geneva talks to properly represent the south – only the French.

A referendum was held in October to decide whether the State of Vietnam should continue under the rule of Bao Dai or become the Republic of Vietnam under Diem. Having rigged the results to achieve an impressive 98.2% of the 605,000 votes cast – by an eligible electorate of 405,000 people – Diem declared himself president and commander-in-chief of the republic. Eisenhower's feelings about this were mixed since although he did not want to be seen supporting a dictator, he privately felt that had the unification elections gone ahead, Ho Chi Minh would have received 80% of the votes.

American military aid was now formally and publically pledged and MAAG, limited by the Geneva Accord to not more than 342 people, set to work training the Republic of Vietnam's soldiers and reorganising its armed forces. This process continued throughout 1956 while Diem began implementing a series of controversial land reforms which upset many South Vietnamese people living in outlying rural areas and resulted in the beginnings of a low level insurgency against his rule. This grew and gained strength in 1957, developing into a campaign of terrorist bombings and assassinations including several attempts on Diem's life. By the end of the year, 400 Republic of Vietnam officials had been killed although the deaths were publically ascribed to the Viet Minh rather than internal factions of the south itself.

The early months of 1958 saw the north conducting raids against the south and in March Ho Chi Minh appealed for all Vietnamese to unite under his rule and declared a People's War against Diem's government. The raids continued to grow in intensity until the south found itself fighting a small war against guerrillas along its northern borders. At the same time, infiltrators from the north began to organise the insurgency which had already arisen among Diem's opponents among his own people.

MAAG had organised the Army of the Republic of Vietnam (ARVN) along American lines – a conventional force set up to fight battles against a conventional foe – but now it faced a threat from within as well as without. US Special Forces were therefore brought in under the umbrella of MAAG to train ARVN forces in counterinsurgency techniques.

January 25, 1960, saw the first large scale assault on the south by communist forces. An ARVN base at Tay Ninh was attacked and 23 soldiers were killed. American intelligence specialists believed that the north now had three main objectives – to incite a revolt within the ARVN, to establish a 'popular front' government in the south and to force Diem into taking such Draconian measures to remain in power that the South Vietnamese would rise up and overthrow him.

This latter objective seemed to be achieving itself. Diem's critics and even his own advisors pleaded with him to reform his government, which was dictatorial and corrupt – but he simply responded by shutting down several opposition newspapers and arresting the journalists who produced them. Attacks from the north continued and on May 5, 1960, at the end of Eisenhower's second and last term as president, MAAG strength was finally increased from 342 to 685 personnel.

John F Kennedy beat Richard Nixon in November to become the 35th president of the United States and inherited the deteriorating Vietnam situation. Kennedy was preoccupied with matters elsewhere but was keen to pay the communist north back for the terrorist attacks it was perceived to have been carrying out in the south. He gave the order after his inauguration on January 28, 1961, but by mid-March very little had been achieved. The order was given again, and this time Kennedy expressly required the CIA to begin its own guerrilla attacks over the border in North Vietnam.

As a result, a new unit code named 'Jungle Jim' but formally known as the 4400th Combat Crew Training Squadron was established to begin a series of strikes on the north in support of ARVN ground forces, Operation Farm Gate, while ostensibly training South Vietnamese air crew. The squadron consisted of 350 men equipped with 16 C-47 Skytrain transports, eight B-26 Invader bombers and eight T-28 Trojan propeller-driven trainers which had been re-equipped for ground attack missions. The Viet Minh became known as the Vietcong at around this time, to distinguish between the force founded to oust the French and the insurgents now faced by the ARVN, although in practice they were one and the same.

Frustrated with the CIA's lack of progress in Vietnam and its failure during the Bay of Pigs fiasco in Cuba, Kennedy transferred responsibility for operations such as Farm Gate to the Department of Defence in June 1961.

December 22 saw the death of the first American soldier officially killed in action in Vietnam – Specialist Fourth Class James Thomas 'Tom' Davis. He was about 12 miles west of Saigon with 10 ARVN soldiers on a mission to monitor Vietcong radio transmissions when their truck hit a mine in the road, the subsequent explosion wrecking its rear end. It rolled a further 30 yards before stopping and was then sprayed with machine gun fire. The ARVN soldiers died as they tried to escape. Davis, in the cab, grabbed his rifle and leapt out, firing off a few rounds before he was shot in the head. Years later, President Lyndon B Johnson would describe him as "the first American to fall in defence of our freedom in Vietnam".

Quang Duc, a Buddhist monk, burns himself to death on a Saigon street on June 11, 1963, in protest at the persecution of Buddhists by the South Vietnamese government. This iconic image by Malcolm Browne won a Pulitzer prize and horrified President Kennedy.

The Strategic Hamlet Program

The day after Specialist Davis's death, 82 US Army Piasecki CH-21 Shawnee helicopters – better known as 'flying bananas' due to their distinctive shape – were committed to Operation Chopper, the first airborne assault of the war in Vietnam. They carried 1000 ARVN paratroopers to the location of a suspected Vietcong base about 10 miles west of Saigon, not far from where Davis was ambushed, resulting in the capture of a radio station.

While this overt US military support was being freely given to the Republic of Vietnam, a far more ambitious project intended to keep the Vietcong out of the south was being drawn up. The Strategic Hamlet Program was the brainchild of British counterinsurgency specialist Sir Robert Thompson, a veteran of the successful British effort to win 'hearts and minds' and defeat communists in Malaya between 1948 and 1960. He had been sent to the Republic of Vietnam by Prime Minister Harold Macmillan at the personal request of President Diem to lead the British Advisory Mission to South Vietnam. Here he met Kennedy's representative, the director of the State Department's Bureau of Intelligence and Research Roger Hilsman.

Thompson's idea was to take existing villages, reorganise them and fortify them to create a defensive perimeter across the north of the republic. The villagers themselves would be given guns and taught how to use them against Vietcong forces while manning the defences – which would consist of walls and earthworks. The peasants would also get a radio to call in ARVN reinforcements at the first sign of trouble. A mobile ARVN response team would then be scrambled and sent to quickly relieve the besieged village, fighting off the Vietcong attackers.

These hamlets would work in cooperation with one another, the programme slowly being expanded in what was described as an 'oil blot' fashion. Once the defensive system was in place, the secure villages could then become centres where peasants' lives could be improved through education, financial support and trade and their leaders could be linked directly to the central government.

Kennedy liked the idea, which was presented to him in a policy document entitled A Strategic Concept for South Vietnam, and gave it his seal of approval. Diem also liked the sound of it and began rapidly implementing it at the beginning of 1962. By September 1962, 3225 strategic hamlets had been built – most of them from scratch rather than being upgrades of existing villages. To populate these new settlements, around 4.3 million people were uprooted from their homes and forced to relocate. Ten months later, in July 1963, 8.5 million people were estimated to be living in 7205 hamlets.

Many of these people had had their own homes burned to the ground in front of them prior to resettlement and to make matters worse many were ancestor worshippers who were forced to leave behind their ancestors' graves.

The original Thompson plan had called for any peasants who had to be relocated to be financially compensated but in many cases the government troops doing the resettling pocketed the money and shot anyone who resisted. The geographical location of some hamlets was found to be unsuitable due to poor soil or flooding and the settlements had to be abandoned as quickly as they had been established.

The incredible rate of hamlet growth completely overwhelmed the government and prevented the ARVN offering any meaningful defence for the hamlets' inhabitants. Vietcong forces armed with assault weapons were able to overrun the settlements while the villagers' frantic calls for support went unanswered. It wasn't long before the villagers were simply handing over their US-supplied weapons to the guerrilla fighters and keeping quiet about it whenever the ARVN did show up. Roger Hilsman himself said that the project leaders appointed by Diem were operating under a "total misunderstanding of what the programme should try to do" and by the end of 1963 it was estimated that just 20% of the newly constructed hamlets were still under Republic of Vietnam control.

Even where hamlets remained loyal to the government, there was a simmering resentment among the millions who had been forced to leave their homes behind. It was clear by mid-1963 that the Strategic Hamlet Program, which had seen a total of 8600 hamlets constructed, had been a failure. The full extent of this failure was only revealed later when the US acquired Republic of Vietnam documents showing that only 20% of hamlets supposedly completed by the government actually met the minimum required standard of readiness to repel an attack. The beginning of 1964 saw all mention of the programme quietly dropped from official US correspondence and most hamlets were abandoned as their inhabitants either returned to their former homes or fled to escape the Vietcong

ABOVE LEFT: A pair of CH-21 Shawnee helicopters of the 57th US Army transport company flying an early morning mission loaded with South Vietnamese soldiers over rice paddies on November 16, 1962. Along with the M113 personnel carrier, the CH-21 was the mostly commonly used American military vehicle during the early stages of the war in Vietnam.

ABOVE: US Marines Captain William F Bethel, right, shows South Vietnamese marines how to use a flamethrower during exercises held near Saigon. When America entered the war in Vietnam it brought with it a vast array of modern weaponry.

LEFT: President Ngo Dinh Diem reviewing his forces. Diem controlled all the key military appointments in South Vietnam and it was common practice for officers to convert to his religion, Catholicism, if they wanted a promotion.

LEFT: Troops under the command of rebel generals fire heavy machine guns at the presidential palace in Saigon during a battle to overthrow regime of President Ngo Dinh Diem on November 1, 1963. The attack ended in the collapse of the Diem Government and left a power vacuum which America was forced to fill.

A South Vietnamese soldier almost entirely equipped with US-supplied gear pictured inside the reception room of the captured Presidential Palace. The jubilation on his face at the fall of Diem was a reflection of popular feeling at the time.

The first major battle

The arrival of large numbers of US helicopters and M113 armoured personnel carriers (APCs) in South Vietnam at the end of 1961 enabled ARVN forces to strike rapidly at the Vietcong wherever they showed themselves. Equipped with a mixed bag of guns captured from the French during the early stages of the conflict and even from the Soviets and Japanese during the Second World War, the Vietcong lacked anything that could punch a hole in an M113 and were forced to retreat whenever one turned up.

During the course of 1962 this superior mobility resulted in a number of victories for the ARVN and the most successful of its fighting forces was the 7th Infantry Division under Colonel Biu Ding Dam and US advisor Lieutenant Colonel John Paul Vann.

Radio transmissions intercepted between December 28 and 30 indicated a Vietcong headquarters in a strategic hamlet called Ap Tan Thoi in Dinh Tuong Province – not far from where the 7th was based – and Dam was ordered to attack. The plan, Operation Duc Thang I, was simple. The ARVN would attack from three directions at once. Three companies of the 11th Infantry Regiment would join Dam's 7th in attacking from the north by helicopter, a regiment of civil guards would approach from the south and more infantry in M113s would come up from the southwest. Reinforcements would be available by helicopter if needed.

Thanks to intelligence operatives working in Saigon, the Vietcong knew they were coming and prepared concealed positions both at Ap Tan Thoi and Ap Bac, another strategic hamlet a mile away to the south. They also made preparations to take on M113s and helicopters.

At 7am on January 2, 1963, the first ARVN troopers arrived by helicopter and the civil guard began their approach on foot. When the latter got within 100ft of Ap Bac, the Vietcong opened fire and shot dead several men including the company commander. The rest were pinned down. Soldiers from the 11th were also attacked at close range and forced to take cover.

At 9.30am, Vann was flying overhead in a light aircraft and Dam asked him to point out suitable landing zones for his reinforcements east and west of Ap Bac. Vann picked a site 1000ft to the west of the hamlet and gave instructions to another L-19 that was leading 10 CH-21 helicopters with the ARVN reinforcements on board. The pilots of these aircraft however landed just 600ft from the hamlet – close to foxholes where Vietcong machine guns had been dug in. All of the aircraft suffered multiple hits. Five UH-1 Huey helicopter gunships escorting the transports strafed the Vietcong with rockets but could not deter them from shooting up the CH-21s as the troops tried to get out.

One 'flying banana' took so much damage it couldn't get off the ground so a second came back to rescue its American crew. This too was grounded. Next a Huey flew in but concentrated fire blew off its main rotor. It flipped over and crashed as a third CH-21 was grounded.

The pinned down ARVN soldiers were refusing to move by 10.30am. Air strikes were called in and two Douglas AD-6 Skyraiders dropped high explosive bombs and napalm on Ap Bac's small thatched houses but the Vietcong held their ground.

Next it was the turn of the M113 APCs. Boggy terrain delayed their advance while a fourth CH-21 was downed during another rescue attempt. When the M113s finally arrived at 1.30pm, Vietcong snipers inside the hamlet picked off their exposed gun crews one by one until 14 crewmen were dead. The trapped airmen were finally rescued but a frontal assault with M113s failed and they withdrew at 2.30pm.

Vann flew to the regional capital and asked General Huynh Van Cao to help by sending in airborne troops to the east. Cao agreed to send the 8th Airborne Battalion in, but to the west rather than the east, and at 4pm 300 ARVN paratroopers arrived on board C-123 Provider transports. At the moment before their jump, the pilots of the aircraft turned to dodge fire coming from the ground but in doing so they succeeded in dropping the paratroopers and their American advisors right in front of the Vietcong positions and they suffered heavy casualties – 19 killed and 33 wounded. The survivors launched several attacks but failed to dislodge the enemy.

As night fell, the Vietcong escaped to the east across the site where Vann had wanted to land the paratroopers. Asked about Operation Duc Thang I later, Vann said: "It was a miserable damn performance, just like it always is. These people won't listen. They make the same mistake over and over again in the same way."

ARVN casualties included 83 dead and more than 100 wounded. Three Americans were killed and eight wounded. The Vietcong lost 18 men and 39 were wounded. It was the South's first major defeat but would not be its last and the Vietcong, having proven they could take on the South and win, gained considerable prestige.

US servicemen lift one of six flag covered caskets of fallen comrades from a truck on October 15, 1963. Casualties among the ever growing team of US military advisors were beginning to mount towards the end of the year.

The sacred heart

Having been immolated for the cause of religious freedom in Vietnam, Thich Quang Duc's body was taken away by his fellow monks and given a proper cremation. After 10 hours in the furnace however, it was found that while the rest of him had turned to ashes, his heart had remained. The charred but intact organ was taken to a temple and put in a glass chalice. Its miraculous survival came to symbolise the unbreakable heart of the Buddhist movement in South Vietnam and Duc came to be regarded as a Bodhisattva or 'enlightened being'. The heart itself was captured by ARVN Special Forces soldiers shortly after being taken to the temple and eventually put in a vault by the Vietnamese State Bank. It still exists today at a museum in Ho Chi Minh City.

The Buddhist Crisis

President Diem's Catholic faith put him in a religious minority in a country which was more than 70% Buddhist but he persecuted Buddhists at every turn. His government was openly biased in favour of Catholics and the Catholic Church was Vietnam's largest landowner. Its members got tax cuts, preferential treatment in the handing out of civil contracts, greater land allocation and a far greater share of the US aid that was pouring into the country by 1963. ARVN officers converted to Catholicism if they wanted to get on and some entire villages converted to avoid resettlement to a strategic hamlet.

On May 7, 1963, Major Dang Sy, the Catholic commander of the Hue garrison banned Buddhists from flying their flag the following day, which was Phat Dan – the birthday of Buddhism's founder Gautama Buddha – but Vatican flags put up for a Christian celebration weeks earlier were allowed to remain in place.

On the day itself, 3000 people took part in a demonstration calling for religious equality in the centre of Hue. The demonstrators were quickly surrounded by civil guardsmen in M113s and tension grew. The soldiers were ordered to disperse the crowd and then there were two explosions. Major Sy fired his pistol into the air and his men opened fire on the crowd. Grenades were thrown and the soldiers then waded in with weapons drawn. Nine protestors were killed and among them were two children who had been crushed under the tracks of M113s.

The government blamed the explosions on Vietcong insurgents but the Buddhists held further demonstrations on May 9 and 10. Buddhists in Saigon staged a demonstration calling for religious equality on May 30 and on June 3 demonstrators in the capital were sprayed with tear gas from old French stockpiles. In Hue, tear gas was used in conjunction with attack dogs. When this failed to disperse monks who were seated in prayer, ARVN soldiers poured the liquid contents of tear gas canisters that had failed to vapourise over their heads – hospitalising 67 with chemical burns.

Eight days later, Buddhist monk Thich Quang Duc and two other monks drove into central Saigon where a demonstration was already blocking the road. The three got out. Duc sat on a cushion in the middle of the road while the second monk took a five gallon petrol can out of the boot and emptied its contents over his head. Duc said a prayer, lit a match and dropped it on to himself. He burned to death and his body remained seated upright for 10 minutes while the flames consumed it before finally falling backwards onto the road.

Vietnam's US backers and President Kennedy himself were horrified by this event. Images of Duc on fire were published in newspapers across the globe. Diem declared himself deeply troubled but Vietnam's first lady Madame Nhu, the wife of Diem's brother and chief advisor, since Diem himself had taken a vow of celibacy, declared that she would clap her hands to see "another monk barbecue show".

Protests continued and on August 21 a series of attacks on Buddhist pagodas saw more than 1400 monks arrested or killed. Martial law was imposed, all commercial flights out of Saigon were cancelled and censorship was imposed on all South Vietnamese newspapers.

Kennedy issued a message to the US embassy at Saigon ordering ambassador Henry Cabot Lodge Jr to look for alternative leadership options to Diem. On November 1, senior ARVN officers led by General Duong Van Minh assembled a large military force on the outskirts of Saigon before sending it into the city. Diem and his brother Nhu were captured and executed and a military government was installed. As the situation worsened, particularly following the death of Kennedy later that month, thoughts turned to what support might be offered in Vietnam by America's allies, Britain being chief among them.

Tran Le Xuan, otherwise known as Madame Nhu, was President Diem's first lady despite being his brother's wife rather than his own. She despised Buddhists and was notoriously unsympathetic to their plight, earning her the nickname 'Dragon Lady'.

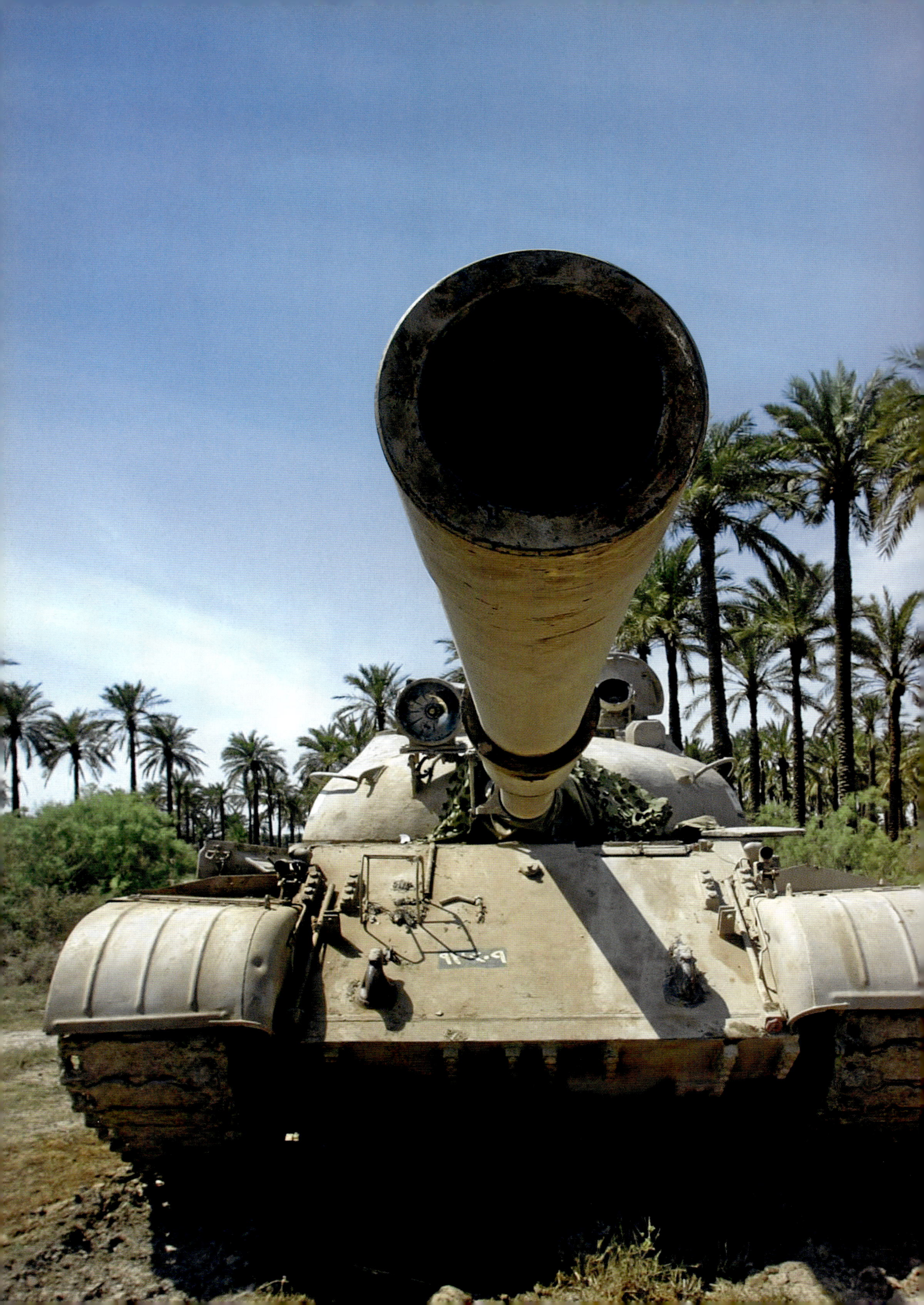

CHAPTER 6

BEHIND THE IRON CURTAIN

The Soviet threat

The Soviet military of 1963 was the largest fighting machine in the world. Universal conscription with a three year minimum period of service ensured a seemingly inexhaustible supply of manpower and vast factories turned out deadly missiles, tanks, aircraft and naval vessels in huge quantities. The West was justifiably fearful of the weapons arrayed against it but just how potent were they?

Military might: a Soviet T-62 tank. It was the USSR's most advanced armoured vehicle in 1963, by which time hundreds were already in service.

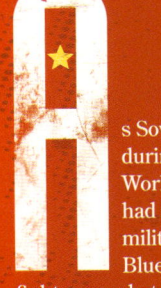

As Soviet units advanced on Berlin during the closing days of the Second World War, an undignified scramble had already begun to salvage the military secrets of the Third Reich. Blueprints for newly developed jet fighters, rockets and missiles were plundered and sent back to the USSR along with, wherever possible, the scientists and engineers who had created them.

Among the spoils were production facilities for the unstoppable V-2 rocket, advanced submarines and a collection of newly developed jet fighters but for the USSR the greatest prize was what remained of the German atomic weapons programme.

Teams of scientists and military intelligence officers were sent in right behind the Red Army to scour Berlin for the technology and they succeeded in capturing both scientists and a stockpile of uranium. Unfortunately most of the key figures in German atomic research ultimately ended up in the hands of the Americans.

Nonetheless, the Soviet atomic programme benefitted hugely from both German research and the uranium in particular and also from spies within the joint American, British and Canadian Manhattan Project. Its first successful test of a nuclear fission weapon, an implosion bomb codenamed First Lighting which was similar to the American Fat Man bomb dropped on Nagasaki during the Second World War, was carried out on August 29, 1949. From this point on there was a nuclear stand-off between East and West which lasted throughout the Cold War.

ABOVE: A brightly coloured MiG-17 is towed from its hanger. The type had a gunsight which was reverse engineered from that of a captured North American F-86 Sabre.

RIGHT: An SA-2 Guideline missile similar to the one that wrecked Gary Powers' Lockheed U-2 spy plane. The SA-2's entry into service marked the beginning of a new phase in the Cold War. High-flying NATO bombers, such as the Avro Vulcan, and reconnaissance aircraft such as the U-2 were no longer safe from attack.
US National Archives

Short to medium range missiles

The years that followed the Soviets' first atomic detonation saw both sides dashing to develop an even more powerful weapon using nuclear fusion which scientists had theorised would be possible – the hydrogen or thermonuclear bomb. The Americans got there first on November 1, 1952, with the 62 ton 'Ivy Mike' experimental hydrogen bomb and the Soviets followed on August 12, 1953, with a device bearing the even odder name Sloika – a type of puff pastry.

These devices were initially too bulky to be fitted atop the Soviet copy of the German wartime V-2, the R-1, which was in any case too inaccurate and short-ranged to be of much strategic use.

During the 1950s the USSR experimented with numerous nuclear bombs designed to be delivered by bomber aircraft, with the drawback that these could potentially be shot down by NATO fighters or anti-aircraft systems.

Development work on V-2 derivatives continued however and on June 2, 1956, the first R-5M or SS-3 Shyster missile was deployed. This was the USSR's first missile capable of carrying a nuclear warhead, albeit a fission-based one. It had a maximum range of around 750 miles – not enough to hit Britain from within the borders of the USSR but certainly enough to wreak devastation on much of Europe. A total of 48 were based at sites along the western fringes of the Soviet Union and it would have taken five hours to get one into the air from a normal state of readiness or one hour if they were on alert.

The real threat to Britain came in the form of the R-12 or SS-4 Sandal medium range nuclear missile – the covert delivery of which to Cuba in October 1962 sparked the Cuban Missile Crisis.

From March 4, 1959, the Soviet military had the ability to launch a missile equipped with a newly developed hydrogen warhead from within its own borders directly on to targets within the UK.

By 1963 there were several hundred of these missiles directed at Britain. It was estimated that it would take one to three hours to get them airborne from a 'soft site' – an above ground airbase – or just five to 15 minutes from a hardened silo. The first regiment with silo-based missiles was put on high alert in January 1963.

A larger and much improved version of the SS-4 Sandal, the SS-5 Skean, was also developed. It had twice the Sandal's 1250 mile range thanks to bigger fuel tanks but was just as accurate. Flight tests started in July 1960 and it began deployment on April 24, 1961, with the first surface-based Skeans being put on alert on January 1, 1962, with a similar readiness time to the Sandal. Just under 100 were built.

A long line of Soviet Army rockets move into Moscow's Red Square towards St Basil's Cathedral during a parade marking the 46th anniversary of the Bolshevik Revolution in Russia on November 7, 1963.

Moscow's umbrella

As their own missile capabilities were enhanced, the Soviets became increasingly aware of just how vulnerable they themselves were to attack. America was developing a new system, the rather heroic sounding MIM-14 Nike Hercules surface-to-air nuclear missile, to blast enemy missiles out of the sky before they could detonate – a sort of precursor to the Patriot missile system of the Gulf War – and the Soviets decided that they desperately needed a version of their own.

The first attempt at providing a missile screen above Moscow was known as System A. This used the newly developed V-1000 Griffon missile which carried a high explosive charge. It was successfully tested on an SS-4 Saddler fitted with a dummy warhead on March 4, 1961, having been guided to its target by three homing radars known collectively as Hen Egg by NATO. A new system using small nuclear warheads to knock out incoming missiles, A-35, was begun in 1959 but was nowhere near completion by 1963.

Intercontinental ballistic missiles

When the Soviets developed their first hydrogen bomb, they also started work on a delivery system which could get it to America. The world's first intercontinental ballistic missile (ICBM), the R-7 or SS-6 Sapwood as it was known in the West, was successfully tested for the first time in 1957. A derivative of it, the R-7A, entered operational service on December 31, 1959, but this was still largely an experimental prospect.

The Americans, meanwhile, had perfected their Atlas ICBM and this entered operational service just a few months ahead of the R-7A, in September 1959.

Further Soviet research and development ensued and the R-16 or SS-7 Saddler ICBM, the USSR's first true production model intercontinental nuclear missile, was accepted for service on November 1, 1961.

During the Cuban Missile Crisis of 1962, the Soviets had between 20 and 50 Saddlers operational but that number was set to soar during 1963 as production was increased.

Meanwhile, development work was ongoing on a third intercontinental missile type, the R-9 or SS-8 Sasin, which would enter service in 1964.

While all three missiles represented a real threat to the US, the R-7A was the least potent. Once fitted with a nuclear warhead, it would only have been able to launch between eight and 12 hours after the order to fire had been given.

The Saddler missile had a maximum range of 6800 miles with 5-6 megaton thermonuclear warhead or 8000 miles with a three megaton warhead. The distance from Moscow to New York is about 4500 miles.

Launch sites for the Saddler were initially out in the open, with missiles being stored in hangers. After a decision had been made to launch, it would take just one to three hours to make them ready. The missiles could not be kept fuelled up all the time because their highly corrosive fuel would eventually eat its way out of them. Assuming a decision to launch was expected in advance and the missiles were fuelled up and ready to go when the launch codes came through, it still took 20 minutes to prepare their guidance systems before they could be fired off.

During 1963, it became apparent that keeping Saddlers out in the open made them highly vulnerable to attack and work began on siting them within purpose built silos.

The SS-8 Sasin, still unfinished at this stage, was designed to be highly accurate, to within one nautical mile, and could carry a similar payload to the Saddler about the same distance. The difference was, however, that the Sasin could be fitted to a mobile launcher.

ABOVE: DA-SN-85-13055 Yak 28 US Nat Arch
A Soviet Yakovlev Yak-28 Brewer-C bomber. This aircraft type, which first flew in 1958, was developed into the underpowered Yak-28P Firebar interceptor. US National Archives

RIGHT: A parked up Tupolev Tu-22 Blinder bomber. It could fly extremely fast but doing so caused its skin to overheat and control surfaces to warp. Makiwo Chew

Bomber fleet

Prior to the advent of ground launched missiles, the USSR had relied on its fleet of bombers to carry nuclear weapons to their targets in the event of war with the West. The first such aircraft was the Tupolev Tu-4 Bull, a direct copy of the US Air Force's Boeing B-29 Superfortress strategic bomber.

Lacking a decent heavy bomber of their own during the Second World War, the Soviets became increasingly aware of the importance of strategic hitting power during the closing stages of the conflict and decided to solve the problem in the simplest way possible – by using a proven design, even if it was someone else's.

Having been refused access to B-29s by the Americans as part of the Lend Lease programme, it seemed too good an opportunity to miss when four of them were forced to make emergency landings on Soviet soil during 1944. A fifth crash landed. Aircraft firm Tupolev was given the task of reverse engineering the B-29 and producing 20 copies of the result within two years. Its engineers therefore rapidly set about dismantling one of the captured bombers and used another for flight tests. The finished product differed only slightly from the original in that it used a different radio, based on an earlier US model acquired under lend lease, and engines – also developed from an earlier American model.

The first one flew on May 19, 1947, and it was in service by 1949. Requiring 11 crew members, its top speed was a lumbering 347mph and its service ceiling was a touch under 37,000ft – decidedly unimpressive by 1949. A total of 847 were made but it was outdated before a single example was completed.

What the Soviets, and Stalin in particular, really wanted was a jet bomber and they got one with a little help from the British Government. Immediately after the Second World War in 1946, with the Tu-4 Bull already in development but before the Cold War deep freeze had really set in, Soviet jet designers asked Stalin for permission to approach the West and buy a working jet from them to help overcome some particularly thorny technical issues.

Stalin, incredulous, reportedly replied: "What kind of fool will sell you his secrets?" He let them try it though, and the answer to this rhetorical question was, it seems, Labour MP Sir Richard Stafford Cripps who was the then president of the Board of Trade. The Soviet designers travelled to Britain, met him and secured a number of working Rolls-Royce Derwent and Nene jet engines on the understanding that they would not be used for military purposes. Back in Russia, these were disassembled, studied, copied and modified to produce the Soviet Klimov VK-1 jet engine.

This process took time though, so the prototype of Stalin's hoped-for jet bomber, the Ilyushin Il-28 Beagle, had to be powered by two RD-10 turbojets based on captured German Junkers Jumo engines from aircraft such as the Arado 234 Blitz jet bomber when it first flew on August 8, 1948.

In 1950, with two unlicensed copies of the Rolls-Royce Nene slung beneath its wings, the first Beagle was delivered to the Soviet Air Force and by the time production ended in 1960, around 6700 had been built. Each was capable of travelling at 550mph, reaching a ceiling of 40,355ft and dropping a small nuclear bomb. The aircraft's range of 1355 miles would have been enough to reach the UK.

For the bigger and therefore more powerful bombs being developed, the Soviets needed an aircraft which was itself bigger and more powerful.

The backbone of USSR's nuclear bomber fleet in 1963 was comprised of the versatile and adaptable Tupolev Tu-16 Badger. First flown in

A line-up of Tupolev Tu-4 Bull bombers pictured on January 8, 1951. The Tu-4 was a very close copy of the USAF's B-29 Superfortress and was used to drop the first Soviet atomic bomb during testing.

Soviet Ilyushin Il-28 Beagle bombers on the runway at Oranienburg Air Base in East Germany on August 26, 1956. Powered by two unlicensed copies of the Rolls-Royce Nene jet engine, the Beagle could carry a nuclear payload.

What's in a name?

The menagerie of names given to Soviet bombers – Bull, Beagle, Badger, Bison, Bear and Bullshot or Blinder – are those given to them by NATO rather than those used by the Soviets themselves. The idea was to provide the Western military with an easy English language way of referring to aircraft which were frequently given names that were difficult to pronounce let alone write down. Although not every bomber had a Russian name beyond its official military designation, e.g. Tu-16, some did, such as the M-4 Molot or 'Hammer'. Over the years, hundreds of different names had to be picked by NATO for Soviet hardware, ranging from the obscure to the downright insulting. The Su-25 ground attack aircraft, for example, ended up with the unlikely name 'Frogfoot', while the AS-4 surface to air missile was the 'Kitchen'. The AT-8 antitank missile, known to the Russians as the macho sounding Kobra was the 'Songster' in the West.

1952 and accepted for service in 1954, the turbojet powered Badger could carry a hefty nuclear payload around 3000 miles at 42,000ft with a top speed of 650mph – making it easily capable of attacking the UK assuming it wasn't shot down on the way over. From 1952 to 1962, more than 1500 Badgers were built in three factories, providing the Soviet Air Force with an extremely potent fleet. By way of comparison, just 136 Vulcan bombers were built by Avro in the UK.

A year after the Badger, in 1955, came the Bison followed by the Bear. Although the Tu-16 was fine for striking at European targets, the Russians needed something that could go all the way to America. Developed almost in parallel with the Tu-16 were the Tu-95 Bear and the Myasishchev M-4 Bison. The latter was an enormous aircraft with four jet engines at its wing roots capable of carrying a substantial payload at 560mph with a ceiling of 49,200ft but its designers found to their dismay that it couldn't actually reach America. Its engines were too thirsty and it couldn't carry enough fuel for the job. A new version, the M-4/3M, entered service in 1958 with more powerful engines and a bigger fuel tank which could get it deep into enemy airspace and back out again but by then nuclear missiles were starting to replace bombers in the minds of those considering war with America. Overall, just 93 Bison of all types were made.

The Bear was a different matter however. Unusually, the Tu-95 was not a jet. It had four Kuznetsov NK-12 engines, each with two sets of propellers rotating in different directions. These were based on the wartime German Jumo 022 turboprop and were in fact designed by a German team who had previously worked for Junkers before being captured and hauled off back to Russia by the invading Red Army. These gave it a remarkable turn of speed for a propeller-driven aircraft. Later versions had a top speed of 575mph, a ceiling of 45,000ft and most importantly an off-the-bat range of 7949 miles. Full scale production began in January 1956 with the Tu-95M. In addition to its hugely capacious bomb bay, capable of carrying 19,809lb of ordnance – nearly as much as nine Tu-4s rolled into one – it had two radar-controlled turret-mounted AM-23 guns for self-defence. Front line units began receiving this formidable piece of kit in October 1957, at around the same time as early SS-6 Sapwood missiles were being tested. More than 500 were made. The USSR now had the ability to attack on an intercontinental scale.

On October 30, 1961, a Tu-95 dropped the Tsar Bomba or 'Emperor Bomb', the most powerful nuclear device ever detonated, on the Novaya Zemlya archipelago at Sukhoy Nos off the north coast of Russia. It was designed to produce a yield of around 100 megatons but this was reduced by half to reduce the threat of drifting nuclear fallout and prevent the Tu-95 itself from being destroyed in the almighty blast. Only one Tsar Bomba was ever built. Today the Tu-95 is still in service with the Russian Air Force and acts as a potent reminder of the Cold War era, having been regularly photographed under escort by British fighters ranging from English Electric Lightnings in the 1960s and 1970s right through to Eurofighter Typhoons in the 2010s.

A sixth Soviet nuclear bomber joined the Cold War in 1962 having first flown in 1959 – the supersonic Tu-22. NATO initially gave it the rather unflattering and thinly veiled codename Bullshot. This was quickly deemed inappropriate and Beauty was picked instead but this in turn seemed too nice so in the end the Tu-22 had to settle for Blinder.

The Blinder was intended to fly higher and faster than any previous bomber, allowing it to bypass all enemy defences along the way. Unfortunately, this is exactly what ballistic missiles could, by now, already do. As a result, the aircraft was almost cancelled. To add insult to injury, the Tu-22 sacrificed almost everything to achieve its top speed of 1242mph. Its range and payload were inferior to that of the ageing Tu-16 Badger and it suffered horrendous technical problems. Its skin rapidly overheated at supersonic speeds, causing its control surfaces to warp and its handling to become extremely tricky as a result. It had to land at speeds that were significantly faster than previous bombers and its tail tended to scrape along the ground in the process. About 300 were made.

A MiG-15 jet fighter takes off from Finsterwalde airbase in East Germany on August 27, 1956. The MiG-15 was the first in a line of highly successful Soviet fighters.

The Yak-23 Flora was an early Soviet jet design that looked very similar to the Yak-15 Feather, with the single turbojet mounted underneath. Makiwo Chew

A Romanian Air Force Russian-made MiG-21. The USSR sold thousands of examples to its satellite states. The type was highly advanced and also relatively cheap to manufacture.

Jet fighters

The defence of the Soviet Union against attacking enemy bombers, the defence of Soviet bombers against attacking enemy fighters and the defence of Soviet interests in any conflict where nuclear weapons were not an option largely fell to the USSR's legion of jet fighter squadrons. Between the end of the Second World War in 1945 and the events of 1963, the Russians had faced the same desperate race to arm themselves with modern jet fighters as every other would-be world power. They had ended the war with some powerful piston engined designs but had nothing of their own to compete with the German Messerschmitt Me 262, the British Gloster Meteor or the American P-80 Shooting Star. As with missile and bomber technology, the Soviets turned to captured German technology to get the ball rolling.

They were fortunate in being able to capture not just examples of operational German jet aircraft but also experimental designs which would have formed the Luftwaffe's second generation fighters had the war continued, such as the Focke-Wulf Ta-183, plus a set of engines including the BMW 003 and the Jumo 004.

When frontline units turned in the first captured engines in 1944, all of the leading Soviet aircraft designers were told to get working on original fighter designs for them to power.

Mikoyan and Guryevich or 'MiG' began developing a new design known as the I-300 with two jets mounted inside the fuselage and a big almost round air intake for them both at the front. Sukhoi played it safe by producing something that looked very much like a Messerschmitt Me 262, the Su-9, with a smoothly rounded fuselage and a jet under each wing. Yakovlev created the Yak-15 by removing the piston engine from its successful Yak-3 piston engined fighter and inserting a turbojet in its place, with the jet venting directly under the body of the plane. The last designer, Lavochkin, created something similar to the Yak-15 in its La-150.

These four designs, each of which flew powered by one or more hastily assembled Russian variants of a captured German engine, suffered from teething troubles.

The Yak-15, undergoing early tests in 1945, was found to burn the skin off its own underbelly and melt its own rear tyre with the heat of its exhaust. This problem was solved by fitting a heat shield and a tail wheel made of solid steel. When the machine finally got into the air, pilots discovered that it had a nasty habit of filling their cockpit with noxious fumes, due to fluid leaks in the engine. Nevertheless, it was easy to fly so around 280 were made between 1946 and 1947. During this time a more advanced design based on the same layout, the Yak-23, was also introduced. The La-150, which also required underbelly heat shielding, was found to be difficult to control and cramped. A series of engine difficulties also made it unpopular and just eight were made. That left the Su-9 and the I-300.

The Su-9 handled well and had good range. It suffered from fewer of the mechanical problems which had beset the other designs and was recommended for production. However, Pavel Sukhoi, the founder of the Sukhoi Design Bureau, fell out of favour with Stalin and not only were his jet designs canned and the prototypes scrapped, he was also forced to close his firm entirely. It would, however, reopen after Stalin's death in 1953.

The MiG I-300 first flew on April 24, 1946, and as tests progressed it was found that when approaching its top speed it suffered from horrendous vibrations. Engineers traced the cause to the jet from its engine buffeting the fireproof sheathing under the rear fuselage. Then, during a low level test flight, the first prototype of the aircraft suddenly dived into the ground and crashed, killing the pilot. Another pilot flying another prototype was doing around 600mph when the nose pitched down without warning. He managed to recover the dive and land but on the ground he discovered that the tailplane of the aircraft had become distorted. The same pilot, on another test run at 2000ft, found the aircraft suddenly vibrating madly and climbing out of control. He reduced power, looked back, and saw that this time one of the tailplanes was actually missing entirely and the other was warped. Fuel started leaking into the cockpit too and the flyer had no choice but to switch off his engines and glide the aircraft home.

In spite of all this, the I-300 had a decent turn of speed and was approved for production as the MiG-9 Fargo. Around 600 were built but it suffered from engine flameouts and poor reliability. It was at this point that Sir Richard Stafford Cripps' gift of jet engines revolutionised Soviet fighter jet design, resulting in one of the best jet aircraft of the early Cold War operated by any nation. The Russians had struggled to develop their assortment of captured German equipment into anything more powerful but with the Rolls-Royce Nene jet, all the hard work had already been done. The designers at Mikoyan-Guryevich, using the MiG-9 as a starting point, built a much more advanced airframe to house the Nene and the MiG-15 Fagot was the result.

It had swept wings and a tail which resembled that of the German wartime Focke-Wulf Ta 183 design but it also looked oddly similar to the American F-86 Sabre fighter jet. The first mass produced MiG-15 flew on December 31, 1948, and front line squadrons had it before the end of 1949.

It was a highly successful design and possibly even the best fighter in the world at that point. It had sufficient firepower to knock out contemporary bombers such as the B-29 with ease, could fly at up to 668mph, and came as a nasty surprise to American pilots during the Korean War when it was flown by Russian and Chinese pilots. Around 12,000 were made – all of them before 1963 – but even better aircraft were to follow.

The MiG-17 Fresco, based on the MiG-15, appeared in 1952. It did not carry air-to-air missiles but was highly manoeuvrable and had a radar gunsight based on one reverse engineered from that of a captured F-86 which made its trio of cannons even more deadly. A huge total of 10,603 were built.

The ultimate development of the Fagot lineage was the MiG-19 Farmer, introduced in 1955. Now the Soviets had a fighter which by 1962 could also be fitted with modern air-to-air missiles in the form of the AA-2 Atoll, a copy of the American AIM-9 Sidewinder. The USSR managed to obtain the missile from captured Taiwanese F-86s and as usual wasted no time in taking it to bits to see how it worked.

Also entering service in 1955 was the Yakovlev Yak-25 Flashlight but this was relatively slow and suffered from engines failures. The withdrawal and retirement of the meagre 483 made was just beginning in 1963.

There was one more fighter available by that year which would give the West its greatest cause for concern. The MiG-21 Fishbed was the Soviet Union's most advanced fighter up to that point – so advanced in fact that it is still in service in 2012 with around 20 nations around the world such as Romania. Its delta-winged design was influenced by experiences of the Korean War and as a result it handled well, was highly manoeuvrable and could pack a considerable punch. It could hit Mach 2 and it was simple to fly but perhaps most importantly – it was cheap. It did everything it did for a fraction of the financial cost attached to most of its contemporaries, particularly American fighters such as the F-104 Starfighter – and this helped it to reach an overall production figure of more than 10,000, although perhaps only 1000 or so had been built by the end of 1963.

A trio of Sukhoi Su-9s parked up on an airfield. Powered by a single Lyulka AL-7 turbojet, the Su-9 could hit Mach 2 and carried up to four AA-1 Alkali air-to-air missiles. It was designed specifically to knock out bombers like the Avro Vulcan. US National Archives

The powerful Sukhoi Su-15 Flagon interceptor. It was the USSR's best interceptor in 1963 but had yet to achieve full front line service status. It could reportedly reach an altitude of 55,000ft in just 75 seconds. US National Archives

High speed jet interceptors

Keeping its own airspace free from enemy bombers was a key concern of the Soviet Union. As soon as they were available, it deployed hundreds of surface-to-air missile units across its vast landmass and Moscow had its System A defence system. The mainstay of its defences, however, was its fleet of jet interceptors. These were short range, limited duration aircraft designed to get airborne within minutes, reach the altitude of enemy bombers even quicker and destroy them before they could deliver their cargo of death to its intended destination.

These duties were initially performed by the USSR's standard front line fighters such as the MiG-15 family but US bombers and reconnaissance aircraft were becoming ever more sophisticated, flying at incredible speed and at nearly unreachable altitudes. The Soviets were therefore forced to produce ever more powerful and elaborate specialist aircraft to intercept them. The dart-like Sukhoi Su-9 Fishpot entered service in 1959 with exactly that mission in mind. Its sleek delta-winged design enabled it to get into the air fast and climb like a rocket until it was within range of any incoming enemies. Powered by a single Lyulka AL-7 turbojet, it could hit Mach 2 and carried up to four primitive AA-1 Alkali air-to-air missiles. It was so powerful that a modified version achieved a new world record on September 4 of its first year in service by zooming up to an altitude of 94,658ft – the highest a manned aircraft had ever been up to that point.

Yet the speed of advances in bomber technology meant that it was quickly outdated. The newest interceptors in 1963 were the Yakovlev Yak-28P Firebar, the Sukhoi Su-11 Fishpot-C and Su-15 Flagon. The Yak-28 medium bomber first flew on March 5, 1958, but an interceptor version, the 'P' model, was developed from 1960 to 1964. It was barely supersonic, being just about able to hit Mach 1 at high altitude, and its service ceiling of 54,954ft would have been scarcely enough to reach an Avro Vulcan cruising at 55,000ft. It carried just two AA-3 Anab air-to-air missiles. The Su-11 Fishpot-C, an upgrade of the Su-9, did better with a maximum altitude of 55,760ft and a top speed of Mach 2.2 but just 108 were made because the Flagon was on the way. A thoroughbred interceptor, the Su-15 Flagon had first flown in 1962 and it entered service testing on August 5, 1963. Its pair of powerful Tumansky R-13-300 turbojets could propel it to speeds up to Mach 2.5 and it reportedly took just 75 seconds to reach an altitude of 55,000ft – the maximum service ceiling of an Avro Vulcan bomber – from takeoff. It could even go higher, up to 59,383ft. Like the Firebar, early versions could carry just two Anabs but it could get them to the target much more quickly. Nearly 1300 were built.

Submarine fleet

The concept of hitting America at long distance with newly developed nuclear missiles had just barely become a reality by 1963 even if striking at Britain that way had been possible for around four years. The Soviets still wanted, if it came to it, to be able to get in and blitz their enemies at close range with as much high powered ordnance as they could possibly muster. They had an effective means of doing it too. Under the Potsdam Agreement at the end of the Second World War, the Soviets had received four advanced Type XXI German U-Boats. This made little difference though, because they had already captured a number of factories which made parts for the Type XXI during their advance into the Third Reich and the Type XXI assembly facilities at Danzig into the bargain. Most submarines of that era were designed to sail around on the surface and only submerged as a means of avoiding detection when enemies were close by. The Type XXI, however, was intended to operate underwater for extended periods of time. It was so advanced that even the Americans operated a pair of them, captured in 1945, for a number of years after the war and the British used one for tests.

The Soviets used their Type XXIs for tests too – and used the blueprints, parts and factory equipment they had taken to build a large number of copies. Between 1949 and 1958, the

K-19: The Widowmaker

The first Hotel class nuclear submarine launched was designated K-19. It entered active service on April 30, 1961, and even then it had already gained a reputation as a killer. During construction of its ballast tanks in 1959, a fire broke out killing three people, and during its launch ceremony on October 11 of the same year the champagne bottle failed to break – never a good sign. A series of accidents and misfortunes befell the ship thereafter. A reactor control rod was bent during a confused exchange, its rubber hull coating came off requiring a complete repaint, water leaks appeared in the reactor compartment and the galley waste system clogged up causing floods. This 'bad luck' continued after the vessel was officially launched and Captain Nikolai Vladimirovich Zateyev took command. During its first independent exercise, a loss of coolant and subsequent internal damage resulted in week-long repairs out at sea. Then a sailor was killed when a missile hatch swung shut unexpectedly.

The incident for which the K-19 later became most notorious, however, happened on July 4, 1961. The submarine's long-range radar system had been accidentally disabled during exercises in the North Atlantic near Southern Greenland. K-19 continued on its way but then suffered a major reactor coolant leak. Water pressure in the nuclear reactor fell away and the reactor's coolant pumps then failed – which was a serious problem. Attempts were made to shut the reactor down but its temperature continued to rise, reaching 800°C (1470°F), which was perilously close to the point at which the fuel rods would melt.

Captain Zateyev sent a team of eight men into the areas of highest radiation to set up a new coolant system by welding a water supply pipe to part of the air ventilation system. There were no radiation suits available, so the men had to make do with chemical protection suits, which really offered very little protection under the circumstances – although the engineers were unaware of that. Radioactive steam was drawn into the ventilation system and circulated to other parts of the ship but the new jury-rigged coolant system worked like a charm and the submarine was saved. The entire crew, however, received a huge dose of radiation – particularly the repairmen.

His vessel crippled and his crew on the verge of mutiny, Captain Zateyev had most of the sub's small arms thrown overboard, except for five pistols which were given to his most trusted officers. Abandoning his original mission, he headed south and managed to meet up with another Soviet submarine, the S-270. The eight men of the repair crew, now sick and incapacitated with their faces swollen and deformed, were transferred to the other ship on stretchers and 'decontaminated' with scalding hot water. Another 79 non-essential personnel were then evacuated, leaving 60 on board. Attempts to tow the K-19 failed because it was too heavy for the tow cables available and eventually it had to be brought back to port by a Soviet ship.

All eight of the repairmen were dead within three weeks of the incident from radiation poisoning and 15 more crewmen died over the next two years.

K-19 was then extensively decontaminated and put back into service in 1964. Eight years later, a fire caused when hydraulic fluid leaked on to a hot filter claimed the lives of a further 28 men on board. K-19 was eventually decommissioned in 1991 and scrapped in 2002.

Russians turned out 215 Whiskey class vessels plus 26 Zulu and 20 Romeo class subs which also owed their existence to wartime technology. The Whiskey class boats were intended primarily as patrol vessels, although a small number were converted to carry nuclear cruise missiles horizontally in large cylindrical containers on their backs.

In 1952, two further types of Soviet submarine were launched – the Zulu and Quebec classes. Thirty Quebec submarines, a small attack type armed only with traditional torpedoes for sinking enemy submarines or shipping, had been launched by 1957. The Zulu class machines were an improvement on the Whiskey class and following tests in 1955, six were converted to carry the SS-N-1 Scud-A mobile launch ballistic missile – the forerunner of the missile used by Saddam Hussein's forces during the Gulf War. Work on these, the world's first ballistic missile-equipped submarines, was completed in 1956.

Development of this concept proceeded rapidly. Meanwhile, an advanced version of the Zulu, the Foxtrot, was launched in 1957 with torpedoes rather than missiles as its armament. The following year, no fewer than three cutting-edge new types of vessel were launched. June 1958 saw the commissioning of the first November class nuclear-powered submarine, followed in December by the first Echo I class boat, also powered by an on-board nuclear reactor. As the Americans had already discovered four years

A Whiskey class submarine pictured with HMS Rothesay – a British warship which appeared for 30 seconds in the 1965 James Bond film Thunderball, actor Sean Connery even going aboard. The Soviet Whiskey class boats were copied from an advanced German type of the Second World War. US National Archives

earlier with USS Nautilus – the world's first nuclear submarine – if you didn't have to rely on regular top-ups of diesel fuel for your engines you could stay submerged for weeks or even months at a time. Now this power was within the Soviets' grasp. The November class vessels were designed to fire thermonuclear torpedoes into enemy naval yards, whereas the Echo I class was equipped with equipment for firing nuclear SS-N-3 Shaddock cruise missiles at land targets.

The third type launched in 1958 was the Golf class. It didn't have a reactor but it did carry a payload of three ballistic nuclear missiles mounted in silos behind the bridge on the submarine's 'sail'. These could be fired while the submarine was moving but it still had to surface. The first three Golf class submarines built were equipped with Scuds but the next 20 had the SS-N-4 Sark missile. This was the first dedicated submarine missile, a liquid-fuel rocket with a range of about 370 miles compared to the Scud's 110 miles. It carried a warhead of up to two megatons and was reasonably accurate.

In 1961, the first of 29 Echo II class submarines designed to knock out enemy aircraft carriers was launched. These each carried eight Shaddock cruise missiles which had to be fired from the surface and guided to their target by the submarine itself. All eight missiles could be launched within half an hour but the sub couldn't dive before the weapons had entered the final phase of their journey to the target.

Six months earlier, the most dangerous Soviet submarines of 1963 had begun to enter service. Based on the nuclear-powered November class body shell, the Hotel had the missile silos of the Golf class fitted into it. Modified to Hotel II standard it could fire its three missiles, the new SS-N-5 Sark/Serb, from a depth of 16m without ever having to break the surface. The Sark/Serb itself had a range of 800 miles – far better than either the Sark or the Scud.

The USSR now had its own Polaris style system fitted to a submarine which could go for months without having to refuel. These vessels may have lacked the reach of land-based or air-launched nuclear weapons but once submerged they were almost impossible to find let alone stop.

This Golf class submarine is a command and control variant. The Golf I could carry three nuclear missiles in silos behind its 'sail'. US National Archives

Tanks and missile launchers

Defeating Germany during the closing stages of the Second World War had involved large numbers of armoured fighting vehicles – particularly the T-34 tank and its successors. Without its legions of tracked and heavily armoured tanks, the Soviet Union might never have stopped Hitler's invasion of 1941 let alone reversed it to the point of eventual victory. Creating those legions in the first place, not to mention their fuel, bullets and shells, required a huge amount of infrastructure in terms of raw materials, refineries and factories. All of this was set up and optimised for massive production overkill as the Red Army drove the Germans back to Berlin.

Tank production was one area of technological arms development where the Soviets scarcely needed the help of captured German equipment – the T-34 was already among the most advanced armoured fighting machines in the world. By the end of 1943 it had evolved into the T-34/85 with a larger turret housing a new 85mm gun designed to punch through the armour of Tiger and Panther tanks. Between them some 84,000 examples were built – making it the second most produced tank of all time. Despite being a Second World War tank, the USSR still had it operating in front line service in 1963. Although it was replaced in the Red Army, dozens of other countries used it and many still use it today. The North Vietnamese used it during the latter stages of the Vietnam War and some of Saddam Hussein's forces were equipped with it during the Gulf War.

The next step was the T-44 with uprated engine, suspension, transmission and armour that was significantly thicker than that of its T-34 forebears. Its gun remained the same though, and it lacked a decent internal heating system which meant its crews often suffered frostbite during the harsh Russian winter. Comparatively few were made – 1823. It did, however, pave the way for the most produced tank of all time, the T-54/55.

Development of the T-54 began in 1944 and incorporated all of the lessons learned by Russian tank crews during fierce engagements against German panzers. When it entered service in 1946, the T-54 had a rifled 100mm main gun, increased fuel capacity over previous designs, a new 38.88 litre V12 diesel engine,

The crew of a T-55 could generate a smoke screen by injecting vaporised diesel fuel into the exhaust system – as demonstrated here.

The frontal armour of a T-54 tank is 100mm thick and angled at 60°. The armour on the front of the turret is even thicker at 205mm.

thicker armour than a Tiger tank, wider tracks and a modernised gun sight.

The T-54 itself, Soviet scientists worked out in 1956, could survive a small nuclear blast of up to 15 kilotons if it was more than 980ft away. The crew, however, would be burned to a crisp inside unless the tank was more than 2300ft away. Protecting crews from the effects of a nuclear attack was something which had not been seriously considered before but now it was deemed essential.

An effective NBC (nuclear, biological and chemical) tank defence system required a host of innovations intended to keep the vehicle operational while protecting it from hazardous heat and radioactive fallout effects. It was initially decided that the T-54's NBC system would need to start operating just 0.3 seconds after a spike in gamma radiation levels was detected. The system would prevent irradiated particles from entering the tank and defend its crew from the effects of the blast itself. Once this was ready, it was decided that the ageing T-54 could also do with a few upgrades in other areas.

The vehicle's main weakness was its unreliability. This would be cured by installing a more powerful engine with an electric starter. Ammo for the main gun was increased from 34 to 45 shells, night-vision scopes were installed and frontal armour was thickened. All of this was added at the same time and the level of improvement was such that the T-54 was rechristened the T-55, entering service on January 1, 1958. It was smaller and more lightly armoured than America's main battle tank at the time, the M48 Patton, and the British Centurion, but it carried a bigger gun than either of them.

Further work was done in 1961 to improve the T-55's NBC system. A plasticised lead antiradiation lining was fitted to the interior to prevent radiation from penetrating into the crew compartment. A chemical filtration system was also added, giving the tank protection against poison gases and other chemical hazards. In total more than 86,000 were built and some estimates place the figure closer to 100,000.

While the bulk of the Soviet tank armies consisted of T-34s and T-54s in 1963, another model had emerged in 1961 which added yet more improvements but also some disadvantages. The T-62 had an even bigger gun – a 115mm cannon – which necessitated a bigger turret and a larger hull. Ammo was up to 40 rounds but weight was also increased and since the T-62 had the same engine as the T-55 it was less manoeuvrable. Around 22,700 were built but at twice the cost of the T-55.

The T-34, T-54/55 and T-62 were all medium tanks. The Soviet Union did have a selection of heavy tanks on its inventory too, but machines like the IS-2, IS-3, IS-4 and T-10 were produced in low numbers – perhaps no more than 7000 altogether. The last of these, the T-10, was a ponderous 52 tonne monster with a 122mm gun.

The Soviet army was notorious for its use of mobile rocket-launching artillery – particularly the Katyusha or 'Stalin organ', so called for the screeching noise it made when the rockets were launched. The latest version, the BM-21, was just entering service in 1963. Its rockets were mounted in tubes on a lorry's rear flatbed and it took just 20 seconds to fire off all 40 of them before manual reloading, which took 10 minutes. The Cold War also saw the introduction of the Scud-A and Frog-7 missile systems. The Frog was a single large unguided rocket fitted to a launcher on the back of a ZIL-135 8x8 truck.

It could carry a payload of 1200lb – which meant it could deliver either conventional or nuclear warheads. Six of these were deployed in Cuba during the crisis of 1962, each fitted with a nuclear warhead, and Saddam Hussein's forces fired high explosive Frog missiles at American forces during the Invasion of Iraq in 2003. Where the Frog was unguided, the Scud-A was controlled in the air by four graphite vanes in the engine exhaust. It had a 50 kiloton nuclear warhead and entered service on April 1, 1958.

Borrowed, stolen and deadly

Much of its most advanced equipment may have been based on 'borrowed' technology but the incredible ability of the Soviet Union to mass produce its weapons had endowed it with a military machine of awesome power on all fronts by 1963 with just one notable exception. The Soviet Navy had no aircraft carriers. It has been argued that it simply didn't need them, that it couldn't get any to copy or that they were simply too expensive. Whatever the reason, the Russians had no carriers 50 years ago.

What they did have were several hundred medium range surface-to-surface nuclear missiles pointed at air force bases, military installations and cities across Western Europe; around 2300 bombers available to carry nuclear payloads; more than 30 submarines capable of launching short-range nuclear missiles; more than 20,000 fighters more or less capable of shooting down bombers and around 100,000 tanks spread across the various Warsaw pact nations bordering the West.

Many accounts of the Cold War, particularly those written from an American perspective, highlight the fact that during the Cuban Missile Crisis, the Russians had very few missiles capable of hitting the US, besides those being delivered to Cuba. President Kennedy, it is pointed out, called Khrushchev's bluff and sent him away with his tail between his legs. Some historians have even pointed out that Kennedy's advisers almost had him sending surveillance photos of all Russia's 20 or so ICBMs to Khrushchev to point out how few missiles the Russians had that were capable of striking at the US. What this fails to account for, however, is the threat that the USSR posed to Britain and other European nations. Had the 'hawks' within Kennedy's administration succeeded in pushing for war, America might have survived relatively unscathed but it is doubtful that Britain would have been nearly so lucky.

A Soviet Maz 543P Scud missile launch vehicle. The SS-1 Scud medium range ground to ground missile could carry a 50kt nuclear or conventional high explosive warhead.

A captured V-2 missile being unloaded at RAF Hendon shortly after the end of the Second World War. British forces set out to grab as many V-2 components as possible as Germany collapsed but the nation ran out of money to develop the technology further.

At the same time, the postwar government of Clement Attlee quietly set up the Gen 75 Committee to begin the development of Britain's own atomic bomb under the guidance of the British scientists who had been part of the Manhattan Project. The Atomic Energy Research Establishment was set up in 1946 and the first British nuclear reactor, GLEEP, which stood for Graphite Low Energy Experimental Pile came into operation or 'went critical' on August 15, 1947.

All the while Britain's coffers were running on empty. The financial burden of attempting to develop a nuclear capability while lacking key areas of knowledge that had been the responsibility of American scientists during the Manhattan Project was immense and Britain's other defence programmes and even other areas of government suffered as a result.

Just when it seemed as though Britain's financial predicament was about to catch up with it, the US stepped in with a lifeline. The Marshall Plan saw billions of dollars handed over to the British government in 1948 and yet more cash was forthcoming in the form of loans with very favourable rates of interest. Although the money was nominally intended to help rebuild Britain's flagging economy and modernise its creaking infrastructure, America turned a blind eye to the fact that most of it was, instead, pumped into defence projects including the British atomic bomb.

The following year, President Harry S Truman even started talks with Prime Minister Attlee with a view to making Britain a full partner in the ongoing American atomic development programme. When it was learned that the USSR had built its own nuclear weapon in 1949, there was even more reason for the Americans to arm their main ally with A-bombs. These talks hit a major stumbling block the following year however, when German-turned-British nuclear scientist Klaus Fuchs was arrested. Fearing for their national security, the Americans rapidly drew back from the negotiating table.

They did, however, station their own nuclear weapons on British soil. Strategic Air Command, the branch of the United States armed forces responsible for operating America's fleet of long-range heavy bombers, rotated dozens of squadrons equipped with B-29/B-50 Superfortresses and B-47 Stratojets carrying nuclear bombs through British air bases such as RAF Lakenheath in Suffolk and RAF Marham and RAF Sculthorpe in Norfolk between 1948 and 1953.

After 1953, Strategic Air Command began to shift its bomber forces westwards to place them behind RAF fighter defences and give them the best possible chance to get airborne before being annihilated in the event of a nuclear strike. Bases including RAF Brize Norton, RAF Greenham Common, RAF Upper Heyford and RAF Fairford periodically hosted B-36 Peacemaker, B-52 Stratofortress and B-58 Hustler squadrons between 1953 and 1963. These were equipped with a variety of American atomic and thermonuclear bombs.

Seated, from left, are British Prime Minister Clement Attlee; President Harry S Truman and Canadian Prime Minister Mackenzie King pictured shortly after it was announced that despite British and Canadian contributions to the Manhattan Project, America would be keeping the technology to itself.

Brown Bunny – the chicken powered atomic bomb

Less than two years after Operation Hurricane saw Britain detonate its first nuclear device, plans were drawn up to use the same technology in a radical defence project for Germany.

The project, codenamed Brown Bunny, would involve a series of low-yield nuclear devices being buried or submerged at important industrial facilities such as oil refineries and power stations along the border with East Germany which could then be either remotely detonated or set off using an eight-day time delay trigger in the event of a Soviet invasion. The resulting devastation would not only annihilate the invaders' supply lines and follow-up forces, it would also make large areas difficult to traverse and impossible to occupy due to radioactive contamination.

The British Army ordered 10 of the bulky 7.2 ton devices, subsequently renamed Blue Bunny and then Blue Peacock, in July 1957. Development continued but one major problem was identified – if the temperature below ground or underwater dropped too far, the concealed device's electronics were likely to fail. One suggested solution to the problem was to wrap them in 'pillows' made of glass fibre. Another was to secrete a number of live chickens and sufficient feed to keep them alive for a few days within the weapon's casing. The birds' accumulated body heat would keep the mechanism from freezing up, it was believed. The project was cancelled in 1958 after only two devices had been built because the government decided that the idea of hiding atomic weapons in an allied country was "politically flawed". A smaller tactical nuclear device, Violet Vision, was worked on but none were built.

The first British atomic bomb to enter service was Blue Danube. It was similar to the American Fat Man device, pictured here, although its outer casing was much more streamlined.

The Avro Blue Steel nuclear stand-off missile looked purposeful but was highly unreliable. Its lower fin is folded up here for display at the RAF Museum, Cosford. Author

Blue Streak from above. The missile would have taken four and a half minutes to fuel up ready for launch – enough time for a concerted Soviet missile strike to annihilate all Blue Streak launch sites.

Britain gets the bomb

Britain finally became a nuclear power on October 3, 1952, when Operation Hurricane saw an experimental device similar to the American 'Fat Man' bomb detonated off the Australian coast. The success of this device led Britain to rapidly move on to a production version and by November 1953 it was ready. Named Blue Danube, it was to be dropped from the V-force aircraft – the Avro Vulcan, Vickers Valiant and Handley Page Victor. Its yield was low at around 10-12 kilotons, although this was roughly the same explosive force as the bomb that had devastated Hiroshima in 1945. Plans were drawn up to build 800 of the weapons and each of the V-force bombers had its bomb bay designed around Blue Danube's streamlined shape and large dimensions. The Americans then promptly made the bomb obsolete by developing the dramatically more powerful hydrogen bomb.

It wasn't just Blue Danube's explosive power that was behind the times either – its method of delivery was also being called into question. By 1954 it had become clear that Soviet air defences – both fighter aircraft and ground-to-air missiles – were rapidly being developed to a point where they would stand a good chance of destroying Britain's bombers long before they could reach their targets and drop their Blue Danubes.

Plans were therefore drawn up to develop thermonuclear weapons and the means to deliver them. A supersonic 'stand-off' missile would be built which could be launched several hundred miles from the intended target and its defenders. Avro, still working on developing the highly complex Vulcan bomber, was given the task of developing the missile, which would need to reach speeds of up to Mach 3 and be able to carry a nuclear warhead. The size and shape of the new missile, codenamed Blue Steel, were determined by the latter which was to be one of two projects then being worked on by the Atomic Weapons Research Establishment – Orange Herald or Green Bamboo. Neither of these had yet been successfully tested but the larger of the two, Green Bamboo, required a spherical space with a diameter of 45in. In order to accommodate this within its casing, Blue Steel had to be 48in in diameter, giving it a rather portly appearance.

Avro started work in 1955 but the project suffered numerous delays due to difficulties in developing the guidance system and problems constructing a fuselage capable of withstanding extremely high speeds. The warheads also proved problematic and the project stalled.

While Avro struggled with Blue Steel, De Havilland was given the task of developing what was seen as the eventual successor to the V-force bombers – a ballistic missile with a 2000 mile range. The US still refused to divulge any of its nuclear secrets but it approached Britain in April 1954 with a plan to jointly develop ballistic missiles. The US, it was proposed, would develop an intercontinental ballistic missile while Britain would develop a medium range missile. This made perfect sense since Britain was geographically much closer to the USSR. Naturally, Britain jumped at the chance and an agreement was signed in August. At around this time it was agreed

The liquid oxygen tank from De Havilland's Blue Streak medium range ballistic missile seen from below. Its steel walls are not much thicker than those of a fizzy drinks can and it has no internal structure to save weight. Author

that the US would supply Britain with 113 MGM-5 Corporal tactical missile systems, which could be fitted with small nuclear warheads, though it would be another four years before these entered service with Royal Artillery units.

Meanwhile, the De Havilland team designed a missile using licensed American technology that was powered by a pair of liquid oxygen and kerosene-fuelled Rolls-Royce RZ2 rocket engines. Like Avro, De Havilland rapidly hit problems, the solving of which saw the cost of its missile project soar. The guidance system, in an age before microprocessors, had to make sure the missile was pointing in the right direction by making fine adjustments to the missile's moveable engine thrust chambers while compensating for a rapidly lightening fuel load. If the engine cut out at the wrong moment the missile, with its thermonuclear warhead, could have been left pointing in the wrong direction. Vibration was also a serious issue.

As the De Havilland design took shape, it also became apparent that operating Blue Streak would pose its own problems. It took four and a half minutes to fuel up ready for launch – meaning incoming Russian missiles would be able to wipe out all British missile sites before one could get off the ground. The solution to this was to place all Blue Streak launchers in vast concrete silos underground. These would cost £2.3 million each, £45.5 million each in today's money, and 60 would have to be built to accommodate the number of missiles regarded as being sufficient for Britain's defence.

Blueprints for these K11 silos, 150ft deep and lined with half an inch of mild steel to protect against the electromagnetic pulse of a nuclear detonation, were drawn up. Blue Streak's development costs, projected to be £50m in 1955, continued to rise.

Joining the thermonuclear club

With Blue Steel and Blue Streak under development, work continued on efforts to create a powerful warhead, ideally a thermonuclear one, that was small enough for them to carry. In the meantime, a freefall bomb successor to Blue Danube was developed that was smaller and could be carried by fighter bomber aircraft such as the Supermarine Scimitar, De Havilland Sea Vixen and Blackburn Buccaneer as well as the V-bombers.

Red Beard was half the length of Blue Danube at just 12ft, a fifth of the weight at 2000lb and 3ft in diameter compared to 5ft. Its destructive force was between 10 and 15 kilotons. It entered production in 1959 and 110 were made. Preparations to test different hydrogen bomb prototypes were made but it was decided that a more powerful interim bomb was needed.

The result was Violet Club, a 9000lb free fall bomb with a warhead codenamed Green Grass based on one of the devices due to be tested with the H-bomb prototypes. Its projected yield was 500 kilotons and its casing was similar to that of Blue Danube. Fewer than five were made.

Britain finally conducted its first H-bombs tests, Operation Grapple, in May and June 1957. Two prototype H-bombs, Short Granite and Purple Granite, were detonated at Malden Island in the Pacific Ocean but gave disappointingly low yields so a second attempt was made over nearby Christmas Island in November. This time the device, Grapple X, was a success – achieving a yield of 1.8 megatons and ushering Britain into the thermonuclear 'club'.

The last truly British made nuclear weapon was called Yellow Sun Mk.I – a Green Grass warhead inside a new casing that was smaller than that used for Violet Club. Thirty-seven were made including five with warheads transferred from the Violet Club project. By now though, events had made these devices obsolete.

When the results of the Granite tests were shown to the Americans, President Eisenhower's administration realised that now was the time to finally put an end to 12 years of denying Britain access to US nuclear support. The 1958 US-UK Mutual Defence Agreement made a wealth of new test data available and gave Britain access to the huge range of advanced nuclear weapons already designed and built in the US.

The American W28 thermonuclear warhead was adapted for use in British systems and codenamed Red Snow for use in a new weapon, Yellow Sun Mk.II. The RAF was also issued with 'off the shelf' US-made Mk.5, Mk.7, Mk.28 and Mk.43 nuclear bombs for its aircraft under an arrangement known as Project E. Two Royal Artillery regiments could finally be equipped with the American-made Corporal missile, now available with a W7 nuclear warhead from the Mk.7 bomb. MGR-1 Honest John rockets, which could launch a 20 kiloton warhead up to 15 miles, were also brought into Royal Artillery service and plans were drawn up for the siting of 60 American Thor intermediate range ballistic missiles with W49 1.44 megaton thermonuclear warheads at British bases.

The Red Snow warhead proved to be ideal for Blue Steel and using it meant the project could finally advance. It entered service in February 1963 looking like a small pilotless aircraft with its own little wings and a tank full of volatile rocket fuel for its Armstrong Siddeley Stentor Mk. 101 engine. Despite the many technical advances it embodied it was extremely unreliable. In its first year of operational testing, the RAF estimated that up to 50% of all Blue Steel weapons taken into action would fail to operate correctly.

Ridiculous but effective — British Cold War codenames

Codenames have been used in military operations around the world since before the First World War but during the Second World War it became apparent to British intelligence that codenames chosen by Germany often alluded to the nature of the top secret operations they were intended to disguise. A long range radar project was named Heimdall – a Norse god with the power to see things before they happened – and a radio navigation system which used only a single beam was called Wotan, a Germanic god who only had one eye.

It was therefore deemed particularly important that the secrecy of British projects should be protected using codenames which were distinctive and easy to remember, but which gave absolutely no clues as to the project itself. A system was established which paired a colour chosen at random from a list with a second random word. This resulted in some of the oddest codenames ever given to military hardware. Blue Badger was a truck-portable nuclear bomb, Green Hammock was a navigation system, Orange Poodle was a radar system, Violet Friend was an anti-ballistic missile system and Purple Possum was a deadly nerve agent now outlawed and classified as a weapon of mass destruction by the United Nations.

Servicemen wearing protective suits remove the highly corrosive fuel from an MGM-5 Corporal surface-to-surface missile operated by the 47th Guided Weapon Regiment in Hampshire on May 3, 1958. The Corporal was among the weapons made available to Britain by the US.

The Red Beard nuclear bomb was small enough to be carried by aircraft such as the Supermarine Scimitar, De Havilland Sea Vixen and Blackburn Buccaneer. Author

Three members of the 47th Guided Weapon Regiment, Royal Artillery, strip off their protective suits after removing the fuel from their MGM-5 Corporal missile. Corporal was inaccurate but by 1963 its British made replacement, Blue Water, had been cancelled.

A British Army MGR-1 Honest John rocket being fired on a NATO shooting range in Hohne, West Germany, on January 13, 1961. The unguided Honest John was short on range, just 15.4 miles, but could be fitted with a small nuclear warhead.

Thor and the Skybolt Crisis

The delivery of Douglas PGM-17 Thor ballistic missiles from the US, Project Emily, commenced in August 1958 as the Blue Streak programme continued to founder. They were split into groups of three, each trio sited at one of 20 RAF stations along the eastern side of the country where they'd be closest to their targets in Eastern Europe.

These massive 65ft liquid-fuelled missiles were stored horizontally at ground level on hydraulic erector/launchers beneath rail-mounted shelters. For a launch, the shelter had to be rolled back and the missile raised into a vertical position prior to fuelling. The process took 15-20 minutes. Once launched, a Thor's main engines would burn for around two and a half minutes and accelerate it up to a speed of 9800mph or 13 times the speed of sound. After a further seven and a half minutes, a re-entry vehicle containing the nuclear warhead would separate from the main missile fuselage and begin its descent towards its target, which would be hit eight minutes later. Once the order to launch had been given, it would therefore take between 33 and 38 minutes for the missile to actually hit its intended target.

All 60 'British' Thors were in place by the end of 1959 and in April 1960 the Government abruptly pulled the plug on the development of Blue Streak as a means of delivering nuclear warheads. Given the huge sums already spent on the project, this prompted heated debates in the House of Commons and the effectiveness of Thor as even a stop-gap replacement was brought into question. While the politicians argued over Thor, English Electric was test launching its new Blue Water surface-to-surface tactical nuclear missile. This was intended to replace the Royal Artillery's inaccurate Corporal missiles and short range Honest John rockets. It was 25ft long and had a range of 55 miles fitted with a British version of the American 10 kiloton W44 nuclear warhead.

While publicly defending Thor's effectiveness, the Government understood that the missiles were probably too slow to prepare for launch and would indeed be knocked out on the ground in the event of a Russian attack. It was believed that there would be just four minutes between incoming Soviet missiles being detected and hitting their targets in Britain. This left the RAF's fleet of V-bomber's as Britain's best front line nuclear strike force, since Vulcan bombers could be kept in a state of constant readiness and their crews could get them airborne within three minutes of the take-off command being given.

Once they were in the air, however, they had little chance of surviving long enough to reach their targets in the USSR and drop their bombs on them. The Blue Steel standoff missile was still more than two years away from entering service in 1960 and it was already clear that it was unlikely to live up to expectations even when it did.

An interim solution was badly needed so in March 1960 Prime Minister Harold Macmillan met President Eisenhower and agreed that Britain would buy 144 Skybolt air launched ballistic missiles. Douglas Aircraft had started work on the GAM-87 Skybolt in 1959 and it seemed to be exactly what Britain was looking for. It had a range of 1150 miles compared to Blue Steel's meagre 150 miles – enabling bomber crews to launch it at Moscow from the edge of the Iron Curtain over Germany rather than deep inside Soviet airspace. It was slightly longer than Blue Steel at 38ft but slimmer with a diameter of 35in and this would require the V-force bombers to undergo some modifications but this was still much cheaper than continuing with Blue Streak.

It was decided that the Avro Vulcan would carry Skybolt with two mounted externally near the outer edges of its enormous delta wing. A newly built Vulcan, XH563, was flown to the Douglas facility in Santa Monica in January 1961 to begin electrical compatibility tests. Further tests took place throughout the year and in December Vulcans XH537 and XH538, fitted with inert Skybolts, conducted air drop experiments. In 1962, the Americans carried out live fire Skybolt tests but these proved to be a huge disappointment with the weapon failing to operate properly during four tests out of four.

This convinced the US Secretary of Defense Robert McNamara to cancel the Skybolt programme. The British government, now having grave doubts about Blue Steel's effectiveness and having cancelled both Blue Streak and Blue Water, was stunned when it heard the news. President Kennedy agreed to an emergency meeting with Harold Macmillan in the Bahamas to discuss the way forward and over the course of three frantic days of negotiations, Macmillan managed to secure an incredible coup – he persuaded Kennedy to let Britain buy Polaris.

This revolutionary new system was designed for use with highly advanced nuclear submarines. A Polaris submarine could remain undetected near its target for months and wouldn't even have to surface to launch its payload of 16 missiles, each with three nuclear warheads. The president also allowed the Royal Navy the option to buy the latest version of the missile in development, the A-3, which it duly did.

The American made Polaris missile, seen here undergoing tests, was the answers to Britain's prayers. It became the mainstay of the nation's nuclear deterrent from the mid-1960s.

It had been thought that the Douglas GAM-87 Skybolt missile represented the future of Britain's nuclear deterrent. It had a much greater range than Blue Steel and Prime Minister Harold Macmillan agreed to buy 144 of them. Author

Skybolt, seen here from the rear, would have been carried by Britain's fleet of Avro Vulcan bombers but the programme was cancelled by the US government in 1962 – causing a defence crisis for the British government. Author

Britain's nuclear arsenal

As Britain entered 1963, it did so with an eclectic collection of deadly nuclear weaponry. Blue Danube had been retired the year before but both the RAF and Royal Navy had access to a stockpile of 110 Red Beard freefall nuclear bombs for their V-force bombers, Canberras, Sea Vixens, Scimitars and Buccaneers, each with a yield of either 15 or 25 kilotons depending on the version used.

The RAF could also call upon 37 Yellow Sun Mk.I bombs fitted with 400 kiloton Green Grass warheads, although these were withdrawn later in the year, and a small number of Yellow Sun Mk.II bombs fitted with US ordnance-derived Red Snow warheads capable of producing a 1.1 megaton thermonuclear yield. Yellow Sun Mk.II had entered service in 1961 and production was still under way. Royal Artillery regiments were operating MGM-5 Corporal missiles, fewer than the original 113 now since a proportion of these had been used in test firings, fitted with W7 warheads that could produce a variable yield of between eight and 61 kilotons. They also had a limited number of short range Honest John rockets that could carry nuclear warheads.

The Project E arrangement, which continued until 1965, meant that British armed forces in 1963 could also call upon a wide range of American made and owned nuclear bombs. Under Project Emily, Britain continued to operate 60 Douglas PGM-17 Thor intermediate range ballistic missiles from 20 RAF bases. This arrangement finally came to an end in September 1963, when these weapons were finally returned home to the US.

The first Blue Steel standoff missiles entered service with the RAF's Vulcan and Victor bombers in February 1963. Each device had a Red Snow 1.1 megaton thermonuclear warhead and each aircraft could carry just one, slung beneath the centre of its fuselage.

Even with this seemingly wide range of nuclear weaponry at its disposal, Britain still lacked an effective means of getting any of it to potential targets within the USSR. RAF bombers stationed in Britain or Germany would have had to run a lethal gauntlet of high speed enemy interceptor aircraft and surface-to-air missiles before they could even get close and in all likelihood the 60 Thor missiles would have been destroyed on the ground by a Soviet strike. Everything now depended on Polaris and the submarines that would carry it.

Its protective shelter removed, one of RAF Feltwell's three Thor missiles is raised into launch position. The British government initially argued that these weapons were worth spending taxpayers' cash on because they would enable crews to train for the Blue Streak programme.

A Polaris missile fired from *HMS Revenge*. It was a long road from the end of the Second World War to the launch of Britain's most successful nuclear deterrent. US National Archives

CHAPTER 8

RULING THE WAVES

— Britain's first nuclear submarines

Submarines powered by nuclear reactors and carrying missiles armed with nuclear warheads were a terrifying Cold War development. They could remain hidden underwater for months on end and didn't even have to surface to fire off their deadly payload. Britain's first nuclear sub entered service in 1963 with a little help from across the pond...

The story of Britain's fleet of nuclear submarines begins, in common with most Cold War developments, at the end of the Second World War. Germany and its U-boats had made it plain that an underwater armada was essential for both destroying enemy ships and preventing enemy subs from destroying yours. As part of the Potsdam Agreement, the treaty that decided what should happen to Germany and its remaining war gear after the conflict, the Russians had got their hands on four Type XXI U-boats. Britain got one too, France got one and America got another two.

The Type XXI was a revelation to the victorious allies. It had highly advanced batteries which enabled it to remain underwater for much longer than conventional submarines – which at that time generally travelled around on the surface and only dived when approaching a target – and gave it much greater range. It was also streamlined, resulting in a high underwater speed, had better crew equipment such as a freezer for storing food, featured an automatic torpedo loading system and had a very sensitive sonar array for detecting other vessels.

All four nations began running these submarines as part of their own fleets, U-3017 being commissioned into the Royal Navy as the snappily named *HMS N41*, and their value became clear. It also gradually became all too apparent that the Russians were using their Type XXIs as a blueprint for hundreds of new submarines which formed the Whiskey and Zulu classes between the late 1940s and the late 1950s. This was a significant threat to NATO shipping and as a result much thought was given to Britain's response.

A second radical German submarine design was also obtained by the British at the end of the Second World War and this resulted in experiments on an alternative source of fuel for Royal Navy submarines which had the potential to give them even greater staying power underwater.

The 'blonde' submarines

German scientist Hellmuth Walter was an early pioneer of rocket propulsion, particularly using a highly concentrated form of hydrogen peroxide known as high test peroxide or HTP. One of the fruits of his research was the Messerschmitt Me 163 Komet rocket propelled interceptor aircraft and another was a high-speed submarine known as the V-80 which was completed in 1939 and underwent trials in 1940. It could reach speeds of 32mph below sea level – a feat unheard of at a time when most submarines struggled to top 20mph while submerged.

An order for four development versions of the V-80 was placed in January 1942. The first two, now known as the Type XVIIA, were completed in October 1943 and the second pair in April 1944. Earlier duo managed 23mph submerged while the latter two managed close to the experimental prototype's top speed. Unfortunately, they were very difficult to handle at top speed

CRISIS AND SCANDAL THE COLD WAR 61

British servicemen scramble over the hulls of partially constructed German submarines at the Blohm & Voss shipyard in Hamburg on May 5, 1945. Britain benefited from capturing so much German naval technology.

and suffered from mechanical problems. Nonetheless, 24 production examples, the Type XVIIB, were ordered. Just three were complete by the time the war ended and all three were scuttled by their crews to prevent them from being captured by the allies.

One of these sunken treasures was allocated to the US at Potsdam and a second to Britain. Britain also kept two uncompleted examples it found at the shipyard of Blohm & Voss in Hamburg. While the Americans showed little interest in their badly damaged hulk, the Royal Navy salvaged and recommissioned its Type XVIIB, U-1407, as the *HMS Meteorite* and then built two of its own HTP boats – the *HMS Excalibur* and the *HMS Explorer*.

The recommissioning was supervised by Professor Walter himself and trials were carried out in 1946 with a view to HTP becoming the fuel of the future for the Navy. Meteorite though, was unpopular with its crews who regarded the HTP itself as highly dangerous. This view was echoed by the crews of both *Explorer* and *Excalibur*, these being known as 'blonde' submarines because of hydrogen peroxide's use as a hair bleaching agent.

The HTP fuel, stored in special bags outside the inner pressure hill, was prone to exploding unexpectedly, flames sometimes appeared on top of the combustion chamber in the engine room and on at least one occasion the crew of *HMS Explorer* were forced to evacuate the pressure hull and stand on the upper casing to avoid fumes which had suddenly filled the vessel. It later became known as 'HMS Exploder'. When it was learned that the US Navy had successfully developed a submarine powered by a nuclear reactor, *USS Nautilus* in 1954, the project and HTP were abandoned.

US developments

Having launched the world-beating *Nautilus* in 1954, the Americans were stunned when, the following year, the USSR successfully launched an SS-N-1 Scud-A ballistic missile from a submarine at sea. The Russians had modified a Zulu class submarine – based on the German Type XXI – to carry a single missile externally. To launch it, the boat had to go through the laborious process of surfacing and raising the missile from its sail but nevertheless Zulu class vessel B-67 successfully test fired its Scud on September 16, 1955. Six of the 26 Zulus produced were converted into missile carriers and the US Navy, which had no ballistic missile programme at that time, was deeply disturbed.

It had been concentrating on developing a submarine launched nuclear cruise missile, the Regulus, which looked something like a small cockpit-less jet fighter. In 1953 a modified Second World War diesel submarine, the *USS Tunny*, carried out the first deck launch of a Regulus missile, and a second vessel, the *USS Barbero,* was also modified to carry them in an ungainly pod attached to its back. These became the first submarines in the world to carry nuclear weaponry.

Now, however, the modified Zulus and what was likely to come after them represented a serious threat to the mainland United States and the US government's science advisory committee recommended rapid development of a sea based ballistic missile for the navy to counter them.

The US Air Force was already working on its Atlas and Titan intercontinental ballistic missiles and its Thor intermediate range

Regulus and the missile mail

Since the 1930s the United States Post Office Department had been searching for an easy way of transporting important post over large distances in a very short time. This had led to experiments with 'rocket mail' in 1936 and on June 8, 1959, *USS Barbero* fired a Regulus cruise missile at the Naval Auxiliary Air Station in Mayport, Florida, its nuclear warhead having been replaced with two very carefully sealed mail canisters containing around 3000 letters and packages.

The missile hit its intended target and the canisters, having survived, were opened and the post sent on to a post office for sorting and delivery. This was hailed as a historic breakthrough in postal delivery services and some predicted that the process would quickly be adopted for high value items. Sadly though, at a cost of nearly a million dollars each, no further Regulus missiles were used for delivering the post.

ABOVE: First Sea Lord Louis Mountbatten pictured in 1955 during a visit to the US to review naval developments. Mountbatten was instrumental in winning over Admiral Rickover and securing British access to American submarine technology.

LEFT: The world's first nuclear submarine, *USS Nautilus*, was launched in 1954. When the Royal Navy heard about it, efforts to create an HTP powered submarine were abandoned.

missiles while the US Army was developing shorter range liquid-fuelled Jupiter missiles. The navy therefore approached the other services about the possibility of working with them on a ship-launched 1500 mile range missile. The air force gave the idea short shrift, it being the navy's chief rival for funding, but the army entered into discussions and suggested that the Jupiter could fulfil both land and sea roles.

The two services arranged a timetable to have the naval Jupiter ready for ships by 1960 and submarines by 1965. This lengthy gestation period stemmed from the Jupiter's cumbersome size and massive weight. Each one was 60ft tall and weighed 50 tonnes. It would take a monstrous submarine of some 8500 tonnes to carry even four of them and the corrosive liquid fuel would make operating them at sea hazardous. After doing some research and preliminary design work the navy decided that a smaller missile with solid fuel propellant would make more sense.

Its contractors came up with a design which used solid fuel and the navy was given leave to abandon its joint Jupiter project and proceed instead with what ended up becoming the Polaris missile system. Early on, it was suggested that the Polaris missiles would be about 28ft tall and would weigh about 14 tonnes each. With this in mind, naval planners set about deciding what sort of submarine would be required to carry them. Feasibility studies showed that, given the technology then available, a submarine could be developed which could hold anywhere between four and 48 missile launcher tubes. At first, the favoured option was 32 tubes. This would mean more missiles could be put to sea on board fewer submarines, thereby saving money.

As with the Jupiter project however, 32 tubes would result in a hulking behemoth of a submarine which, while technically possible, would probably be a nightmare to operate and maintain in practice. Naval officers who saw the 32 tube designs baulked at the idea of such a mammoth underwater machine and recommended a smaller sub with just 16 tubes. This was agreed. It was also agreed that the missiles would be launched while the vessel was still under water, in contrast to the Russian surface launch approach. This was because the same naval officers pointed out that a calm undersea platform could operate with greater reliability and effectiveness than one forced to launch its incredibly potent weapons while being tossed about in the middle of a raging storm.

Having been stunned for a second time when the Soviets put the first satellite into orbit, in 1957 the Americans redoubled their efforts to get Polaris into service early. The requirement for the missile to have a range of 1500 miles was dropped to 1200 to speed things up. Work on the dedicated Polaris submarine was shelved and an existing nuclear attack submarine already under construction, the *USS Scorpion*, was effectively cut in half and had a 130ft long missile launcher section inserted in the middle. As a result of this dramatic modification the *USS Scorpion* was renamed the *USS George Washington*.

A host of additional electronic systems were quickly added to the submarine's layout including launch and guidance systems for the missiles as well as fire control and many more.

The *George Washington* was launched in December 1960 and the Regulus programme, which had entailed the construction of two dedicated Regulus submarines – the *USS Growler* and the *USS Greyback* – was phased out. By February 1962, the US had six operational Polaris capable submarines with a further 31 either under construction or in the advanced planning stages. The first successful test of a Polaris missile in operation was carried out by the *USS Ethan Allen* in the South Pacific.

A shopping bag full of secrets — the Portland spies uncovered

Ethel 'Bunty' Gee was a bit of a sad case. Aged 44 in 1958, she was an unmarried virgin working full time as a filing clerk. She didn't get out much and spent most of her spare time caring for her elderly mother, aunt and uncle.

On January 7, 1961, she was arrested by Special Branch detectives in London. The shopping bag she was carrying was found to contain large quantities of photographic film and developed prints of classified material about the inner workings of HMS Dreadnought – all of it destined for the Russians.

Bunty's filing was done at the Admiralty Underwater Weapons Establishment at Portland, Dorset, and in 1958 she met Harry Houghton. Harry was born in Lincoln, Lincolnshire, in 1906 and joined the Royal Navy at a young age. He rose through the ranks and in 1951 joined the naval attaché at the British Embassy in Poland. Here he developed a taste for the black market, buying and selling coffee and medicinal drugs. He drank heavily too and soon came to the attention of the Polish Secret Police. What happened then is unknown but in 1952 Harry went to work at the Admiralty's Portland facility and by 1956 he was passing information back to the Poles who sent it on to the USSR.

When Harry met Bunty he gained access, through her, to some much more sensitive secrets. Harry and Bunty had an affair – Harry was married but separated from his wife – and often met up at hotels where Bunty would pose as his wife. In July 1960, Harry introduced Bunty to a man he called

Peter and Helen Kroger kept spy equipment at their home in Cranley Drive, Ruislip, North-West London.

'Alex Johnson' who was apparently a commander in the US Navy. This was actually Gordon Lonsdale, a Canadian businessman, or to give him his real name, Konon Trofimovich Molody, a KGB agent.

Meanwhile, in 1959 the CIA had received information from a mole codenamed Sniper that the Russians were receiving details of HMS Dreadnought's development from inside the Portland facility. MI5 was informed and Harry Houghton immediately fell under suspicion. He earned a meagre salary yet owned four cars, had just bought his house and was well known for his generosity in buying rounds at the pub.

Harry and Bunty were put under surveillance, as was Gordon when the MI5 saw them frequently meeting up with him. Gordon led them to another couple, Peter and Helen Kroger of Cranley Drive, Ruislip,

Ethel Gee found love aged 44 but ended up giving away Britain's submarine secrets into the bargain.

North-West London. The Krogers were then also watched.

All five were arrested and Gee's shopping bag full of secrets was found. Helen Kroger's handbag contained a series of microdots which turned out to be letters sent between Lonsdale and his wife – who lived in the USSR with their children – but MI5 realised that the same microdot method was being used to move classified naval secrets out of the country. The Krogers also had lots of cash, code pads, fake passports and a radio transmitter. Harry, Bunty and Gordon all had large piles of cash at their homes too.

Harry and Bunty got 15 years in prison and married when they got out. The Krogers got 20 years but went back to the USSR in 1969 as part of a prisoner exchange. Lonsdale got 25 years but he was exchanged for a captured British spy in 1964.

The formidable Admiral Hyman Rickover boards the USS Nautilus on August 25, 1958. He was initially unwilling to hand over any nuclear know-how to the British.

Abandoned submarines at the Blohm & Voss yard in Hamburg. In the background three more submarines rest in the cradles awaiting launch. It was here that British troops found unfinished German experimental high test peroxide submarines.

HMS Dreadnought

As the US forged ahead with nuclear weapons for its nuclear powered submarines, Britain was stuck in the technological doldrums. *USS Nautilus* had been a game changer for the Royal Navy and during joint manoeuvres it had amply demonstrated its ability to overcome existing anti-submarine technology and wowed several high-ranking Admiralty staff. The Royal Navy, it was felt, had to have its own *Nautilus*. The problem was that the Americans were still operating under the Atomic Energy Act of 1946, which prohibited any sharing of secrets regarding nuclear technology. This meant that Britain would have to go it alone no matter the cost.

The first British Magnox nuclear reactor was under construction by 1955 at Windscale in Cumbria and it was a case of working out how to cram such a hugely complex piece of machinery into the relatively compact body of a submarine. Vickers Armstrong Engineering and Foster Wheeler were brought in to begin design work and the first step was to create an experimental reactor suitable for a submarine on shore. The Government approved this project in 1956 and construction of a test reactor began at Dounreay in Scotland.

Progress was slow to begin with, since the British scientists and engineers involved lacked the necessary expertise with nuclear technology and had to make everything up as they went along. The project soon fell behind its projected timetable and thoughts turned to the US Navy which, by now, had built itself a small fleet of nuclear submarines. *USS Nautilus* was followed by *USS Seawolf*, which used a one-off sodium nuclear reactor, in 1955, and by 1956 work had begun on the *USS Skipjack*, *USS Skate*, *USS Swordfish*, *USS Sargo*, *USS Seadragon* and *USS Triton* with many more planned.

Britain had been working to have the Atomic Energy Act of 1946 amended or overturned for a decade but it seemed as though the American

HMS Dreadnought moves slowly through the Devonshire dock, Barrow-in-Furness, escorted by the tug ST Roa while being prepared for sea trials on November 7, 1962.

opposition to sharing the secrets of its nuclear capability was finally melting.

The man in charge of the US Navy's submarine fleet was Admiral Hyman Rickover, a man who had a reputation for fearsome intellect, blunt speaking and a willingness to do whatever it took to get a job done. He had little interest in handing American nuclear know-how over to Britain until he came up against another equally powerful personality – Lord Louis Mountbatten, the First Sea Lord. Mountbatten was determined that the Royal Navy should have a nuclear capability and was not shy about telling Rickover so. In 1956 he met Rickover in Britain and secured an invitation from him for a British team to visit the US and see first-hand what nuclear technology could do.

Meanwhile, the British design team had begun to make some real progress. It was determined that the best possible shape for the new submarine would be similar to that of the American *USS Albacore* – a streamlined teardrop which stretched to make it also resemble a cigar. By the end of 1956, Rickover was so won over by Mountbatten that he suggested to the US government that Britain should be sold a nuclear reactor for its submarines. The arrival of Harold Macmillan as Prime Minister in 1957 marked a sea-change in the overall attitude of the American government to Britain and in mid-1958 the Atomic Energy Act was amended to allow sharing of nuclear secrets.

Now Britain, with Rickover's full support, was in a position to take full advantage of its ally's technology and Rolls-Royce signed a £10 million deal with US firm Westinghouse for an S5W reactor and all the associated equipment it needed to function effectively. The S5W, used to power the *USS Skipjack*, was cutting edge technology – certainly more advanced than the experimental reactor powering the *Nautilus*.

The reactor was somewhat different in its design and dimensions from the home-made reactor originally envisioned by the British design team so alterations had to be made to accommodate it. In addition, the S5W was so advanced that the tentative and primitive British reactor designs were simply binned. This led to the rear of the projected nuclear submarine, with the engine room and reactor compartment, being largely American in design while the front half, where the accommodation, sonar rooms, control sections and torpedo rooms were located, was mostly British.

Engineers then devised ways of bringing the two sections together while paying particular attention to structural strength, which had been identified as a weakness in the American Skipjack design. Vickers Armstrong was picked as the shipyard to build the submarine. It had built dozens of diesel powered submarines before but even so, the new boat presented a significant challenge. Welding in the tight spaces demanded by a nuclear reactor, the need for absolute cleanliness and having to bond lead to steel and other metals created significant difficulties for the engineers at Vickers' Barrow-in-Furness shipyard.

At the same time, the Russian nuclear submarine programme had already been successful – producing the first November class boat. This gave added impetus to the British development programme and by July 1959 work was progressing so well that the vessel was named *Dreadnought* after a revolutionary battleship of the same name launched in 1906. As the name was being chosen, a group of British submariners was being selected to undergo training in the US on how to manage the S5W reactor. They each spent six months aboard the *USS Nautilus*, the *USS Skipjack* and the *USS Skate*.

HMS Dreadnought's nuclear power plant was complemented by a host of other innovations built into the boat. The control room featured a joystick control column and an aircraft style instrument panel for the 'pilot' and there were hitherto undreamt of

Russian sailors do calisthenics on the deck of a typical trawler spy ship, the Barograph.

Something fishy going on – Soviet spy ships

During the 1960s Russia maintained a fleet of around 60 spy ships dressed up as fishing trawlers. Their chief function was, operating exclusively in international waters, to record the sound signatures of Western submarines. Every submarine makes a unique sound as it passes through the water and recording this allows hidden submarines to be identified even if they cannot be seen. This information is invaluable for anti-submarine warfare since it can give the top speed and maximum dive depth of an enemy vessel in a combat situation.

HMS Dreadnought out at sea. The vessel's crew could take a shower, launder their clothes, eat in a cafeteria style mess and even watch films on board.

Nuclear submarines including HMS Warspite, in the lead, and HMS Valiant pass the royal yacht Britannia during a naval revue. Valiant and Warspite were Britain's second and third nuclear submarines, respectively.

levels of comfort for the crew. They could take a shower, launder their clothes, eat in a cafeteria style mess and even enjoy films thanks to the submarine's on board cinema equipment. Fixtures and fittings were designed to look attractive too.

The nearly competed vessel was officially launched by the Queen on October 21, 1960, but the reactor core was not loaded until 1962. Surface trials began in December of the same year and the submarine's first dive took place in January 1963, closely monitored by a Russian ship disguised as a fishing trawler.

While HMS Dreadnought was entering the final phase of its pre-service testing and trials, plans were being drawn up for the next generation of British nuclear submarines. The S5W reactor having been carefully studied, development of the first all-British reactor was begun by Rolls-Royce in collaboration with the Atomic Energy Authority and the Admiralty Research Station HMS Vulcan at Dounreay. This, the Rolls-Royce PWR1, was to be fitted to Britain's second nuclear sub HMS Valiant, which was ordered on August 31, 1960. A third nuclear submarine of the same design, HMS Warspite, was ordered in 1962.

Dreadnought, with its American reactor now up to full speed, was commissioned into Royal Navy service on April 17, 1963.

The Polaris platform

The two Valiant class submarines were closely based on the tried and tested Dreadnought design but were lengthened by 20ft. Lessons learned from the earlier vessel were also applied to making the Valiants quieter. They each had a Paxman diesel-electric generator which could be used for true silent running – an idea which was later adopted by the US Navy despite the initial scepticism of Rickover.

As a development of both the original American designs and the British innovations embodied by Dreadnought, the Valiants were highly successful and well regarded by their crews. This made them an ideal starting point for Britain's next nuclear submarine development – the Resolution class.

With Skybolt cancelled and the effectiveness of the RAF's V-bombers and their soon-to-enter service Blue Steel stand-off missiles called into question, President Kennedy offered Polaris as the best possible solution. Britain was given leave to buy the system as part of the 1962 Nassau agreement. Now all that was needed was a suitable vessel to launch it from. Naturally, naval designers turned to the Valiant type as a starting point and again British teams visited the US to reap the benefits of information sharing. They were given complete details of the US Navy's Benjamin Franklin class submarine design both in terms of ship-building and equipment requirements. They also received permission to visit the Electric Boat Company, the contractor supplying much of the machinery and electronic systems associated with Polaris. The firm said it would be willing to give design support and supply everything necessary for the British Polaris programme. This led to the British effectively receiving the exact same hull mounted missile launchers as those employed on the Benjamin Franklin class.

The design team for what would become the Royal Navy's Resolution class nuclear ballistic missile submarines decided that it would take every opportunity possible to learn from the Americans' mistakes in designing their nuclear subs and improve on existing designs wherever possible.

As a result it was decided that all hull valves would be ball valves capable of being rapidly closed by a 90° movement in the event of an emergency. Welding would also be used throughout construction rather than the brazing process – similar to soldering – employed by the Americans. Shortly after this decision was taken, a US nuclear submarine,

The second Resolution class vessel built by Vickers Armstrong – *HMS Repulse*.

ABOVE: British nuclear submarine *HMS Renown* test fires a Polaris missile. US National Archives

the *USS Thresher*, sank with the loss of all its crew after a brazed pipe joint ruptured in the engine room.

Fitting the American Polaris launch system to the basic Valiant frame was no simple task either. More crew space was needed to accommodate missile specialists, extra power systems were needed and additional ballast tankage was required. Carrying 16 missiles, each weighing 16 tonnes, and the equipment needed to launch them was a problem in itself, not to mention the strain that high powered underwater launches put on the vessel's structure.

Two pairs of the new Resolution class nuclear submarines with ballistic missile launching capability were ordered in May 1963. Vickers Armstrong was able to handle the first pair, HMS *Resolution* and HMS *Repulse*, but lacked the manpower for the second two, HMS *Renown* and HMS *Revenge*, which were contracted out to Cammell Laird at Birkenhead in Merseyside.

Resolution and *Renown* were laid down in 1964 and *Repulse* and *Revenge* followed in 1965. Vickers, with its greater experience at building submarines, rapidly overtook Cammell Laird with both of its vessels being launched before even the *Renown* – *Resolution* in 1966 and *Repulse* in February 1967. Each was 427ft long, 33ft wide and 30ft high compared to *Dreadnought's* 266 x 31 x 26ft dimensions and the *Valiant's* 285 x 33 x 27ft. Top speed submerged was 29mph compared to 32mph for the two earlier types. In addition to their 16 Polaris A3 missiles, the Resolution class boats also had six 21in torpedo tubes at the bow firing Tigerfish wire-guided torpedos. They had 143 crew compared to *Dreadnought's* 113 and *Valiant's* 116. While plans were laid for the future of Britain's nuclear deterrent, in 1963 the nation's ultimate defence against the Soviet Union lay elsewhere.

Experiencing minor difficulties – the sudden loss of *USS Thresher*

During a test dive on April 10, 1963, alongside the submarine rescue ship *USS Skylark*, the *USS Thresher* had reached the required depth of 1000ft when the *Skylark* received a garbled message via underwater telephone: "…experiencing minor difficulties, have positive up angle, attempting to blow." Two brief and still more garbled messages followed: "900 N," and "…exceeding test depth." Then silence. After repeated requests for clarification it became clear that something had gone seriously wrong aboard the *Thresher*.

A minute later, the *Skylark* detected a high energy, low frequency noise with the characteristics of an underwater implosion.

Investigators later determined that around nine minutes earlier, at 9.09am, a brazed pipe joint had failed in the engine room, spraying sea water on to an electrical panel which shorted out, causing the nuclear reactor to shut down. The vessel's ballast system froze when the crew tried to use compressed air to push out the water in its tanks, causing it to fail. By 9.13am the engine room was becoming flooded and the additional water was weighing the sub down, causing it to dive tail first. It is believed to have imploded at a depth of between 1500ft and 2000ft as the pressure on the hull caused it to collapse.

All 129 men on board, including crew and civilian technicians, were killed as the ship broke into six pieces. The wreck, off the US east coast, was too deep to recover.

The *USS Thresher*. Britain's submarine designers were determined to avoid making the same mistakes as the Americans in putting together vessels like this.

V-bombers and Centurions

Britain's conventional armed forces

Britain poured huge resources into maintaining its military strength after the Second World War and by 1963 still had a powerful arsenal. While much of Western Europe was helpless and entirely reliant on the US for protection, Britain could pack a nuclear punch and had a conventional fighting force that was the envy of the world...

CHAPTER 9

ABOVE: A striking yellow De Havilland Sea Vixen naval jet fighter. It was one of Britain's best Cold War aircraft but just 145 were made.

OPPOSITE: A shiny Gloster Meteor – Britain's first jet fighter. Small numbers were still being used for training even by 1963.

Britain had joined the Americans and the Russians in grabbing as much German technology as it could lay its hands on as the Second World War drew to a close. Advanced aircraft were either flown back to the Royal Aircraft Establishment at RAF Farnborough for study or dismantled in situ and crated up, ready for transport back to home. Records of these examinations were made and catalogued but there was little follow-up work to do – Britain had already developed the world's first jet engine and had one of the first production jet fighters, the Gloster Meteor, in service by August 1944. Other designs followed with the first De Havilland Vampire jet fighters joining the RAF in 1946.

By then, British military planners had determined that the future of the nation's defence lay in high flying bombers carrying air-dropped nuclear bombs. January 1947 saw the Air Ministry issue a requirement for just such an aircraft and the foundations for what would later become the V-force were laid. Handley Page and Avro came up with advanced designs which would evolve into the Victor and Vulcan bombers respectively. Vickers-Armstrong submitted a third design which later went into production as the Vickers Valiant.

The V-force

While the designers and engineers of the three firms tasked with creating Britain's next generation jet bomber fleet went to work, the air crews of RAF Bomber Command were equipped with the final development of the Avro Lancaster bomber – the Lincoln. It was longer and wider than the Lancaster, its bomb bay could carry a bigger load and its four Rolls-Royce Merlin 85 V engines developed a whopping 1750hp each. The Lincoln remained in service for far longer than the Lanc too – the last examples only being phased out in March 1963.

The RAF also had the English Electric Canberra, Britain's first jet bomber. The prototype flew on May 13, 1949, and it entered service at RAF Binbrook in Lincolnshire with 101 Squadron two years later. Lots of Canberras were needed so English Electric's rivals including Avro, Handley Page and Shorts had to build them too. They were too small to carry Britain's earliest nuclear weapons but they dropped conventional ordnance over Korea and during the Suez Crisis in 1956. They were later used to carry US-owned Mk.VII tactical nuclear weapons. Around 750 Canberras were built, although by 1963 most of the bomber versions had been retired and the only Canberras in service in the UK were being used for reconnaissance and training. These remained on active duty until July 2006.

Having been bought some time by the ultimate development of the Dambusters icon and the versatile Canberra, Vickers-Armstrong spent four years on the Valiant. The design had initially been rejected by the Air Ministry due to its lack of advanced features but Vickers had argued that it would be available sooner than the other two aircraft and that if their revolutionary designs proved to be unworkable, the Valiant would still be ready to fill the gap. The prototype, known as the Vickers Type 660, first took to the air on May 18, 1951.

Its appearance was futuristic compared to the Lincoln yet it still had two wings attached to a fuselage and a normal looking tail section. Its four Rolls-Royce Avon turbojet engines were buried in the roots of its wings with their intakes blended into the wing leading edges. This improved the aircraft's aerodynamic profile but it made engine maintenance work difficult and increased the risk of a single engine fire spreading rapidly to the others.

The Air Ministry placed an order for 25 Valiant B.1s in April 1951, and the first completed production aircraft of the 107 made flew on December 21, 1953. It had a service ceiling of

CRISIS AND SCANDAL THE COLD WAR 69

A Supermarine Scimitar lands on the deck of *HMS Victorious* on June 1, 1959. Just 76 were made, 39 of which were lost in accidents.

The Australian 'Atomic Tank'

During a British nuclear test in Australia as part of Operation Totem in 1953, an Australian Army Centurion Mk.III was positioned around 1500ft from the epicentre of a nine kiloton blast. It was left with its engine running.

When it was examined after the explosion, it was found to have been pushed about 5ft backwards. Its radio antennas were missing, its cloth mantlet cover had been burned away and its lights and periscopes had been rendered unusable by heavy sandblasting. The tank was then driven away from the site and later used for driver training.

Had the tank been fully crewed, it is likely that they would have been killed by the blast shockwave but even if they survived the detonation, they would have been incapacitated by neutron and gamma radiation within a matter of hours.

This amalgam would be posted by two Bristol-Siddeley Olympus turbojets – an advanced version of those used on the Avro Vulcan. High wing loading enabled the aircraft to fly extremely fast at low level without being affected by thermals and other ground-related weather phenomena. The aircraft's systems included ground-following radar that allowed for an innovative autopilot which adjusted for terrain features – significantly reducing the air crew's workload. The TSR.2 also had a head-up display, a canopy coated with gold alloy to reflect the flash of a nuclear detonation and an emergency back-up mechanism which would cause the aircraft to climb rather than crash in the event of a total systems failure.

Developing all this resulted in spiralling costs. Further problems were caused by the project's disorganised funding structure. Some contributing manufacturers worked directly for the Air Ministry rather than BAC, which caused communication difficulties, and equipment for the project was supplied by the Ministry from further contractors even though it was being designed by BAC. There were, officially, no prototypes – just an initial batch of nine production airframes. Four years into the project though, the first few airframes were being used as testbeds nonetheless.

By 1963, the first two development aircraft were competed but engine and undercarriage problems delayed their first flight. Questions were now being raised as the cost per aircraft rose to £16 million on the basis of 30 being ordered. The year ended without a single test flight. A TSR.2 finally flew on September 27, 1964 at Boscombe Down in Wiltshire. During the first supersonic test flight, the aircraft reached Mach 1 on dry power only. The pilot then activated the reheat unit on one engine and the aircraft accelerated away from the Lightning which had been flying behind it. The Lightning's pilot Wing Commander James Dell had to use reheat on both his engines to catch up. When Dell flew the TSR.2 himself, he said it handled "like a big Lightning".

Further flights followed and a number of issues such as undercarriage vibration were resolved. The last of 24 test flights took place on March 31, 1965. Although it was winning praise from pilots, the TSR.2 was falling short of the originally agreed service requirements. It couldn't manage a short take-off and it couldn't carry enough fuel to travel 1200 miles. It was therefore agreed that the acceptable range would be reduced to just 750 miles and allowable take-off distance was increased to 1000 yards.

Time though, had run out. The newly elected Labour Government of 1964 asked the RAF to consider the American General Dynamics F-111 Aardvark instead of the TSR.2, which it was believed would take a further three years to reach front line service. The Minister of Defence, Denis Healey, was clear in his scepticism about continuing with the TSR.2 and at a cabinet meeting on April 1, 1965, the aircraft would be cancelled. The completed TSR.2s ended up in museums and the RAF never did get its F-111s. It did, however, get the Buccaneer.

Battle tanks and APCs

The greatest threat posed by the Soviet Union in 1963 came from its nuclear missiles but the abiding image many held of its armed forces was one of vast armoured legions parked up just behind the Iron Curtain in Eastern Europe. The USSR had around 100,000 tanks in service that year, although many of them were beginning to show their age.

Britain therefore had to have the very best tanks and armoured fighting vehicles if it was to have any chance at all of holding off a Russian attack involving 'conventional' ground forces. Fortunately, after a series of lacklustre designs produced during the Second World War such as the Crusader, Matilda and Churchill, British tank designers had finally got it right with the A41 Centurion medium tank.

The first mock-up was created in May 1944 but prototypes were not ready to begin trials until May the following year. It had been designed to withstand a direct hit from the deadly German 88mm gun – the weapon carried by the infamous Tiger tank – but had to be no heavier than 40 tons. Other requirements were protection from mines, agility and the ability to reverse at high speed.

The first Centurion had a Rover-built 650bhp Rolls-Royce Meteor engine, Horstmann suspension, a hull with sloped welded armour and a partially cast turret fitted with a 76.2mm '17 pounder' main gun plus a 20mm cannon in a separate mounting. During work on the prototypes it became obvious that the 40 ton limit, set so that the tank could be carried on existing trailers, was impractical so it was decided to get new trailers instead and allow a heavier tank to be built. The Centurion was better armoured than far heavier tanks yet had the speed and manoeuvrability of much smaller armoured fighting vehicles. It was Britain's first 'universal tank' and it was a great success.

The Centurion Mk.I was quickly superseded by the Mk.II which had thicker armour and the tank entered service in December 1946. It didn't take long for a better main gun to become available either – the 84mm '20 pounder' – and it was decided that a Browning machine gun would be more effective against infantry than the 20mm cannon. In addition, a new automatic stabilisation system had been invented which allowed the Centurion's gun to fire accurately while the tank was moving, where all previous tanks had been forced to stop before firing.

These improvements were bundled together with a more powerful engine and a new gun sight and incorporated into the next version of the Centurion, the Mk.III, which entered service in 1948. In fact, the level of improvement was so dramatic that all Mk.Is and Mk.IIs were withdrawn from front line service and either upgraded to Mk.III standard or converted into the Centurion Armoured Recovery Vehicle. The Mk.III was also the most numerous version produced, with more than 2800 being built. During the mid-1950s it was determined that the Centurion's 84mm main gun was insufficiently powerful to defeat the armour of the Soviet T-54 and work was begun on an even more powerful weapon. The powerful 105mm L7 rifled gun entered service with the Centurion Mk.VII in 1959 but was designed to fit into the turret mountings of the 84mm gun so the entire British Centurion fleet, numbering more than 3000 by this point, could be up-gunned.

The Centurion was the main British and Australian battle tank for the Korean War between 1950 and 1953. It also served during the Suez Crisis of 1956 and by the time production ceased in 1962, 4423 Centurions of all types had been built. The typical Centurion had a crew of four – commander, driver, gunner and loader – a top speed of 22mph, an operational range of 280 miles and weighed 52 tons.

The second primary British tank serving during 1963 was the FV 214 Conqueror heavy tank. Reports of the extremely heavy Russian JS-3 tank, which boasted a 122mm main gun, convinced British military planners that a similarly heavy tank was needed. Work on a completely new series of tanks was begun in 1946 based on a platform known as the FV200 Universal Tank – the most basic version of which was the FV201. This in turn became the basis for the Conqueror which first appeared in 1955, entering service the following year. It was powered by a 810bhp Rolls-Royce Meteor and had modified Horstmann suspension. Its main gun was a 120mm monster based on an American design which was itself based on an anti-aircraft gun. Heavy armour – up to 7in thick in the horizontal plane at the front – meant that even the powerful Meteor engine was heavily stressed causing numerous mechanical and electrical malfunctions that plagued the tank throughout its service career. Production continued until 1959 but just 185 Conquerors were built. It weighed 65 tons, had a top speed of 21mph and a range of 95 miles. Its crew of four manned the same positions as those aboard the Centurion.

A third British main battle tank had just entered service in 1963. The Chieftain was originally designed in 1956 by Leyland Motors and three prototypes were produced. Numerous design changes ensued and six more prototypes were built between 1961 and 1962. The following year, the Chieftain entered service with the British Army but a number of flaws, mainly related to its Leyland L60 engine, had yet to be ironed out if it was to face a potential onslaught from the East.

The L60 engine was designed so that it could run on either petrol or diesel but this useful feature was undermined by the fact that it was constantly breaking down. Problems included cracking of cylinder liners, fan drive trouble, failure of lip seals, poorly routed pipework and piston ring breakages. Fixes were gradually introduced which resolved many of these issues.

As with its predecessor, the Centurion, the Chieftain had Horstmann suspension with large armoured side plates to protect the tracks. It had

An early version of the Chieftain tank that would eventually replace the Centurion in British Army service. This photograph was taken in 1962 but the tank did not enter full service until 1966 after a number of design flaws had been ironed out.

The Soviet Cruiser Sverdlov.

Naval diver Lionel 'Buster' Crabb pictured in 1950.

Buster Crabb and the Sverdlov menace

A new type of warship was introduced by the Soviet Navy in 1950 which gave British naval planners cause for serious concern. The Sverdlov class cruisers, of which four were launched in 1950 alone, were large, fast and well-armed. Their speed was such that they would be able to avoid anti-shipping torpedoes fired by Royal Navy submarines with relative ease. Their anti-aircraft guns – missiles would come later – were highly effective too at close range. The Navy therefore decided that a new type of aircraft was needed specifically to fly from British carriers and take on the Sverdlovs. The resulting requirement produced the Blackburn Buccaneer.

Fear of the huge Sverdlovs was such that any opportunity to take a look at them close up was grasped with both hands. In 1956, a Sverdlov, the Ordzhonikidze, brought Nikita Khrushchev to Britain on a diplomatic mission. While it was docked at Portsmouth, Second World War veteran diver Commander Lionel 'Buster' Crabb was recruited by MI6 to swim down and have a look at its main propellers. He had undertaken a similar mission the year before and come back with valuable intelligence about a smaller propeller in a recess near its bow.

This time however, he vanished. Fearing the worst, MI6 tried to cover up evidence of the operation but the Soviets later released a statement saying that sailors on the Ordzhonikidze had seen a frogman in the water on the same day that Crabb had gone missing – April 19. Fourteen months later, in 1957, a body in a diving suit was found floating in Chichester harbour. Its head and hands were missing, making identification difficult. The inquest on Crabb returned an open verdict but the coroner said he was satisfied that the body was that of Crabb.

Claims about what happened to him have ranged from a Russian sailor cutting his throat, to his being murdered by a diving buddy sent along with him by MI5. The truth may never be known.

The Sverdlov, however, was obsolete by rapidly advancing missile technology and by 1963 was no longer viewed as a significant threat to Western shipping, even by the Russians.

---

a 120mm L11A5 rifled main gun and an NBC system which could protect the crew in the event of a nuclear blast or chemical attack by sealing them off from the outside world. The Chieftain weighed 56 tons, had a top speed of 30mph and a maximum range of 310 miles. It had a crew of four and a total of 2280 were made, although few of these would have been available in 1963. It may not have been a battle tank, but Britain also possessed the FV601C Saladin Mk.II armoured car in 1963 and it was quite capable of knocking out Soviet T-54s as it would later prove during the Gulf War in 1991. The rugged 6x6 vehicle, which had a turret and looked like a tank on wheels rather than tracks, was built by Alvis and entered service in 1959.

Britain also had a wide selection of armoured personnel carriers in 1963. Among them were the charmingly nicknamed Humber 'Pig' 1-ton APC and the Saracen APC, which were gradually making way for the new FV 432 APC. The 'Pig' was a 4x4 truck with an armoured shell. Britain sold off a number of old 'Pigs' in the early 1960s but when the Troubles began in Northern Ireland they were bought back and some 500 were sent to over. They became an enduring symbol of the conflict.

Surface fleet

The Royal Navy ended the Second World War with a huge collection of aircraft carriers – 38 escort carriers, 10 Colossus class light fleet carriers, four large Illustrious class fleet carriers and two Implacable class carriers. By 1963 all but one of these had gone and in their place were modern fleet carriers *HMS Ark Royal* and *HMS Eagle* plus four Centaur class light fleet carriers. The sole Second World War survivor was the veteran Illustrious class vessel *HMS Victorious* making a total of seven.

Tests had shown that it was very difficult to operate jets from a carrier designed for piston engine aircraft. Three key advances in technology made this possible however – mirror landing aids, angled decks and steam catapults. All three were developed by the British but quickly adopted by the Americans and other nations.

These advances were quickly incorporated into the designs of six carriers that were already under construction by the early to mid-1950s. Work was begun on rebuilding Britain's older carriers to the new modern standard but this quickly proved to be prohibitively expensive. Only *HMS Victorious* had the work completed.

British Army Centurion tanks drive through West Berlin on May 21, 1963.

The long-serving Alvis Saracen could transport a squad of 10 soldiers.

HMS Eagle was one of Britain's seven operational aircraft carriers in 1963. The nation had more than 50 at the end of the Second World War.

Commandos climb aboard a Westland Wessex helicopter on the deck of HMS Albion on October 13, 1962.

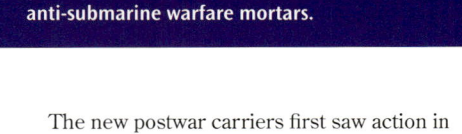

Leander Class vessel HMS Penelope entered service in 1963. It was equipped with Sea Cat missile systems, two 4.5in guns and Limbo anti-submarine warfare mortars.

The new postwar carriers first saw action in 1956 during the Suez Crisis. Aircraft from *HMS Albion*, *HMS Bulwark* and *HMS Eagle* carried out air strikes on Egyptian forces.

In 1963, sister ships *HMS Eagle* and *HMS Ark Royal* had a crew of 2640 including aircraft personnel, a top speed of 31.5 knots (36mph) and could each carry 50 aircraft – Scimitars, Buccaneers, Sea Vixens, Fairey Gannets and Westland Wessex helicopters. The Victorious had a crew of 2200, could hit 30.5 knots (35mph) and could carry 36 aircraft. The four light fleet carriers each had a crew of 2100, a top speed of 28 knots (32mph) and could carry 30 aircraft.

With the advent of missile technology, it was believed that one of the central roles to be played by cruisers was in anti-aircraft defence against bombers. The Royal Navy decided at first that a new cruiser design was needed to carry the newly developed Seaslug surface-to-air missile system but the project was then cancelled in favour of smaller missile carrying destroyers.

In November 1962, the first County class destroyer, *HMS Devonshire*, entered service followed by *HMS Hampshire*, *HMS Kent* and *HMS London* during the course of 1963. These each carried a crew of 471 and could travel at 30 knots (34.5mph). They had two turrets fitted with twin 4.5in guns, two Oerlikon 20mm cannons, one Seaslug missile launcher with 24 missiles, two Sea Cat surface-to-air missile launchers, or at least the mountings for them, two triple-tube torpedo launchers and a single Westland Wessex for anti-submarine warfare.

This flexible mix of weaponry was also adopted for the Navy's new Type 12 or Leander class frigates. These had a top speed of 27 knots (31mph) and a crew of 260. They were intended as general purpose warships which could handle a wide range of missions. The first four, *HMS Leander*, *HMS Dido*, *HMS Penelope* and *HMS Ajax* were accepted into service in 1963. A total of 26 were built. Each had a top speed of 27 knots (31mph) and a crew of 260. They were fitted with Sea Cat missile systems, two 4.5in guns and Limbo anti-submarine warfare mortars, which could basically fire depth charges up to 1000 yards from the ship in any direction.

Britain's defence forces

Britain's armed forces were at a turning point 50 years ago. Developments in missile technology meant much of the nation's Second World War and even 1950s hardware was long past its sell-by date and huge sums were required to create state-of-the-art next generation equipment.

Britain's bombers were technologically advanced but were being made obsolete by missiles. The RAF's fighters were world beaters but were being let down by their own complexity. The 20-year-old Centurion tank was still highly effective but its Chieftain replacement was dogged by teething troubles. The Royal Navy's fleet was small but extremely capable.

In spite of everything though, with Polaris now in the pipeline the country was on course to retain its position at the top table of world affairs for years to come – although the spending cuts and pessimism at the highest levels meant some other nations came around to the idea that Britain had lost its teeth. Argentina would later learn the hard way that this was not the case.

The Bristol Type 188, also known as the Flaming Pencil, looked a little like a British SR-71 Blackbird – which was its near contemporary. Two were made in 1962, XF923 and XF926, and they were used for high speed tests. XF923, pictured here, was later scrapped but XF926 survives at the RAF Museum, Cosford.

ABOVE: Looking down the slender nose of Bristol Type 188 XF926 at RAF Musem, Cosford. It looked fast but its performance failed to live up to expectations. Author

ABOVE RIGHT: It's easy to see why the Type 188 was nicknamed the 'Flaming Pencil' from looking at this rear view. It was an extremely narrow aircraft. Author

RIGHT: The Type 188's cockpit was packed with gauges and readouts in anticipation of the aircraft's flight to Mach 3 and beyond. The 188 never got there. Author

FAR RIGHT: The RAF roundel on XF926's fuselage aft of the cockpit area. The aircraft's uncoated steel skin caused Bristol's engineers some major headaches. Author

CHAPTER 10

The Flaming Pencil

And the nation's other expensive experimental aircraft

Billions were spent on developing high tech weapons systems for the RAF and Royal Navy between the end of the Second World War and 1963 — particularly aircraft. Dozens of innovative prototypes and experimental airframes were produced by British designers and engineers to win an arms race upon which the nation's very survival depended. Among the oddest being testing in 1963 was the Bristol Type 188, otherwise known as the Flaming Pencil...

The Air Ministry decided in 1952 that superfast aircraft were the future and it needed a flying testbed so that research could be carried out on the effects of travelling at several times the speed of sound. It therefore invited all the major aircraft manufacturers of the day to submit designs for "research aircraft for Mach number two". Research at the time suggested that the best shape for such an aircraft was either a very narrow fuselage and small straight tapered wings with an engine positioned in the middle of each wing or a single engine fitted within the fuselage and small straight wings.

Bristol, Armstrong Whitworth and Boulton Paul all came up with designs which took the former shape. Hawker, Vickers and Saunders-Roe came up with aircraft which took the latter and English Electric came up with two designs in each style. Unusually, Bristol decided it would use a complex steel alloy for the construction of its design rather than aluminium. Its skin would be made of very finely rolled steel and its internal structures would be made of steel too. It was to be powered by a Rolls-Royce RA.14R Avon in the centre of each wing.

In the heady days of 1953, when money seemed no object, Bristol was awarded a contract to build its design, the Type 188, and the proposed engine was changed to a Rolls-Royce RA.24. During March 1954 no fewer than eight further types of engine were examined as potential replacements. It was confidently predicted that with the right power plants on board the 188 would easily reach Mach 2 and possibly go well beyond it. Bristol further predicted that the first prototype would be ready in two years.

Serial numbers XF923 and XF926 were assigned for the first two airframes in January 1954. An order for three more followed in 1955. By 1957 however, the firm was still casting around for the right engine and eventually picked De Havilland's PS.50 Gyron Junior. Now the second order was cancelled and it was decided that two Type 188s would be quite enough. There were ongoing difficulties with the type of steel needed for the aircraft's construction but now there were hopes that it would be able to achieve Mach 3 and beyond. As a result, both prototypes were fitted with a wide variety of gauges and instruments designed to measure the stresses of extreme speed on the aircraft. They would examine everything from heating of the steel skin to the action of the wings and tail.

Time dragged on and the first flight did not take place until April 14, 1962, and the 188, nicknamed the Flaming Pencil due to its narrow shape, only managed to reach Mach 1.88 to the great disappointment of all concerned. Worse still, the aircraft could only stay airborne for around 10 minutes due to the incredible fuel consumption of its engines and it was difficult to control. Testing continued throughout 1963 and into 1964 but then the programme was cancelled. It was generally acknowledged that the only lesson learned from the 188 was that aircraft probably shouldn't be made entirely out of steel. The first prototype, XF923, was scrapped but the second still survives at RAF Museum, Cosford.

The Bristol 188 was a classic example of the sort of project that Britain was undertaking during the 1950s with a huge wad of American banknotes burning a hole in its pocket. Another was the Saunders-Roe SR.45 Princess – one of the largest flying boats ever made. Its story began in 1945 when the Ministry of Supply asked the Isle of Wight based firm to submit designs for a flying boat that would be used for transatlantic passenger flights operated by the British Overseas Airways Corporation. The Princess design won the contract and three examples were ordered.

The Princess was huge. It had 10 Bristol Proteus turboprop engines and two decks for up to 105 passengers. Unfortunately, the corporation decided in 1951 that it didn't actually need the Princess after all. The prototype was completed anyway and the Air Ministry decided that the three aircraft it had ordered could be used as military transports by the RAF. The first Princess, registered as G-ALUN, first flew on August 22, 1952, and appeared at the Farnborough Air Show the following year. The two other Princesses, G-ALUO and G-ALUP were built but were mothballed before taking even one flight. By 1963 all three had been cocooned in their hangers for more than six years and the maintenance contract which was in place to keep them airworthy had lapsed. American firm Aero Spacelines offered to buy them and use them for transporting NASA rockets in 1964 but when the cocooning material was removed it was found that the Princesses had begun to rot away. They were scrapped in 1967.

A selection of Cold War prototypes...

Two examples of Hawker's P.1040 were made and these became prototypes for the Royal Navy's Hawker Sea Hawk fighter. The aircraft pictured here, VP401, was used for racing and then as a testbed for the Armstrong Siddeley Snarler liquid fuelled rocket motor. The engine was fitted to the rear fuselage and the last of six test flights resulted in a small explosion in the rear fuselage.

A Saunders-Roe Princess flying boat going through the final phases of assembly at the Columbine Works at East Cowes, Isle of Wight. Three were made but only one ever flew. All were scrapped in 1967.

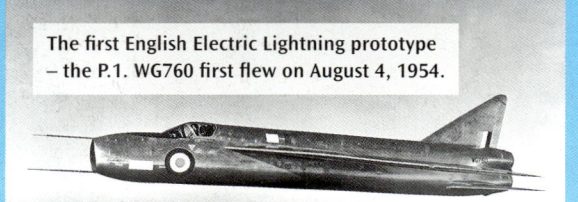

The first English Electric Lightning prototype – the P.1. WG760 first flew on August 4, 1954.

Avro Vulcan VX770, the first prototype of the Vulcan, in flight near London during preparations for a flypast at RAF Odiham, Hampshire, in front of the Queen. VX770 was destroyed in 1958 at RAF Syerston when one of its wings disintegrated during an air show and it crashed, killing all four crew and three people on the ground.

The first Fairey Delta II high speed research aircraft WG774, pictured here, broke the world air speed record by reaching 1132mph over a nine-mile course between Chichester and Ford, Sussex, on March 10, 1956. It held the title for 19 months before an American McDonnell F-101 Voodoo beat it by 75.6mph. Two Fairey Delta IIs were made and both still survive.

The Boulton Paul P.111, VT935, takes to the sky. Its first flight was on October 10, 1950, and its last in 1958.

The Avro 707B was made, like the Boulton Paul P.111, to test delta wing designs. It was one of four prototypes which were used by Avro in preparation for its Vulcan bomber. This aircraft, VX790, is the only one that no longer survives.

The Supermarine 510 prototype VV106 in flight. This was the only one made and its design led to the Supermarine Attacker naval jet fighter. It is now on display at the Fleet Air Arm Museum in Somerset.

The one and only Boulton Paul P.111. It was built to investigate the characteristics of a small delta winged aircraft. VT935 still survives at the Midland Air Museum. Author

The Short Brothers and Harland SA.4 Sperrin jet bomber was produced in 1951 just in case there were delays in the V-bomber programme. There weren't. Both prototypes were scrapped in the late 1950s.

A Saunders-Roe SR.A/1 flying boat jet fighter, moored up on the Thames in London on June 17, 1951. Three were built but two of them were destroyed during accidents. The sole survivor is now at the Solent Sky Museum in Hampshire.

The mushroom cloud generated by a hydrogen bomb detonation. Minutes after a strike on Britain in 1963, any survivors could expect to see more than 100 of these stretched out along the horizon.

CHAPTER 11

DUCK AND COVER

PREPARATIONS FOR A NUCLEAR ATTACK ☢

Hundreds of Soviet nuclear missiles were pointed at Britain by 1963. The Cuban Missile Crisis had made it clear that the nation might be attacked at any time but few had any idea just how devastating such an attack might be. Those at the highest levels of government had few illusions...

The USSR's strategic missile troops probably had several hundred SS-4 Sandal missiles at their disposal at the start of 1963 and more were entering service every month. Deployed along the western edge of the Soviet Union, their 1200 mile range was sufficient to hit Britain and each was fitted with a warhead of either one or 2.3 megatons. It is unknown precisely what they might have been aimed at in 1963 but a Ministry of Defence report in 1967 identified 104 probable targets.

It is likely that a Soviet missile strike would have attempted to knock out all of the RAF's bomber bases and those of the US Air Force's strategic bomber bases as a priority. It would have simultaneously hit military command centres, communications centres, radar stations, naval bases, fighter bases and surface-to-air missile defence bases. Twenty major cities were also on the list: Belfast, Birmingham, Bristol, Cardiff, Coventry, Edinburgh, Glasgow, Hull, Leeds, Leicester, Liverpool, Manchester, Middlesbrough, Newcastle, Nottingham, Sheffield, Stoke-on-Trent, Southampton, Swansea and Wolverhampton.

Every one of these would have been hit by at least one, probably two missiles. Two would be fired at each target in case one failed and London would be hit with eight missiles. Assuming the strikes on fighter bases, radar sites and missile defence bases had been a success and Britain lay ruined and helpless, the next phase of the Soviet plan involved sending waves of strategic bombers over the same 104 targets and dropping two 500 kiloton nuclear bombs on each of them. These, the smallest of the weapons to be used, each had the explosive power of 450 Hiroshimas.

In addition to preparing for a full scale nuclear strike, the USSR was also compiling detailed maps of Britain using Ordnance Survey maps, photo reconnaissance from Zenit spy satellites and information gathered by spies working on the ground. Around 50,000 cartographers were employed to produce the documents which typically showed military structures left off maps made available to the public and in some instances even gave road widths and load bearing characteristics of bridges in the event that the Red Army might need to roll its new 40 ton T-62 tanks across them. A colour coding system was used with industrial structures coloured black, administrative centres in purple and green for military installations. Primary routes of invasion for cities such as London, Birmingham and Manchester were marked in red. These maps were regularly updated throughout the Cold War but it is not clear in what circumstances they were to be used, given the likelihood that a nuclear strike would have reduced many of the buildings and even roadways illustrated to unrecognisable rubble.

KEEP OUT

These suits were the last word in protection against radioactive fallout in 1963. They are seen here being worn by British Army officers and men at the Joint Services Bomb & Missile School. They are equipped with an array of Geiger counters and toxicity meters.

A nuclear strike on London

A thermonuclear missile air burst just above the centre of London, over St James's Park for example, would result in catastrophic damage. The detonation would produce a shockwave of high pressure air radiating outwards, crushing everything in its path. The park's lake, trees and wildlife would be instantly vaporised and all large buildings in the vicinity – Westminster Palace, Whitehall, the Ministry of Defence, Downing Street, Buckingham Palace and so on – would be destroyed in less than one second. People and objects such as cars and lamp posts would be annihilated by the sheer overpressure of the blast. The surface pressure and shock would shatter below-ground structures up to a depth of about 20m.

Everything within a distance of less than a mile from ground zero, all the debris generated, would remain in situ but would be completely unrecognisable. It would pile up to a depth of several hundred feet in places. At the same time, an intense flash of light and burst of heat would affect anyone looking in the direction of the blast, even from miles away. This would produce temporary flash blindness lasting several minutes. Over the next 15 seconds, the blast and firestorm would spread out, covering a radius of up to 10 miles and resulting in more than two million fatalities.

Hundreds of thousands more just outside the immediate radius of the blast would suffer from first, second and third degree burns. A person suffering even third degree burns over more than 24% of their body will enter severe shock which will most likely prove fatal. Dense sources of combustible material such as duvets and sofas would be ignited by the expanding wave of thermal radiation causing numerous fires in even small areas. Anyone caught in but surviving the initial blast would be exposed to a lethal dose of direct radiation.

The greatest hazard to survivors outside the blast zone would come from small particles of debris irradiated by the nuclear explosion and then carried outward by the shock wave or those forming the 'cap' of the mushroom cloud. Particles forming the mushroom cloud's 'stem' would be more highly radioactive but would quickly fall back to earth in areas where most people have already died.

Particles carried away from the point of impact in whichever direction the wind happens to be blowing would form a distended radiation 'hot spot'. Rain causes particles to fall back to earth too so areas of rainfall in the days following the blast are more likely to become heavily irradiated.

In the case of London, with this grim scenario being repeated seven more times across the city,

Effects of a 16 kiloton blast on a house 3500ft away. The time from first to last image is $2\frac{1}{3}$ seconds.

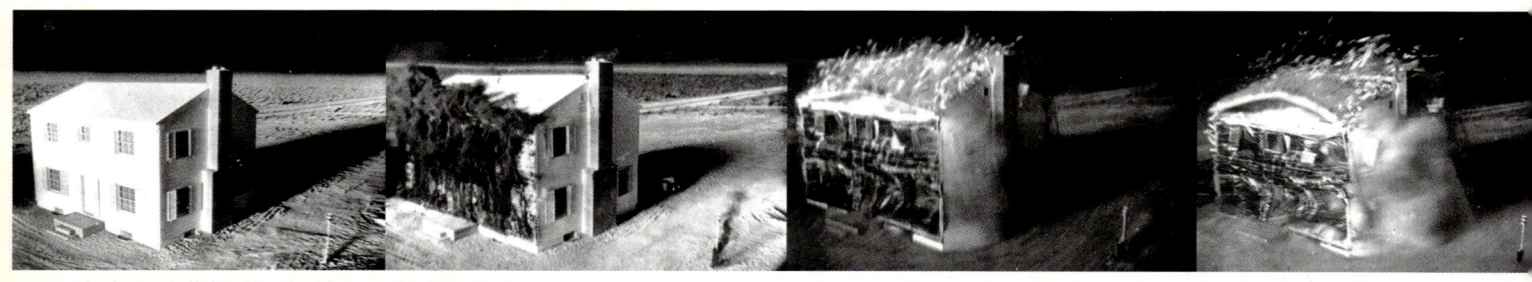

The house is lighted by the blast. | The front begins to burn. | A shockwave blows out the fire. | Disintegration of the house begins.

In the aftermath of a nuclear strike, and assuming it was still able to, the BBC would have broadcast the following message:

This is the Wartime Broadcasting Service. This country has been attacked with nuclear weapons. Communications have been severely disrupted, and the number of casualties and the extent of the damage are not yet known.

We shall bring you further information as soon as possible. Meanwhile, stay tuned to this wavelength, stay calm and stay in your own house. Remember there is nothing to be gained by trying to get away. By leaving your homes you could be exposing yourself to greater danger. If you leave, you may find yourself without food, without water, without accommodation and without protection.

Radioactive fallout, which follows a nuclear explosion, is many times more dangerous if you are directly exposed to it in the open. Roofs and walls offer substantial protection. The safest place is indoors. Make sure gas and other fuel supplies are turned off and that all fires are extinguished. If mains water is available, this can be used for firefighting. You should also refill all your containers for drinking water after the fires have been put out, because the mains water supply may not be available for very long.

Water must not be used for flushing lavatories: until you are told that lavatories may be used again, other toilet arrangements must be made. Use your water only for essential drinking and cooking purposes. Water means life. Don't waste it.

Make your food stocks last: ration your supply, because it may have to last for 14 days or more. If you have fresh food in the house, use this first to avoid wasting it: food in tins will keep. If you live in an area where a fallout warning has been given, stay in your fallout room until you are told it is safe to come out. When the immediate danger has passed the sirens will sound a steady note. The 'all clear' message will also be given on this wavelength.

If you leave the fallout room to go to the lavatory or replenish food or water supplies, do not remain outside the room for a minute longer than is necessary. Do not, in any circumstances, go outside the house. Radioactive fallout can kill. You cannot see it or feel it, but it is there. If you go outside, you will bring danger to your family and you may die.

Stay in your fallout room until you are told it is safe to come out or you hear the 'all clear' on the sirens. Here are the main points again: stay in your own homes, and if you live in an area where a fallout warning has been given stay in your fallout room until you are told it is safe to come out. The message that the immediate danger has passed will be given by the sirens and repeated on this wavelength.

Make sure that the gas and all fuel supplies are turned off and that all fires are extinguished. Water must be rationed, and used only for essential drinking and cooking purposes. It must not be used for flushing lavatories. Ration your food supply – it may have to last for 14 days or more. We shall be on the air every hour, on the hour. Stay tuned to this wavelength, but switch your radios off now to save your batteries. That is the end of this broadcast.

---

with two further bombs being dropped after the initial strikes, it seems unlikely that there would be any survivors. If all 104 targets on the Ministry of Defence's 1967 list had been hit at once, there would have been no safe zones anywhere in Britain. It is estimated that this scenario would have resulted in two thirds of the population dying instantly. Almost the entire country would have been rendered uninhabitable and those few who did manage to survive would face a situation of unimaginable destruction and horror. All facilities such as water and power would have been knocked out. There would be no easy way of telling which areas were irradiated and which, if any, were not and even those hospitals which avoided being destroyed in the first strike would be rendered completely ineffective by the sheer volume of casualties they would be called upon to treat.

Missile alert system

Few people realised in 1963 just how devastating an all-out nuclear attack would be and there was always the possibility that an attack would be less than total. Therefore, Britain had an advanced missile detection and attack early warning system in place. Early in the year, this started with the Jodrell Bank Experimental Station, now known as the Jodrell Bank Observatory. Its radio telescope was regarded as being the only scientific instrument in the world capable of detecting an incoming missile.

Later in the year though, a much more advanced and dedicated missile detection system was installed at RAF Fylingdales on the North York Moors. The Ballistic Missile Early Warning System (BMEWS) consists of three radomes, each measuring 40m in diameter, which look like gigantic golf balls and contain mechanically steered radar equipment. It is still in operation today but even in 1963 it was powerful enough to track incoming missiles and determine what their targets were. Britain would get a maximum of five minutes' warning but the US, which installed the system, would receive 30 minutes.

The second stage of the system was the responsibility of the United Kingdom Warning and Monitoring Organisation (UKWMO) at Royal Observer Corps (ROC) headquarters in Preston. Once it was sent a verified warning by BMEWS, it would immediately put out an alert on all national and local TV and radio networks via an emergency studio at BBC Broadcasting House in London. This would override whatever programme viewers and listeners happened to be tuned in to at the time.

Simultaneously, a second system called Handel would send a verbal warning to 250 major police stations across the country via the

---

The only source of light was from the bomb.

Photos courtesy of National Nuclear Security Administration / Nevada Site Office

Further disintegration takes place.   The house collapses.   Remaining parts of the house fall away.   The house is destroyed.

Operators at the RAF Fylingdales early warning station would have had just seconds to raise the alarm if they detected incoming missiles.

The Ballistic Missile Early Warning System at RAF Fylingdales on the North York Moors. It became operational in 1962.

The hatch leading down to the small underground Royal Observer Corps post at Burgh on Bain in Lincolnshire. Rob Rickels

RAF Stenigot was one of 170 radar sites operated during the Second World War. These were replaced by a system initially known as Green Garlic but later as Type 80. Rob Rickels

Protect and Survive

Public information films designed to help families cope with a nuclear attack and the aftermath were shot in 1975 but similar advice would have been issued in 1963 if an attack had taken place. Here are a few of the instructions given out.

Choosing a fallout room
Families were advised on how to work out which room in their house was most likely to survive a nuclear blast. It would be on the ground floor or in the basement if there was one – whichever room had the least amount of outside wall – and it needed to be as far from the roof as possible. People living in blocks of flats were told to stay in inside passages away from walls and windows and if they lived higher than the fourth floor they were advised to make arrangements to stay elsewhere. Those living in bungalows were told their homes offered little protection and to stay with someone else if possible.

Refuges
It wasn't enough to create a fallout room. Within this you needed a 'refuge'. Making one required a shovel, boxes, cartons or large plastic bags, earth or sand, a hammer, a saw, a screwdriver, nails, screws, string or thin rope and scissors or a penknife. Viewers were advised to "start collecting them now". There were three different ways to make one – firstly by constructing a lean-to made out of wooden doors slanted against a wall and secured to the floor with a wooden strip across the bottom. Bags or boxes filled with sand, earth, books or rolled up clothes had to then be stacked against them from floor to ceiling. The same applied to both ends. The second idea was a cupboard under the stairs. You just put the earth filled boxes on the stairs and around the sides instead. Finally, you could do the same thing with a few sturdy tables.

Sanitation care
Toilet facilities in your fallout room would consist of a bucket lined with a bin bag and covered with a lid. You had to pour disinfectant into it to reduce the smell. Wiping your hands afterwards involved toilet paper soaked in more disinfectant. When it was nearly full, you had to seal it up and put it in a separate container from your food waste.

Food consumption
Naturally, you had to build up reserves of tinned food in your fallout room. These had to be kept under cover to prevent irradiated material from getting on to them but even so, you had to wipe every container before opening it. It was assumed that you'd be 'resting' in your fallout room most of the time and therefore wouldn't need to eat much. Viewers were advised to "eat the smallest amount that you can get by with".

Casualties
If someone died in your fallout room you had to move the body to another room in the house, label it with name and address, wrap it in polythene, paper, sheets or blankets and then tie a second name and address tag to the outside. You then needed to await instructions via the radio. If these didn't come and you'd waited longer than five days you had to bury the body in a trench outside or cover it in earth and mark the spot.

same phone lines that were used by the speaking clock. The operator would hold down a button and give the message: "Attack warning red! Attack warning red!" The system was also wired into 7000 remotely powered air raid sirens across the country which would then be sounded. If this failed, the sirens could be operated manually by the police.

What might happen next has never been clearly defined. The Government created a publication called Protect and Survive but it was never officially published. Later, a series of 20 public information films was produced but never screened. The BBC had instructions only to air it if a nuclear strike looked likely within the next 72 hours.

Prior to 1963, it was assumed that the best way to protect the population was to move it away from large urban areas and potential military targets. April 8, 1962, saw the implementation of Exercise Bluebell. This involved moving 4000 volunteers via the Bluebell Railway to 36 rest centres along its route. It took months to plan and little thought was given to what would happen to the people evacuated if they could not be moved back to their point of origin within a day or two.

Exercise Bluebell was typical of the sort of civil defence planning conducted by the local authorities that had responsibility for it. During 1963 there was a growing realisation that in the event of an attack using thermonuclear weapons there would be very few 'safe' places. In 1966 it was formally decided that attempting to move large numbers of people around shortly before an attack with highly unpredictable consequences was a very bad idea.

There were three organisations in Britain that would have been expected to swing into action in the immediate aftermath of an attack, had any of their members survived long enough to do so. By 1963, the nation's Civil Defence Corps had 122,000 members and the Auxiliary Fire Service had 14,000. The corps, whose members were issued with dark blue uniforms and berets, was expected to form a civilian authority in the aftermath of a nuclear attack. Every county in England and Wales and burgh in Scotland had a 'division'. These were divided up into sections such as headquarters, signals, scientific and reconnaissance, wardens, rescue and ambulance.

The Auxiliary Fire Service was equipped with 1000 'Green Goddess' Bedford RLHZ Self Propelled Pump fire engines and operated alongside the regular fire service during peacetime. In the event of a nuclear strike, it would have operated alongside the Civil Defence Corps in attempting to bring fires resulting from nuclear blasts under control and would have been tasked with rescuing survivors from debris.

The Royal Observer Corps, which had been tasked with spotting enemy bombers during the Second World War, was a third key element of Britain's civil defence. After a nuclear attack its members would have had to report on points of missile impact, the magnitude of the explosion and levels of fallout. A total of 1563 hardened ROC monitoring posts were constructed between 1958 and 1968 and although the number of ROC groups was reduced from 40 to 31 in 1962, those that remained were more professional and better trained.

Britain's nuclear bunkers

For anything other than a direct hit, an underground bunker provided the best defence against the blast and subsequent fallout of a nuclear missile attack and Britain had hundreds of them already built by 1963. The most numerous were the ROC's tiny underground monitoring posts. These were sited about eight miles apart across the whole country and cost about £5000 (£96,000 in today's money) each to build. They were made from a waterproofed concrete shell buried about 25ft down.

The three ROC staff for each post had to climb down a vertical shaft on a steel ladder to get in and once inside they could look forward to living in a single room together with a set of bunk beds, a chemical toilet in a separate compartment and air provided by ventilators at both ends. Power came from a 12v lead-acid battery which would be charged from a portable petrol generator and communication was via telephone, although this was replaced in 1964 first boosted tele-talk units and then radio. In practice, conditions were cramped, cold and often damp – despite the waterproofing.

The ROC monitoring posts were linked to around 30 command centres. These were far more substantial structures that were either above ground or semi-sunken to provide increased protection. They provided living quarters for up to 100 observers and UKWMO warning teams. Men and women had separate dormitories; there were kitchens, decontamination facilities, life support systems, a communications centre and a central operations room.

The ROC was a civilian organisation and its bunkers therefore paled in comparison to what was available to Britain's military. In 1963, preparations were being made to bring the nation's 66 decommissioned Rotor bunkers back into use. Work on Rotor, a code name for Britain's air defence radar system, was begun in 1949. The 170 radar sites operated during the Second World War were drastically reduced in number and the equipment in those that remained was upgraded. The old Chain Home radar technology was replaced by a system initially called Green Garlic but later known as Type 80.

Rotor was established on both the eastern and western sides of the country but those on the eastern side had greater protection since they would be closer to the incoming Russian bombers. These huge underground bunkers, often with as many as three below-ground levels, were disguised above ground by a 'bungalow'. This innocuous looking building served as both a concealed access point and a guardroom for the bunker below. It appeared to have a conventional wooden roof structure with tiles on top but beneath this ordinary exterior sat layers of reinforced concrete.

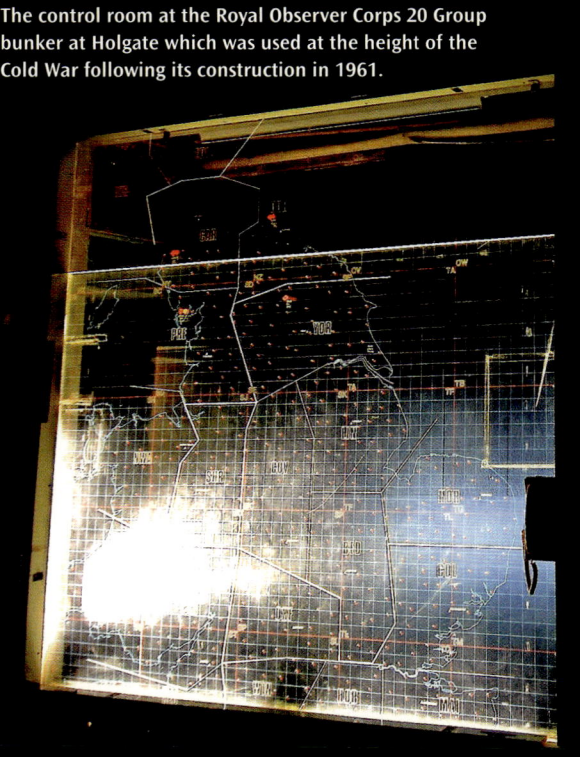

The control room at the Royal Observer Corps 20 Group bunker at Holgate which was used at the height of the Cold War following its construction in 1961.

Beneath this innocuous looking bungalow at Kelvedon Hatch, Brentwood, Essex – 125ft down – lay a hardened Sector Operations Centre for RAF Fighter Command. It could house hundreds of staff for up to three months.

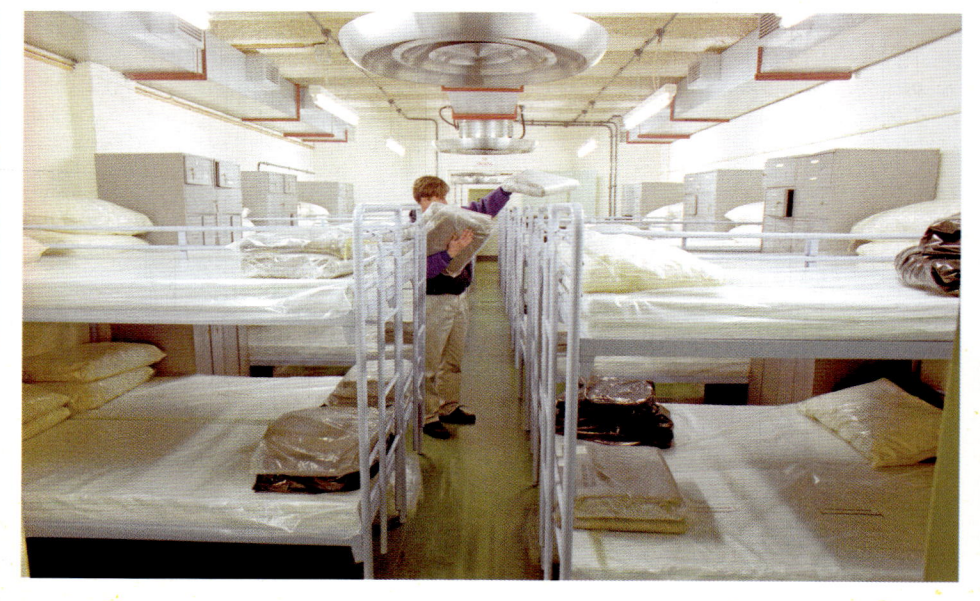

ABOVE: One of the seemingly endless underground corridors at the Kelvedon Hatch bunker in Essex.

RIGHT: A dormitory at Kelvedon Hatch. Conditions following a nuclear strike which irradiated the surface above would quickly have become very uncomfortable.

The bunkers themselves had 10ft thick walls made from concrete laid over a tough skeleton of iron bars, their own generators, air conditioning and boreholes for water. The overall Rotor project entailed the use of 350,000 tons of concrete and 20,000 tons of steel plus hundreds of thousands of miles of telephone lines and electric cabling. In 1953, command and control staffs were transferred to the Rotor bunkers because it was quicker to relay information to them if they were there on the spot. A system of Master Radar Stations (MRS) was set up in 1955 to supersede Rotor and this required far fewer than the 66 stations already built. Many of these were mothballed and the rest were upgraded.

These MRS facilities were themselves in the process of being replaced by a new system – Linesman – in 1963. The advent of missiles with hydrogen warheads and supersonic Soviet bombers meant that the existing system of air defence radar would have to undergo a second upgrade which would integrate the individual stations into a system focused on a single site, known as L1. The staff at L1 would receive data from all Linesman stations simultaneously, giving them a complete picture of the UK's air defence status.

In addition, the powerful but easy to jam Type 80 radar would be replaced by three new systems that would work together. These would be Marconi's new Type 84 radar and AEI's Type 85, also known as Blue Yeoman, and a device produced by Decca to determine the height of incoming contacts called HF200. The two new radar systems would operate on separate frequencies to reduce the chances of both being jammed. The prototype of L1 was established at RAF West Drayton in Middlesex in 1963 but the system did not become operationally active until the 1970s.

The satellite Linesman bunkers at RAF Neatishead in Norfolk, RAF Staxton Wold in Yorkshire, RAF Boulmer in Northumberland and RAF Bishopscourt in Northern Ireland fed their information into L1 enabling its staff to form a 'recognised air picture' covering an area which measured 1024 by 1024 nautical miles over the British Isles. As more advanced computers were added to Linesman the area of coverage increased to 1900 by 1900 nautical miles. L1 also received data from radar sites at RAF Ash in Kent, RAF Ventnor on the Isle of Wight, RAF Clee Hill in Shropshire, RAF Corsham and two sites in London.

Save the Queen — Operation Candid

Plans were drawn up in 1963 for what should happen to the Queen and the Royal Household in the event of a nuclear attack. These plans were codenamed Operation Candid and involved a 1300 strong battalion of soldiers and a signals unit in a fleet of armoured cars escorting the royals to safety. Candid would be activated when it became clear that a state of emergency existed and the royal family would be rapidly taken to an isolated country estate well away from any of their well known residences such as Balmoral Castle in Aberdeenshire, Scotland, or Sandringham House in Norfolk. Although precise details have never been made public it is likely that Prince Charles, as the heir to the throne, would have been moved separately to a second location.

The Queen and Prince Philip in 1963.

The underground city

The largest bunker in Britain in 1963 was reserved for the Government. If nuclear war seemed imminent, there needed to be somewhere safe for the prime minister, his cabinet, high level civil servants and their staff to shelter and continue the work of governing what remained of the nation. This vast but top secret site was known as Burlington bunker or 'Site 3' and it was situated 60-100ft below the surface in a former stone quarry in Wiltshire.

Throughout the 1950s the Government's underground shelter and war rooms had been situated in London but during the age of atomic weapons it was considered that destruction of the capital would be a high priority for the Soviets and the existing shelter, known as Paddock, was not strong or deep enough to withstand a direct hit. Therefore, in 1956, it was decided that a more secure facility would be needed and the Spring Quarry site was chosen. Work began on the 3300ft by 650ft site immediately and was completed in 1961.

When the decision was taken to evacuate the Government from Whitehall, the prime minister and key members of his cabinet would have been flown to Burlington by helicopter. The rest of their staff – up to 4000 civil servants – would join them as soon as possible thereafter by train via a secret branch line off the GWR. The bunker had everything they would need to remain below ground for at least three months. There were dormitories, two kitchens, two canteens, a bakery, a laundry, a medical centre complete with examination rooms, hospital wards, workshops and a library stocked with everything the country would need to rebuild even if all specialists in particular fields were wiped out. It had books on scientific processes, technical manuals, maps and Government documents.

There was an underground lake to keep the bunker's residents supplied with fresh water, a water filtration plant, a telephone exchange which was the second biggest in Britain when it was built, a system of pneumatic tubes so that written messages could be easily relayed across the complex, electric buggies for speedy transportation of personnel along 60 miles of roads, a buggy battery recharging station, a dark room for developing photographs, and even a pub called the Rose & Crown.

There were more than 100,000 individual lights, a public address system with record player for piping music around the bunker and an air conditioning system to keep the climate at a steady 20°C. This was fitted with filters and butterfly valves which could be used to seal the system if there was a risk of fallout or other contamination. The bunker's generators had enough fuel to keep them running nonstop for three months. Accommodation for the prime minister and his family consisted of an ordinary looking room, much like those elsewhere in the bunker but the walls were whitewashed and there was a private bathroom complete with bath whereas most other residents would have been forced to share communal washrooms with long rows of lavatories and basins.

The bunker's storerooms were kept stocked with everything necessary to maintain a 'normal' existence. There were teapots, lamps, toilet brushes, a potato rumbler for removing skins and even equipment for making butter pats. Murals were painted on the walls by artist Olga Lehmann. There was an armoury too, which would have been stocked with the standard issue service weapons of the day – Enfield No. 2 Mk.I revolvers, Browning Hi-Power pistols, Sterling submachine guns and possibly even a Bren gun or two.

A staff of around 50 kept the bunker in a state of readiness throughout 1963 and on into the 1980s until it was mothballed in 1991 and finally decommissioned in 2004. Its future is uncertain with several options apparently being reviewed.

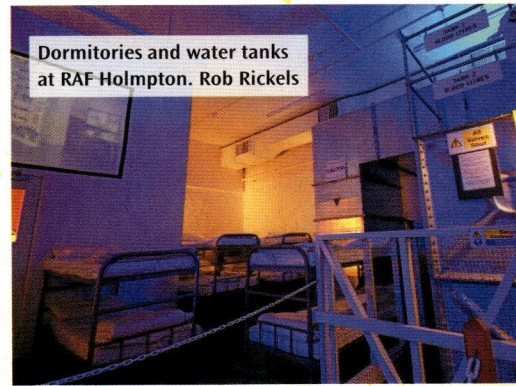

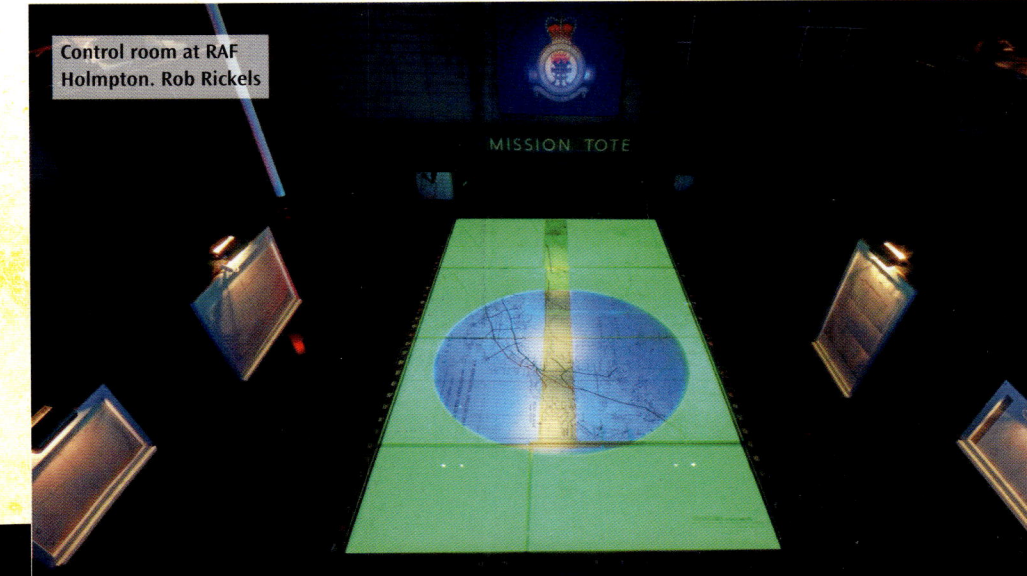

One of RAF Holmpton's many underground offices complete with an array of alert status monitors. Rob Rickels

Dormitories and water tanks at RAF Holmpton. Rob Rickels

Control room at RAF Holmpton. Rob Rickels

The Fab Four in 1963. Paul McCartney, John Lennon, Ringo Starr and George Harrison made 1963 the year of the Beatles and put pop music in the headlines day after day.

Mike Hailwood on his way to gaining a double victory in the Motorcycle Championship at the Sachsenring circuit in Hohenstein, East Germany, on June 30, 1963. Motorcycle racing in 1963 had a strong influence on a generation of young people.

Proud Mods Roy Young and Linda Jarvis with Roy's customised scooter. Mod style was taking off in 1963.

Rockers riding along the sea front at Hastings.

CHAPTER 12

The teenage dream

The rise of youth culture

While the world's leaders rattled their sabres and prepared for the worst, the youth of Britain was enjoying new-found freedom. The pill was available on prescription, young people had more spending power than ever before and pop music was creating the idea of the modern 'teenager'.

The chill of the Cold War permeated all levels of society in 1963 but young people were nevertheless enjoying the dawn of a new golden age of liberty. The baby boomer generation was growing up and there were more teenagers living in Britain than there ever had been before. In 1946, there had been 650,000 births and the following year there were more than 800,000. The death rate each year was roughly 250,000, resulting in a huge population increase. By 1963, there were more than 1.4 million 16 and 17 year olds in a total population of 53.6 million – around one in every 38 people.

These youngsters began to see themselves as different from the generations that had gone before. They were more willing to question the establishment and embrace the changes and challenges of the modern world. It was the beginning of a cultural shift which would eventually alter traditional values and politics to the point where the Cold War, with its Iron Curtain, its deadly nuclear weapons and the paranoid fear it embodied simply ceased to be relevant. The generation which emerged from the ashes of the Second World War would be the generation which ultimately succeeded in ending the conflict that followed – not with guns and bombs but through the unlikely combination of free love, peaceful protest, pop music, fashion and technology.

The contraceptive pill

The first oral contraceptive pill was developed in the US by pharmaceutical firm G D Searle & Company in 1957 and was originally marketed as a treatment for menstrual disorders. It was called Enovid and it had been tested and proven effective on 600 women during clinical trials. Over the next two years it became apparent that Enovid was successful in another way too and on July 23, 1959, Searle applied to the American Food and Drug Administration to have it approved as a contraceptive. Approval came on June 23, 1960, and by the end of 1961 more than one million women were using it in the US although it was not made available in all states.

As Enovid was being made available across the pond, Searle also attempted to sell its product in Britain. Renamed Enavid, it was made available to women suffering from menstrual problems in 1957. During the same year the Family Planning Association, a sexual health charity that was the main provider of family planning services in Britain, set about testing a range of oral contraceptives on animals. As a result of these tests, large scale clinical trials began in 1960 and 1961 in Birmingham, Slough and London. The Birmingham tests involved a version of Enavid called Conovid, which was also produced by Searle, while the Slough trials tested a similar pill called Conovid-E. The London trials, meanwhile, focused on Anovlar, a product of German chemicals company Schering.

As a result of this extensive testing programme, Conovid was added to the Family Planning Association's list of approved contraceptives in October 1961. Less than two months later, the Minister of Health, Enoch Powell, announced that Conovid would be made available on prescription from the NHS. The price would be two shillings a month. Both Conovid-E and Anovlar were approved as contraceptives the following year. At the time it seemed as though the effect of this medical breakthrough was being blunted by the establishment. An article in the Observer published on May 5, 1963, noted that the pill was very difficult for an unmarried woman to get

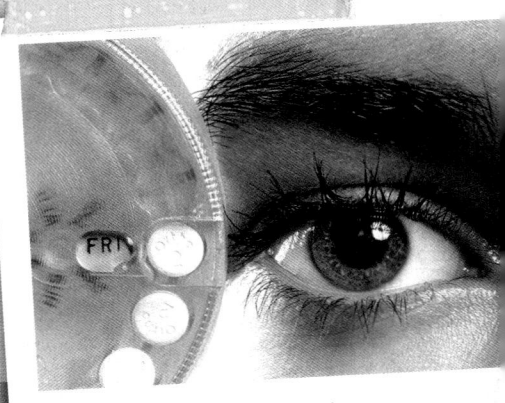

The contraceptive pill began to give young people a new-found sexual freedom in 1963.

Leather clad rocker girls demonstrate a style that, at the time, seemed the antithesis of everything the Mod culture stood for.

Mods gather on the promenade at Hastings in 1964, the year after the youth movement really got going.

French fashion designer Yves St Laurent receives a kiss from model Eva after showing off his fall and winter fashions in Paris on July 29, 1963. Saint Laurent was one of male fashion's trend setters that year.

hold of. It stated: "If she knows the right man in Harley Street she can get fitted for five guineas. If she is able to lie convincingly and stick to her story through often ruthless cross questioning, she can go to the family planning clinics and tell them she is about to get married. If she is confident enough she will go to her GP who may or may not be ready to help her. But he is probably a friend of her parents. The end result is that most girls give up."

However, the somewhat frosty reception that the pill initially received gradually began to thaw as it became an accepted part of everyday life and by the end of 1963 an estimated 480,000 women were using the contraceptive pill. Looking back on the early years of the pill, feminist novelist Angela Carter, who'd been 23 in 1963 having married aged 20 in 1960, wrote: "The introduction of more or less 100% effective methods of birth control, combined with the relaxation of manners that may have derived from this technological innovation or else came from God knows where, changed, well, everything."

A survey carried out in 1960 had shown that the majority of couples already used condoms for birth control but the pill was different. It allowed women to take control of their own fertility and therefore contributed towards an increasing movement towards equality of the sexes. It became easier to have sex for the sake of pleasure without having to worry too much about the potential consequences and this new freedom had an effect that was subtle at first but which gradually changed attitudes towards sex throughout British society.

Changing fashions

During 1963, the economy grew at a rate of 5-6%. Unemployment, which had risen to 7% of the workforce in 1961, was down to an average of 5.5% and continuing to fall. British industry was doing well and this meant young people were more likely to have a degree of disposable income and there were an increasing number of ways in which they could spend it. Motorcycles were enjoying a surge in popularity thanks to the performances of legendary racers such as Mike Hailwood – who won seven 500cc Grand Prix races to win the overall title in 1963 with MV Agusta. Scooters were popular too.

Both forms of transport were linked with two emerging youth cults – the Mods, short for modernists, and the rockers. Mod was a new movement which had begun to form the year before. The boys tended to cut their hair short and wore casual jackets, wool shirts, ankle length trousers and casual shoes or sneakers. The style for Mod girls was to wear their hair in a bob and dress in long leather coats and dresses down to their calves. The rocker movement grew out of existing teddy boy and ton-up groups. They had long ted-style hair, short leather jackets, turned up jeans and winkle pickers.

Clashes between proponents of the two distinct styles began to break out in 1963 in London, although the real antagonism took place at seaside resorts the following year. During 1963, Mods identified most closely with the Beatles and their music but by 1964 the 'in' Mod bands had become the Rolling Stones, the Yardbirds and the Kinks.

Miniskirt inventor Mary Quant was at the top of her game in 1963 and had a powerful influence on the way young people dressed for the rest of the decade.

The Beatles had a far wider impact in 1963 than they're often given credit for. This outfit, pictured on October 29, 1963, supposedly represented the 'Beatle look' for women.

Youth culture and style was also being influenced by a new wave of designers who were rapidly changing fashion in a way that had never been done before. Among them were the likes of Mary Quant and Yves St Laurent. Quant was a home grown talent from Blackheath, southeast London. She started out making hats but in November 1955 she opened her own shop in King's Road called Bazaar with her husband Alexander Plunket Greene. By the late 1950s Bazaar was getting noticed for its stockings and black dresses and in 1963 Quant won the inaugural Dress of the Year Award, which is still presented annually by the Fashion Museum in Bath, the Sunday Times International Fashion Award and the Woman of the Year Award. Her great innovation was the miniskirt which she named after her favourite type of car, the Mini.

Although there had been a trend for skirts to get shorter during previous years, giving women more freedom to move quickly, Quant went further, believing that a shorter skirt would provide practical benefits in allowing women to, for example, run to catch a bus. She also came up with the idea of matching the miniskirt to coloured and patterned tights. In her own words: "It was the girls on the King's Road who invented the mini. I was making easy, youthful, simple clothes, in which you could move, in which you could run and jump and we would make them the length the customer wanted. I wore them very short and customers would say 'shorter, shorter'." She also said: "A woman is as young as her knees."

Yves Saint Laurent, who had a big influence on male fashion in 1963 and beyond, was French but was born in Algeria. As a teenager he designed dresses for his mother and his two younger sisters. Aged 18 he moved to Paris and met Christian Dior who took him under his wing. Dior himself died in 1957 in unclear circumstances – some sources suggest he suffered a heart attack after a strenuous sexual encounter, while others believe he choked on a fishbone – and Saint Laurent, aged just 21, became the chief designer of the House of Christian Dior. He won huge praise for his 1958 spring collection but his subsequent work, which showed the beginnings of his beatnik style, was not so successful and in 1960 he was called up to serve in the French Army during the Algerian War of Independence.

As a young gay man he suffered attacks from his fellow soldiers and ended up in a military hospital, where he found out that he had been given the sack by the House of Christian Dior. As if this wasn't enough, he was then sent to another hospital where he was constantly sedated and forced to undergo electroconvulsive therapy – a series of electrical shocks to the brain. Finally released in November 1960 he took Dior to court for breach of contract and won the case. By 1963 he was at the cutting edge of men's fashion, pioneering safari jackets and tight trousers.

The sound of 1963

While fashion designers were reshaping the baby boomers' clothes, music was starting to become the generation's obsession. Fans of other genres and bands may object but the facts speak for themselves – 1963 was the year of the Beatles.

The group's first single, Love Me Do, was released in October 1962, but John, Paul, George and Ringo's debut album Please Please Me was the real source of their success. It came out on March 22, 1963, and went to number one in the charts – remaining there for 30 weeks before being knocked off the top spot by the Beatles' own second album With The Beatles in November. This stayed at number one for a further 21 weeks – giving the group nearly a full calendar year at the top. No one else has ever managed this feat.

Although the reach of pop music was less all-pervading than it is today, the effect of the Beatles reign in the charts was dramatic. The clothes they wore and their hairstyles influenced high street fashions, their irreverence and offhand manner appealed directly to the baby boomers' sense of being divorced from the British tradition of deference and their rags to riches story inspired young people across Britain to pick up a guitar and attempt to emulate their success.

There were further spinoffs too. There had been 'groupies' before but never on the scale witness by the Beatles. The band members were mobbed wherever they went. A riotous performance at the London Palladium on October 13 resulted in the Daily Mirror coining the phrase 'Beatlemania' to describe the hysterical antics of fans which largely bemused the uncomprehending older generation. The Beatles were also influential in giving a leg up to another band who were beginning to attract national attention in 1963 – the Rolling Stones. George Harrison recommended them to Dick Rowe, the man from Decca Records who had turned down the Beatles before they

Social activist Mary Whitehouse began writing to the BBC after being appalled by what she saw as declining standards on British television in 1963. She is pictured here in 1965 handing a petition over outside the House of Commons calling for the Beeb to have a "radical change of policy".

Prime Minister Harold Macmillan told Postmaster General Reginald Bevins that being laughed at was better than being ignored.

Postmaster General Reginald Bevins had responsibility for the content of BBC television programmes and pledged to take action against That Was The Week That Was for criticising the prime minister until Harold Macmillan told him not to.

Political activism and protests

Successive Conservative governments had ruled Britain for more than 12 years by 1963. Labour's Clement Attlee had held power for a six year spell after the Second World War but then Sir Winston Churchill, Anthony Eden and Harold Macmillan had each been put in charge to guide Britain through the dark days of the early Cold War. Now though, the prevailing breeze was blowing against the Conservatives. Scandals such as the Profumo Affair and constant bickering about the vast sums being spent on Britain's defence had turned the public against them. There was a feeling that change at the top was long overdue but even after Macmillan took early retirement, yet another Conservative rose to take his place – the aristocratic Sir Alec Douglas-Home.

Britain's young people felt the general public dissatisfaction more keenly than most and there was a rise in public protests and activism against the Government's activities – particularly when it came to nuclear weapons. The Campaign for Nuclear Disarmament (CND) had been formed in 1958 during a meeting attended by 5000 people at Central Hall in Westminster. In Easter of the same year the organisation arranged its first 52 mile march from London to the Atomic Weapons Research Establishment at Aldermaston in Berkshire. This event initially attracted a few thousand protestors but by 1963 there were more than 100,000 people taking part. The route had also been reversed so that the marchers were walking from Aldermaston to London.

The 1963 march was the last however, since it had grown too large and unwieldy for its organisers to properly control. Numerous smaller groups such as anarchist organisations and a militant faction, Spies for Peace, had also become involved and there were more disturbances along the way than there had been before. There were, however, further CND protests throughout the year.

Another expression of anti-establishment feeling in 1963 was the formation of the Hunt Saboteurs Association (HSA). Direct attempts to disrupt fox hunting had been made since the late 1950s by the League Against Cruel Sports – which had been going since 1927. In August 1958 it had tried to sabotage the Devon and Somerset hunt by laying false scents and similar efforts were made over the next few years. By 1962 though, the league's members were ready to take more direct action. Activist Gwen Barter made newspaper headlines when she climbed on to the front of a deer cart and brought the Norwich hunt to a halt.

At the league's annual meeting in 1963, the former Conservative MP for Brighton Kempton Howard Johnson told the assembled members: "I have a vision in the coming stag and foxhunting season of whole numbers of you sitting in the roadway at meets of the hunt doing exactly what the anti-nuclear demonstrators do." The founder of the Hunt Saboteurs Association, 21-year-old freelance journalist John Prestige from Devon, took this message to heart and established a more radical wing of the league on December 15, 1963. In an interview with the Daily Herald he said: "We aim to make it impossible for people to hunt by confusing the hounds. The movement is being financed by a small legacy of mine and the 2/6d membership fee."

By the end of the year, Prestige had more than 100 members and had received more than 1000 letters of support from across the country. The HSA's first mission was on Boxing Day 1963 at a hunt in Torquay. Members bought 50lb of meat and managed to feed it to the hounds before the hunt commenced. They also researched how huntsmen blew their horns, bought some horns of their own, and blew them throughout the event, causing chaos and confusion. The following year the HSA started using chemicals to distract the hounds.

Mounted and on foot, police struggle to hold back hordes of anti-nuclear marchers swarming through Whitehall on April 15, 1963. With thousands more young people in attendance, the CND Aldermaston march was in danger of getting out of hand.

A long column of 'ban the bomb' marchers arrive at Hyde Park, London. The march had started from the Atomic Weapons Research Establishment at Aldermaston.

Fighting racism

Young people were instrumental in helping to get the law changed to outlaw racism during and after an incident in 1963. Britain may not have had a Rosa Parks – the black American woman who refused to give up her seat for a white man in Alabama, US, in 1955 – but it did have a bus boycott inspired by Martin Luther King which resulted in moves towards greater equality just the same. Bristol was the scene of racial discrimination and antagonism in the early 1960s. It had a population of some 3000 West Indians, many of whom had settled in the city shortly after the Second World War, and they suffered from attacks by gangs of white youths, difficulty in getting jobs and discrimination when it came to housing.

One of the West Indian community's foremost grievances was the open discrimination practiced by the Government-owned Bristol Omnibus Company. It refused to hire black people as bus crew even though it was struggling to fill its vacancies. Existing bus crew members claimed that a new supply of workers would result in their wages being dropped.

This attitude didn't wash with the West Indian community and four young men, Roy Hackett, Owen Henry, Audley Evans and Prince Brown decided to take direct action with the help of 25-year-old youth worker Paul Stephenson. Stephenson, who had been to college and was well spoken, gathered evidence on the bus company's 'colour bar' by ringing up and arranging a bus conductor job interview for a young man called Guy Reid Bailey. When Bailey turned up for the interview, he was told that the job had gone. Stephenson rang back to ask whether this was the case and was told the position was still vacant. With this evidence in hand, the group decided to stage a bus boycott beginning on April 29.

By the following day it was said to have attracted widespread support from all sections of society. Asked about the Bristol Omnibus Company's response to the boycott, the firm's general manager Ian Patey said: "You won't get a white man in London to admit it, but which of them will join a service where they may find themselves working under a coloured foreman? I understand that in London, coloured men have become arrogant and rude, after they have been employed for some months."

Bristol University students backed the boycott and staged a protest march to the bus station on May 1. The local MP Tony Benn got in touch with the leader of the Labour opposition, Harold Wilson, and he was quick to condemn the position of the Bristol Omnibus Company. The bus workers' union representatives still refused to meet with Stephenson and the others however. There were further demonstrations and at various stages the Bishop of Bristol Oliver Stratford Tomkins, the Lord Mayor of Bristol and the leader of the Transport and General Workers Union were all involved in negotiations.

Finally, on August 27, at a meeting of 500 bus workers it was agreed that the colour bar would be lifted and the city's first non-white bus conductor, Raghbir Singh, started work on September 17. Harold Wilson's Labour Party defeated the Conservatives at the general election the following year and in 1965 Parliament passed the Race Relations Act – the first pieces of legislation in Britain to address issues of racism. It made "racial discrimination unlawful in public places".

While the baby boomers were finding their feet and starting to make their mark, there was plenty going on which would help to form the basis of a burgeoning pop culture for the decades that followed – a pop culture which would eventually help to break the ice of the Cold War.

Elizabeth Taylor, already a Hollywood superstar, in London in August 1963. She had made headlines throughout the year.

1963: The key events

January >

- The big freeze, Britain's worst winter since records began, disrupts services and causes numerous deaths particularly among the elderly, weak and vulnerable.
- Labour Party leader and leader of the opposition Hugh Gaitskell dies aged 56 from autoimmune disease Lupus erythematosus and is replaced by Harold Wilson.
- Comedy shows screened by the BBC are finally allowed to mention sex, politics, religion and the royal family.
- Britain's application to join the EEC is vetoed by French President Charles de Gaulle.

RIGHT: Cliff Richard in Summer Holiday.

- LNER Class A3 Pacific steam locomotive No. 4472 *Flying Scotsman*, operating as No. 60103, hauls its final British Railways service and is sold into preservation.
- Five US helicopters are shot down in South Vietnam during the first significant battle of the Vietnam War.
- Drummer Charlie Watts joins the Rolling Stones.
- Summer Holiday, starring Cliff Richard, gets its British premiere.
- The world's first discotheque, the Whiskey A-Go-Go, opens in the US.
- Ian Fleming begins writing the last James Bond novel that would be published in his lifetime – You Only Live Twice.

CHAPTER 13

Swinging 1963

From the headless man to The Great Escape

While the Cold War threatened to heat up very quickly in 1963, Britain suffered one of its coldest winters on record. The year also saw huge upheaval, sex scandals, classic films, horrific crimes, iconic cars, the first episode of Doctor Who and . . . the touch tone telephone.

The year began with Britain deep frozen by one of the worst winters on record. December of 1962 had seen early snow followed by a very cold blast from Russia and heavy snow blanketed the country on Boxing Day, carrying on into December 27. Temperatures remained low even when the skies cleared a little and two days later a blizzard drove yet more snow over the south. Power and phone lines came crashing down under the sheer weight of ice that built up on them and some roads were covered with drifts up to 20ft deep. Five people died in snowstorms on December 30, two of them due to suffocation while trapped in their cars. Five more died the following day and 2000 ponies became trapped under drifting snow.

By the time January had arrived, Manchester was under 6in of snow, Stafford was under 18in, Kent had some drifts up to 8ft deep and parts of the West Country were under 15ft of freezing white precipitation. Helicopters had to be used to ferry supplies out to communities in the west that were cut off. Four more deaths were attributed to the snow on January 2.

Now that the snow was in place, temperatures dropped still further causing much of it to turn into ice. To make matters worse, the country was shrouded in a pall of freezing fog for much of the month, which was the coldest recorded in the 20th century. The sea froze for nearly a mile around Herne Bay in Kent. Roads and railways were impassable in many cases, airports closed too and the price of fresh food rose 30% due to the difficulty of getting it to the shops. There were no rubbish collections and some people had to get their water supplies from tankers in the street after entire mains pipes froze solid. Farm animals starved to death in their shelters because farmers were unable to get feed out to them. Eleven people died due to gas leaking from frost damaged pipes. On January 18, a woman was found frozen to death outside her cottage and two days later a man was found dead in a stranded car near Blackburn. Two coachloads of people had to be rescued near Derbyshire after spending all night trapped in a snowdrift.

Small icebergs were seen floating in the Mersey on January 22 and pack ice was reported in the Humber and the Solent and in East Anglia. A further seven deaths were attributed to the severe cold. The following day, 200 London buses were put out of action when their fuel froze in their

February >

- The big freeze continues causing the fifth and sixth rounds of the 1962-63 FA Cup to be postponed by the Football Association.
- The Beatles get their first No. 1 single with Please Please Me and record their debut album of the same name in just nine hours and 45 minutes.
- Telstar 1, the world's first privately financed communications satellite, is destroyed in space by radiation just eight months after it was launched.

RIGHT: Telstar 1.

Milkmen use children's sledges to make deliveries in South London during the Big Freeze.

Waves turned to solid ice along a three mile stretch of Kent coastline for a quarter of a mile out to sea.

Ships of the Leigh-on-Sea fishing fleet locked in the ice at their berths in the Thames Estuary, Essex, in January. The last time this had happened was in 1887.

tanks. Those rail services still able to run were thrown into chaos when diesel fuel, coal, water and points were rendered unusable by ice and snow.

A brief thaw at the end of January created more problems than it solved. The National Grid collapsed, with blackouts sweeping the land, particularly the East Midlands, and firemen had to deal with 1473 floods in London alone due to burst pipes thawing out. Ten tons of ice dropped on to railway lines at Caerphilly and Derbyshire County Council used 400lb of explosives to blow up a huge overhang of snow above Snake Pass which had been closed to traffic for 11 days.

There was no relief in February as yet more snow arrived. Another blizzard, this time lasting 36 hours, swept the nation and winds reached speeds of up to 81mph. Children had to be rescued from their school buses by farmers in Midlothian on February 4. A couple of days later nearly 1000 cars became stranded on the Great North Road at Alnwick. On February 8, helicopters ran regular flights to isolated communities in Northern Ireland and farmers there were forced to prepare 1500 pigs for slaughter simply because they had run out of feed for them.

The much longed for thaw finally arrived on March 6. Temperatures rose and the snow gradually disappeared, though the process took as long as two months in some places. It has been estimated that the winter of 1962-63 killed off between 50% and 80% of Britain's wild bird population including 80% of wrens and 98% of all Dartford warblers. The Office for National Statistics estimates that in addition to the well-publicised deaths outdoors, the harsh winter of 1962-63 was directly responsible for a further 89,600 deaths due to vulnerable people such as the very young, the elderly and the sick being exposed to extremely low temperatures for a sustained period. The Big Freeze, as it has become known, is widely regarded as having been Britain's worst winter since records began.

The Duchess and her 88 lovers

The national temperature rose considerably after the snows, particularly when the Duke of Argyll produced naked Polaroids of his wife, the Duchess of Argyll, during their sensational 11 day divorce proceedings.

The duchess, Margaret Campbell, was the daughter of a Scottish millionaire, had wedded her second husband Ian Douglas Campbell, the 11th Duke of Argyll, after meeting him on a blind date in 1951 but it had not been a happy marriage. Margaret was notorious for her wandering eye and Ian, who had fought during the Second World War and been held prisoner by the Germans, decided he'd had enough.

At first he put a bolt on his bedroom door to stop her from getting in. Next he obtained a court order banning her from their home at picturesque Inveraray Castle in Scotland. Margaret launched a legal challenge to this and

March >

- Labour MP George Wigg tells the House of Commons that War Minister John Profumo is sleeping with Christine Keeler – a topless dancer known to also be involved with a Soviet naval attaché. Profumo admits knowing Keeler but denies any wrongdoing.
- Britain has its first frost-free night since the big freeze began.
- British Railways chairman Dr Richard Beeching unveils plans for huge cuts to the national railway network. His plans involve closing more than 2000 stations and are expected to result in more than 60,000 job losses.
- The divorce of the Duke and Duchess of Argyll results in a national sex scandal. During their marriage the Duchess, Margaret Campbell, had numerous affairs and during the divorce proceedings the Duke produces Polaroid photos of her performing a sex act on a naked man, whose head is not visible, while wearing nothing but her signature pearl necklace.
- Lee Harvey Oswald buys a mail order rifle for $21.45 under the alias 'A Hidell' that he will later use to assassinate US President John F Kennedy.
- The Beatles release Please Please Me.
- The Marvel Comics character Iron Man makes his debut in an issue of Tales of Suspense. His armour is metallic in colour.

Omar Sharif in Lawrence of Arabia.

Margaret Campbell, the Duchess of Argyll. During her divorce proceedings, her husband produced photographs of her performing a sex act on a mystery man.

the couple's marital problems came to the attention of the public for the first time. In addition to her challenge, the duchess also claimed that many of the valuable items still inside Inveraray were hers. The duke countered by claiming that his wife had broken into the castle while he was out and taken a painting, photo albums and two boomerangs from his study.

As the case progressed, Margaret was allowed into the castle for one day to collect her things. She took 500 records, a wooden ash tray, a tartan cloth and an engraved paperknife.

Now it was the duchess's turn to launch a fresh legal case. She claimed Lady Jeanne, the duke's daughter, had seized personal property from her house in Mayfair.

There was some truth in this because that's how the duke ended up with the compromising photographs of his wife and the 'headless man', not to mention her diaries covering the preceding four years.

He accused her of infidelity and the photos, which he presented at the proceedings, certainly demonstrated that his suspicions were on the money. The duchess was depicted nude except for her trademark triple strand pearl necklace performing fellatio on a naked man whose head was 'chopped' off by the edge of the photo.

The duke wasn't finished however. He also brought out a list of 88 men he claimed had slept with his wife. It is believed to have included three members of the royal family and two government ministers. As the case rattled on, Sir Winston Churchill's son-in-law Duncan Sandys, a cabinet minister in the Conservative government, approached the Prime Minister Harold Macmillan and confessed that he feared he might be the man in the photographs. If this was the case then the resulting scandal could have toppled the government, which was already teetering thanks to the ongoing Profumo Affair.

Lord Denning was called in to uncover the identity of the 'headless man'. He saw that each of four shots of the man in different states of arousal had a handwritten caption – "before",

April >

- Britain signs an agreement to buy the Polaris nuclear missile system from the Americans prompting more than 70,000 protestors to march from London to the Atomic Weapons Establishment at Aldermaston, Berkshire, in protest.
- Former Prime Minister Sir Winston Churchill is made an honorary US citizen.
- The US nuclear submarine Thresher sinks off the coast of Cape Cod, Massachusetts, with the loss of all her 129 officers, crewmen and civilian technicians.
- Football manager Alf Ramsey leaves Ipswich Town after eight seasons, having guided them from the Third Division South to the very top of English football. Three days later he takes up his new post as England manager. The press are incredulous when he predicts that his squad will win the next World Cup, which is to be held in England in 1966.
- Lawrence of Arabia picks up seven Oscars including best picture at the 35th Academy Awards hosted by Frank Sinatra.
- The Beatles release From Me To You. It is their first No. 1 in some UK charts but their second in others.
- Beatle George Harrison watches unsigned band The Rolling Stones in concert and is unimpressed.
- Filming of Stanley Kubrick's black Cold War comedy Dr Strangelove or: How I Learned to Stop Worrying and Love the Bomb, starring Peter Sellers, begins in England and continues on into the summer.
- The 10th James Bond novel, On Her Majesty's Secret Service by Ian Fleming, is published.

Peter Sellers in Dr Strangelove.

Great Train Robbery ringleader and mastermind Bruce Reynolds. He spent five years on the run after the robbery before being caught and handed a 25-year prison sentence. He served nine.

Ronnie Biggs was a fugitive for 36 years after taking part in the Great Train Robbery, even though he'd initially been caught and jailed. He eventually came home in 2001 and served eight years in jail.

Robber Buster Edwards had a film made about his life in which he was portrayed by Phil Collins. He committed suicide in 1994.

The Great Train Robbery

Just four and a half months after Beeching pronounced sentence on Britain's railways, a gang of criminals carried out one of the most audacious crimes of the 20th century – on a train.

Drawing inspiration from the railroad robberies carried out by the Hole in the Wall Gang of the Wild West a century earlier, armed robber Bruce Reynolds gathered inside knowledge on the movement of valuables through Buckinghamshire on an overnight Travelling Post Office train.

This service regularly went from Glasgow to London with staff on board sorting post prior to arrival. The second carriage from the front was the high value package carriage where registered post was sorted. Reynolds established that around £300,000 was usually carried but every time there was a bank holiday weekend in Scotland the quantity of money on the next train load was increased dramatically.

Having established when this was likely to happen next, August 8, 1963, he came up with a plan to stop the train and drew together a gang capable of grabbing and making off with the money.

On the big day, shortly before 3am, a glove was stuffed into the signal box at Sears Crossing near Leighton Buzzard, masking the correct signal. At the same time, a 6v battery was wired up and used to activate the red 'stop' signal.

When the Travelling Post Office approached the 'red', driver Jack Mills saw it and stopped the train. Co-driver David Whitby got out to see what was wrong but found that the lineside phone cables had been cut and was therefore unable to contact the signalman. While he was doing this, a masked robber jumped into the cab and hit Mills on the head with a metal bar, knocking him out.

More robbers climbed aboard and uncoupled the engine and the first two carriages from the rest of the train. The idea was to move the money a mile further down the track to Bridego railway bridge where it could be safely offloaded into waiting Land Rovers but the robbers soon realised that they were unable to operate the complicated diesel locomotive and had to wake Mills up to do it for them.

July >

- British spy Kim Philby is named as the 'third man' in the Cambridge spy ring and defects to the USSR.
- The Moors Murderers Myra Hindley and Ian Brady claim their first victim, 16-year-old Pauline Read, in the Gorton area of Manchester. Her throat is cut and her remains hidden. Pauline's body is not discovered until July 1987.
- The US and the USSR sign a treaty which prohibits the testing of nuclear weapons in the atmosphere, in space or under water for the sake of the environment.
- The Beatles record She Loves You and begin work on their second album With The Beatles.
- The Great Escape, starring Steve McQueen, opens at cinemas.
- Cleopatra, starring Richard Burton and Elizabeth Taylor, hits cinemas and proves to be a massively expensive flop.
- The Rolling Stones perform at the Corn Exchange in Wisbech, Cambridgeshire. At the bar afterwards Mick Jagger speaks with young fan Roger 'Syd' Barrett, later to become the front man of psychedelic rock band Pink Floyd. Barrett starts busking on guitar with his friend David Gilmour, who will later replace him in Pink Floyd.

RIGHT: A skeleton from Jason and the Argonauts.

Mailbags recovered from the cottage where the robbers had been hiding after the robbery.

At the bridge, the gang members formed a human chain to get the two and a half tons of cash in 120 bags, a total of £2.6 million or £44.7 million in today's money, into their vehicles. They told staff on the train to wait 30 minutes before calling police and quickly fled.

When the alarm was finally raised, police launched a nationwide manhunt. The jubilant robbers quickly divided up the loot at their nearby Leatherslade Farm hideout and played Monopoly with real money, but low flying RAF aircraft gave them cause for concern and, fearing detection, they scattered.

A neighbour who had grown suspicious at all the comings and goings at the farm called police. Officers entering the property discovered large quantities of registered mail packaging, bank note wrappings and post office sacks inside and realised what they had found.

Several fingerprints were recovered from the hideout, some of them on the Monopoly board and others on a ketchup bottle, and police were soon able to pick up most of the criminals involved.

It took five years to capture Reynolds though and he was given 10 years for masterminding the raid. Altogether, members of the gang were sentenced to a total of 307 years of jail time.

Some of the gang, such as Ronnie Biggs – a carpenter by trade before the robbery – managed to elude capture for years. Ronnie was caught soon after the crime but managed to escape from Wandsworth Prison in a furniture van after 15 months on the inside.

He then fled the country, underwent plastic surgery to change his appearance in Paris and then moved from Spain to Australia to Brazil. Every attempt to extradite him back to Britain met with failure.

Another gang member, Buster Edwards, gave himself up after spending three years in exile in Mexico. His story was told in the Phil Collins film Buster in 1988.

Train driver Jack Mills never truly recovered from his injuries. He couldn't go back to work after the robbery and died seven years later. Most of the stolen money has never been recovered.

Murderers on the moors

Teenager Pauline Reade was walking down Foxmer Street in Gorton, Manchester, at around 8pm on July 12, 1963, on her way to a dance at the nearby British Railways Club when a minivan pulled up alongside her. At the wheel was her friend Maureen's older sister. The woman asked her if she could help look for a rather expensive glove of hers which she had lost on Saddleworth Moor. It was still light and Pauline said she wasn't in a great hurry to get to the dance. Off they went, heading north east out of town. It took less than half an hour to reach the moor and the woman then stopped the minivan. A man rode up on a Triumph Tiger Cub motorcycle and stopped. The woman introduced the rider as her boyfriend and said that he had also come to help look for the missing glove. Pauline agreed to follow the man out on to the moor while the woman waited in her minivan. She never came back.

The man, Ian Brady, 25, returned alone and walked up to the woman in the minivan – 20-year-old Myra Hindley. The pair of them then went back out on to the moors to the spot where Pauline lay dying with her throat cut. Hindley later recalled how she had noticed that the 16-year-old's clothes were "in disarray" and surmised that Brady had carried out a sexual assault on her. Brady retrieved a spade he'd hidden nearby during a previous visit to the moor and set about burying Pauline in a shallow grave.

Driving back into Manchester with the Tiger Cub in the back of the minivan, they passed Pauline's mum Joan and her brother Paul out on the street searching for her.

Almost four and a half months later, on November 23, at a market in Ashton-under-Lyne, a town on the eastern side of Manchester, not far from Gorton, Hindley and Brady walked up to a 12-year-old boy, John Kilbride, and Hindley offered him a lift home. It was early evening and it was already getting dark. Hindley told the boy that his parents would be worried about him and then said she had a bottle of sherry and that he could have a drink while she and Brady drove him home. John agreed and got into a Ford Anglia that Hindley had hired.

August >

- The Great Train Robbery sees £2.6 million stolen during a raid on the night mail train from Glasgow to London in Buckinghamshire.
- Guy Burgess, who spied for the Soviets in Britain and was a member of the same spy ring as Kim Philby, dies in Moscow.
- Martial law is declared in South Vietnam and Kennedy gives tacit approval for a coup against the Diem government.
- The Beatles give their final performance at the Cavern Club in Liverpool.
- The Kingsmen release Louie Louie – the song which spawns a thousand garage rock bands.
- Martin Luther King Jr. gives his 'I have a dream' speech at the Lincoln Memorial in Washington.
- Honda's first four-wheeled vehicle, the T360 light truck, is launched.
- Ford Motor Company begins hiring the top men in GT racing to construct what will be unveiled the following year as the GT40.
- Musician David Sutch, aged 23, later known as Screaming Lord Sutch, stands in the by-election caused by the resignation of John Profumo as MP for Stratford-on-Avon. Representing the National Teenage Party he comes last with 209 votes – 0.58% of the electorate.

RIGHT: Syd Barrett.

Child murderers Myra Hindley and Ian Brady.

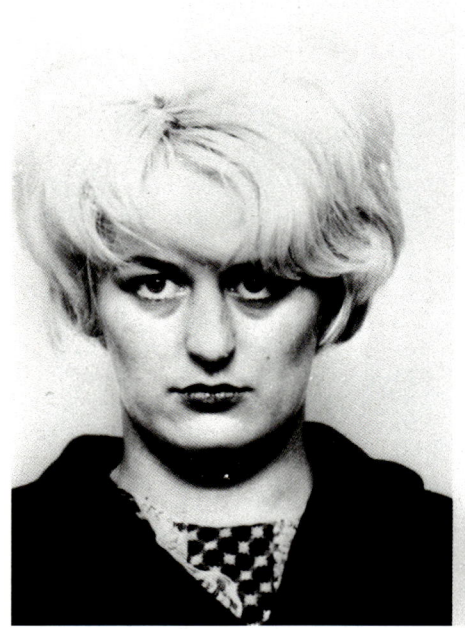

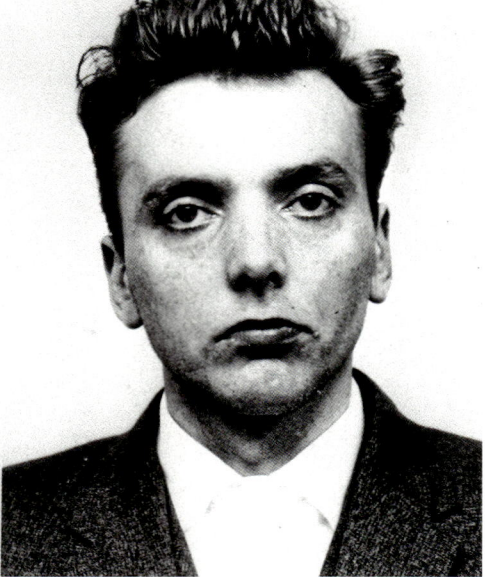

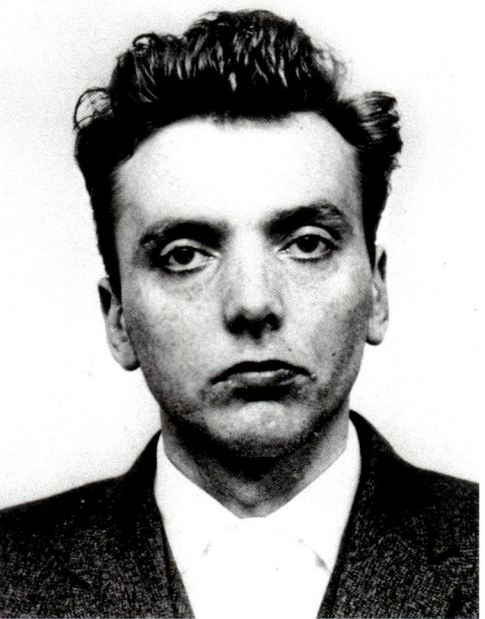

Moors murder victim John Kilbride.

There was no bottle of sherry however. Brady told John that he had left it at home and that they would make a short detour to pick it up before continuing on. A short way further on, Brady suggested that they could instead go to look for a glove that Hindley had lost on the moor. Now it was dark but it took less time to reach the moor, Ashton-under-Lyne being that bit closer. When they got there, Hindley parked the Ford and waited in the driver's seat while Brady took John out with him on to the moor itself.

Brady then sexually assaulted John and tried to cut his throat open with a 6in serrated knife but he was unable to do so, possibly because John was struggling too hard, and settled for strangling him with a piece of string which may even have been his shoelace.

As 1963 drew to a close, both Pauline Reade and John Kilbride were missing but no one had any inkling that they had both been murdered by the same sadistic couple.

Brady and Hindley killed again in 1964, on June 16. Keith Bennett, 12, was lured into Hindley's car with a promise of a lift home if he would help load some boxes. Once again, Brady went through the lost glove routine and left Hindley in the car while he sexually assaulted and killed Keith.

A fourth victim, Lesley Ann Downey, 10, followed on Boxing Day of the same year. This time though, they persuaded her into their car by asking her to help carry their shopping. Then they took her back to their house where she was forced to undress before being tied up and made to pose for photographs before Brady raped and murdered her. The next day, the pair took her body to the moor and buried her naked with her clothing positioned at her feet.

The fifth and final murder took place nine months later on October 6, 1965. Brady met Edward Evans, an apprentice engineer, at a train station and invited him back to his house in Wardle Brook Avenue, Hattersley – an overspill estate built by Manchester City Council – for a drink. He introduced Hindley as his sister and the three of them went home together. At the house, Brady sent Hindley to fetch David Smith, 17, the husband of Hindley's younger sister Maureen. Smith went into the kitchen and then heard a scream, followed by Hindley shouting for him to come and help. In the living room, Smith saw Brady beat Edward repeatedly with the flat of an axe before strangling him with electrical cord. Smith then helped Brady wrap the body in plastic sheets before returning home, having agreed to go back the following day and dispose of Edward's remains.

Away from Brady, Smith rang the police. Police went to the Wardle Brook Avenue house, found Edward's wrapped up body and arrested Brady. Hindley was not arrested but went with him to the police station. Both Brady and Hindley claimed that Edward's death had been the accidental result of an argument that got out of hand. Four days later Hindley was arrested and charged with being an accessory to Edward's murder.

Under questioning, Smith told police that Brady had packed "dodgy" items into suitcases and that he "had a thing about railway stations". This led police to search the left-luggage lockers in every Manchester train station. They found a

September >

- Labour leader Harold Wilson makes his 'white heat' speech at the Labour Party Conference in Scarborough.
- The Denning report on the Profumo Affair is published.
- The first surviving British quintuplets are born in Aberdeen.
- George Best makes his debut for Manchester United aged 17.
- American Express launches the first big name credit card in Britain.
- The Rolling Stones begin their first national tour, opening for Bo Diddley and the Everley Brothers.
- Jimi Hendrix forms his first band after leaving the US Army, the King Kasuals, in Clarksville, Tennessee.
- The Sindy fashion doll, a rival to Barbie, is created by British firm Pedigree Dolls & Toys.
- The first X-Men comic is published by Marvel Comics in the US.
- Porsche unveils its first 911 sports car at the Frankfurt Motor Show. Vauxhall launches its new Viva, a small family saloon that is similar in size to both BMC's 1100 and the extremely popular Ford Anglia model.

Martin Luther King.

suitcase belonging to Brady which contained nine photographs of a young girl in pornographic poses and a 13 minute tape recording of her screaming and pleading for her life. Lesley Ann Downey's mother listened to this and confirmed that it was her daughter's voice. Lesley's body was discovered the following day, on October 16. On the opposite side of the A635 they found the remains of John Kilbride.

Brady and Hindley were each charged with three murders – those of Edward, John and Lesley – which they denied. The 14 day hearing was in April-May 1966. David Smith was the chief prosecution witness. On May 6, the jury found Brady guilty of all three murders and Hindley guilty of murdering Lesley and Edward. They were each sentenced to life imprisonment.

Mr Justice Atkinson, who heard the case, described the couple as "two sadistic killers of the utmost depravity". Both denied any involvement in the disappearances of Keith Bennett and Pauline Reade until finally, in 1985, Brady confessed to murdering them.

Hindley, maintaining her denials, visited Saddleworth Moor with police on December 16, 1986, in an attempt to locate areas where the bodies might have been. David Smith also returned to the moor to try to pinpoint the location of the graves. Hindley finally confessed to involvement in all five cases on February 10, 1987. Pauline's body was found on July 1, 1987, just 100 yards from where Lesley had been found. Keith Bennett's body has never been found.

Triple threat for Ferrari

Italian sports and racing car firm Ferrari was faced with three fledgling challengers to its sports and racing car supremacy in 1963. Work on the first prototype for the British designed Le Mans 24 Hour Race winning Ford GT40, the GT101, was begun, German firm Porsche unveiled its new 911 model and Lamborghini was established. Early in the year, Ford Motor Company chief executive and chairman Henry Ford II heard that Ferrari might be willing to sell its car-making business. Ford had already spent millions reviewing Ferrari's assets when owner and founder Enzo Ferrari abruptly pulled out in a dispute over who would control the motor racing side of Ferrari. Henry Ford II was infuriated by this turn of events and decided that he was going to beat Ferrari at his own game. He opened negotiations with Cooper, Lotus and Lola – all firms with experience of racing. Of the three, the best fit was Lola which was already using a Ford V8 engine for its Lola Mk.VI Le Mans GT car. Ford bought two Lola Mk.VI chassis that had already been built and a development team comprising Lola owner and chief designer Eric Broadley, former Aston Martin team manager John Wyer and Ford Mustang designer Roy Lunn was set up in September.

Their masterpiece, the GT/101, was unveiled in April 1964. It had a 4.2 litre Fairlane engine which had previously been used in both the Lola Mk.VI and the Lotus 29, which had come second in the 1963 Indy 500 race. The car, known as the GT40, was initially a dismal failure but later versions of it went on to win Le Mans four years in a row from 1966 to 1969 – ending five years of Ferrari dominance. Henry Ford II got his revenge on Enzo. The second challenge to Ferrari, which also resulted from Enzo rubbing someone up the wrong way, came in October 1963 at the Turin Auto Show when Ferruccio Lamborghini wowed the world's assembled motoring press with his first car – the Lamborghini 350GTV. Ferruccio, a tractor firm owner, had been an enthusiastic Ferrari buyer but disliked their harshness. When his Ferrari's clutch broke he found it was the same one he used in his tractors and asked Enzo to make a better one. Enzo dismissed Ferruccio as a mere tractor maker who knew nothing about sports cars. Ferruccio thereafter determined to prove him wrong.

He started by commissioning one of the engineers responsible for Ferrari's 250 GTO, Giotto Bizzarrini, to make him an engine. Giotto created a 3.5 litre V12 capable of producing 360bhp. The chassis was produced by another former Ferrari engineer, Gian Paolo Dallara, and the body was by then-unknown designer Franco Scaglione. Construction started in July 1963 and finished in time for the motor show. Ferruccio then bought a 500,000sq ft property at Via Modena and set up his car factory. The production model 350GT was ready in time for the Geneva Motor Show the following year and Ferruccio then sold every one of the 350GTs he

The prototype Ford GT with its designers, from left, John Wyer, Eric Broadley and Roy Lunn. It was funded as part of a plan to defeat Ferrari at Le Mans.

October >

- Prime Minister Harold Macmillan resigns due to ill health during the Conservative Party Conference in Blackpool. Alec Douglas-Home renounces his peerage to be appointed prime minister in his place.
- Kennedy signs National Security Action Memorandum 263 signalling his intention to withdraw US troops from Vietnam.
- Lee Harvey Oswald gets a job at the Texas Book Depository in Dallas.
- The term 'Beatlemania' is used for the first time, to describe fans' reactions during and after a performance at the London Palladium.

- The second James Bond film, From Russia With Love, opens at British cinemas.
- Car manufacturer Lamborghini is founded and unveils its futuristic looking 350 GTV model at the Turin Auto Show.
- Honda's first production car, the S500, is launched.
- The newly formed National Theatre Company, under the artistic direction of Laurence Olivier, stages its first show, Hamlet, with Peter O'Toole in the title role.

LEFT: George Best.

Ferdinand Alexander Porsche working on designs in his studio in 1963 – the year he created the legendary Porsche 911.

ABOVE: Enzo Ferrari pulled out of a deal to sell his firm to Henry Ford II in 1963, infuriating the American company boss and compelling him to create one of the most successful GT cars in history.

made at a loss to make sure they were cheaper than Enzo's offerings.

Porsche's 911 was not a direct challenge to Ferrari in 1963 but it sowed the seeds for what was to come. Based on sketches drawn by Ferdinand Porsche in 1959, the first 911 was displayed at the Frankfurt Motor Show in September 1963.

It was originally called the 901 and the first 82 cars were made bearing that name but Peugeot already held the French rights to car names with a zero in the middle of three digits so Porsche decided to move up a digit. The early 911 had a 128bhp flat-six engine mounted at the rear and four seats, although the two at the back of the car were tiny.

The model was a success and engine sizes continued to rise throughout its existence, output spiking dramatically in 1974 with the introduction of turbocharging. A Porsche 911 derivative, the 935, won at Le Mans in 1979 – roundly defeating every team operating Ferraris, the best of which managed 12th place.

1963's blockbusters

Already on husband number four, Elizabeth Taylor was one of the world's biggest film stars in 1963 and audiences eagerly awaited the much-hyped Cleopatra ahead of its launch on July 31.

The film's spiralling budget and production problems had already been well publicised. Its budget had been just £1.2 million but this rose to £27 million by the time it was in the can – £198 million in today's money – nearly bankrupting 20th Century Fox. The film had some of the grandest sets, costumes and props ever created but its crew was forced to make it all twice due to the production being relocated to Rome.

Filming had begun in 1960 with director Rouben Mamoulian but he bailed out with the film already £3 million over budget and Citizen Kane co-writer Joseph L Mankiewicz took over. He soon discovered that he had been left with no useable footage. Also, Taylor's fame meant that her wage bill was enormous. Thanks to production delays she ended up receiving the equivalent of £28 million – 14 times the film's original overall budget. She had prompted the relocation to Rome after becoming ill in London and having to have a tracheotomy, a hole in her neck to allow her to breath. The cold British weather made her recovery slow and six months later the Rome move was decided upon to keep her happy. Then she began an affair with her Welsh co-star Richard Burton, which made the headlines of newspapers all over the world.

Matters were not helped by the fact that Mankiewicz, now the writer as well as the director, had become very precious about the project and couldn't bear to make his film any shorter than six hours. The studio persuaded him to chop it back to four hours for the premiere but then demanded that he make it three hours so that cinemas could have more than two showings a day. The director tried to persuade the studio to cut the film into two parts – Caesar and Cleopatra and Antony and Cleopatra, but this idea was rejected.

Critics panned the film but Elizabeth Taylor did achieve a Guinness World Record for making an incredible 65 costume changes and it won four Oscars too. It even recouped all the money 20th Century Fox spent on it. Eventually.

The second huge film of 1963 was From Russia With Love starring Sean Connery as James Bond, based on author Ian Fleming's 1957 novel of the same name. As a Cold War thriller it suited the mood of the time perfectly. US President John F Kennedy even chose the novel as one of his 10 top favourite books during an interview with Life magazine.

A Dalek queues for a bus in December 1963.

November >

- US President Kennedy is assassinated by Lee Harvey Oswald after the precise route of his motorcade is published in a Dallas newspaper. Oswald is later shot dead himself by nightclub owner Jack Ruby.
- South Vietnamese leader Ngo Dinh Diem is assassinated following a military coup and coup leader General Duong Van Minh takes over. New US President Lyndon B Johnson confirms ongoing military support for South Vietnam.
- The Dartford Tunnel is opened.
- The Moors Murderers Brady and Hindley claim their second victim, 12-year-old John Kilbride, at Ashton-under-Lyne in Greater Manchester. His body was found in 1965.
- The first episode of Doctor Who, An Unearthly Child, is screened.
- The Beatles' second album With The Beatles is released, knocking Please Please Me off the No. 1 spot after 30 weeks, and I Want To Hold Your Hand becomes the first record in history to sell a million copies before it has even been released. The group perform in front of the Queen during the Royal Variety Show.
- A mining disaster in Germany and the time taken to get equipment to the mine to rescue 50 men trapped underground inspires animator Gerry Anderson to create the Thunderbirds TV series which first appears in 1964.
- Garage rock band The Trashmen release their Surfin' Bird single in the US. It remained an obscure rarity in Britain until 2010 when it reached No. 3 in the charts during a battle for the Christmas No. 1.
- The touch-tone telephone is introduced.

LEFT: Having served in the United States Marine Corps from 1947 to 1950, Steve McQueen was well qualified to play Captain Virgil Hilts in The Great Escape. On one occasion during his time as a marine, McQueen rescued five other soldiers from a tank as it slid through breaking ice into the sea during an arctic exercise.

BELOW: Elizabeth Taylor and Rex Harrison in Cleopatra. The production was a disaster and it became one of the most expensive films in history but it was undoubtedly the biggest box office event of 1963.

The plot involves Bond travelling to Turkey to help a cipher clerk working at the Soviet consulate defect to the West with a valuable Lektor cryptographic device but the sinister SPECTRE organisation decides to intervene. Naturally, the clerk is a sexy young woman; Bond gets a trick attaché case fitted with a tear gas bomb, an AR-7 sniper rifle, a throwing knife and 50 gold sovereigns; there's a helicopter chase and a mysterious bad guy – Number 1.

Much of the filming took place on location in Istanbul, Turkey, with additional footage shot at Pinewood Studios in Buckinghamshire. Principal photography began on April 1, 1963, and wrapped on August 23 with Connery having done most of his own stunts.

The Great Escape, starring Steve McQueen, was another cinematic hit of 1963. Set during the Second World War, it was based on a book by Aussie Spitfire pilot Paul Brickhill who had been shot down in 1943 and held prisoner in Stalag Luft III, a German PoW camp. During Brickhill's time at the camp there had been a mass breakout attempt involving a tunnel dug 9m down from a prisoners' hut and then 102m towards and then under the camp's barbed wire perimeter fence. It took 600 men to dig it but only 76 were able to successfully use it during the escape on March 24, 1944. The 77th man out was spotted by the camp guards. During the escape the prisoners used 90 double bunk beds, 635 mattresses, 192 bed covers, 161 pillow cases, 10 single tables, 34 chairs, 76 benches, 1212 bed bolsters, 1370 beading battens, 1219 knives, 478 spoons, 582 forks, 69 lamps, 246 water cans, 30 shovels, 4000 bed boards, 1000ft of electrical wire, 600ft of rope, 3424 towels, 1700 blankets and 1400 cans.

Just three of the escapees evaded capture. Fifty of the remaining 73 were executed on the personal orders of Adolf Hitler. Brickhill himself took part in neither the tunnelling nor the escape, being claustrophobic. The film alters the facts a little – there were no Yanks involved in real life for a start and the thrilling climax, where McQueen attempts to jump his motorcycle over a wire fence, was, sadly, make-believe.

Chitty Chitty Bang Bang.

December >

- The Berlin Wall is briefly opened for Christmas.
- The trial of 21 former Auschwitz death camp guards begins in West Germany.
- Kenya declares independence from Britain.
- The Beatles release their first Christmas record for fans.
- The Daleks make their first appearance in an episode of Doctor Who – The Dead Planet.
- James Bond author Ian Fleming begins writing his last book, Chitty Chitty Bang Bang, about a customised chain-driven Mercedes with a six-cylinder 23 litre Maybach aero engine.
- The Rolling Stones perform at St Mary's Hall in Putney with opening act The Detours – who later become The Who.
- Marvel Comics' Iron Man makes his first appearance in red and gold armour.

Kennedy expresses his solidarity with the people of West Berlin in no uncertain terms.

CHAPTER 14

The assassination of JFK

Paranoia seizes America

It is Dallas, Texas, 1963, and Lee Harvey Oswald is holding a high-powered 6.5mm Carcano rifle. Crowds are gathering and he knows they will help to cover his getaway after he shoots his target dead. He raises the weapon, takes careful aim, and squeezes the trigger. He misses. Then he runs back to his car, drives away and buries the weapon in his back garden. The assassination attempt has failed...

President John F Kennedy was on top of the world in early November, 1963, but the world was starting to crumble away beneath him. His presidency had seen him prevent the Soviets from swallowing up west Berlin, facing down Khrushchev during the Cuban Missile Crisis and signing a nuclear test ban treaty – eclipsing the failures of the Bay of Pigs and the Vienna summit.

His summer had been spent travelling around the world. During a visit to Berlin on June 26 he had expressed his solidarity with the city by proclaiming: "Ich bin ein Berliner." He had then gone on to visit Ireland and then Britain – which was at that time in the grips of the Profumo Affair – where he received the warmest of welcomes from a besieged Harold Macmillan.

But he now faced growing unrest at home and the beginnings of a serious problem abroad as he began preparations to run for re-election as president in November 1964. The burgeoning civil rights movement had expressed its feelings about the state of American politics during the March on Washington for Jobs and Freedom in August, one of the largest political rallies in US history, and the situation in Vietnam was getting out of hand with upwards of 16,000 US military 'advisors' now actively involved in the South's battles.

Worse still, Kennedy had tacitly approved the assassination of South Vietnamese President Ngo Dinh Diem and his replacement by a group of generals. The nation was left unstable and vulnerable, forcing even closer US involvement.

With all this to think about, he was unaware that on April of that year, a former US marine who had defected to the Soviet Union for over two and a half years before returning to America in June 1962, had tried and failed to assassinate retired General Edwin Walker at his home in Dallas, Texas, with a 6.5mm Carcano rifle. The general was wounded when an unknown shooter fired a bullet that missed him by inches, hitting a window frame instead and peppering his forearm with fragments of debris. The would-be assassin was Lee Harvey Oswald.

CRISIS AND SCANDAL THE COLD WAR 113

Another shot taken seconds before the shooting, this time from restored film footage.

The Texas School Book Depository where Lee Harvey Oswald worked. On November 22, at 12.29pm, he was on the sixth floor, firing his Carcano rifle at President Kennedy.

Jackie Kennedy moves to cradle her husband seconds after the first bullet hit him in the back and exited through his throat. No-one else moves, not realising that anything is wrong.

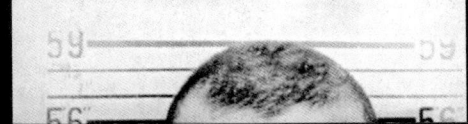

The presidential limo, now with Secret Service agent Clinton Hill riding on the back, accelerates away from Dealey Plaza. The second bullet has already fatally injured Kennedy.

Jackie Kennedy stands over her husband, covered in his blood, as limousine driver Secret Service agent Bill Greer guns the Lincoln's V8 engine.

Bloodstains on the seat of Kennedy's Lincoln Continental limousine after the shooting.

Comrade Oswaldskovich

Accidentally shooting himself in the elbow with a .22 handgun was enough to get Private First Class Lee Harvey Oswald court martialled and

Houston Street and Elm Street. Once the route was finalised, it was published in Dallas newspapers several days in advance so the maximum number of people would have the opportunity to see the president.

In keeping with their schedule, the president and the First Lady, Jackie, flew to Houston on November 21 and toured a NASA facility before giving speeches to the League of United Latin American Citizens at the Rice Hotel. They then returned to Air Force One and flew to Fort Worth where they touched down just after 11pm, as planned. On Friday, November 22, having spent the night in another hotel, the couple got up, got ready and attended a breakfast appointment with the Fort Worth Chamber of Commerce before climbing back aboard Air Force One at 11.10am and flying to Love Field, arriving at 11.25am. After briefly speaking to the crowd gathered to meet him on the airfield, Kennedy and his wife got into the back of their uncovered and unarmoured 1961 Lincoln Continental four-door limousine with the recently elected Governor of Texas John Connally, and his wife Nellie, sitting in front of them and set off for their journey through Dallas at 11.40am. There were three rows of seats in the car and the front row was occupied by Secret Service agents Bill Greer and Roy Kellerman. Greer was driving. Progress through the streets was slow but by 12.29pm the motorcade was just five minutes away from the trade mart.

The bullets that changed America

Entering Dealey Plaza, Nellie turned to Kennedy and told him: "Mr President, you can't say Dallas doesn't love you." The limo turned off Houston Street on to Elm Street, passing the Texas School Book Depository, heading for the exit onto the Stemmons Freeway. President Kennedy had his right arm up, waving to the crowds on his right. Then a shot sounded. Most of the crowd ignored it, thinking that it was just a car backfiring. In fact, a bullet had hit Kennedy in the back of his neck. It damaged his spine on the way in and clipped the top of his right lung before punching out through the centre of his throat, just below his larynx, nicking the knot of his tie on the left side. In shock and sudden agony, he clenched his fists and brought his elbows up, putting his hands in front of his face and neck before leaning forward. Jackie put her arms around him, not yet knowing what was happening.

The same bullet travelled on into Governor Connally, who was sitting in front of the president. It hit him in the back on his right side below his armpit, collapsed his right lung and smashed his right fifth rib bone before exiting just below his right nipple, leaving a 2.5in oval chest wound. It then entered his right wrist, broke his right radius bone into eight pieces, exited on the inner side of his right palm and entered his left inner thigh. Then there was a second gunshot and badly wounded as he was, Connally then shouted: "Oh, no no no. My God – they're going to kill us all."

The second bullet hit the back of Kennedy's head on the right side, creating an oval hole. Blood, skull fragments and brain matter exploded outwards onto the car's interior, the Secret Service car following behind, its driver's left arm and the police officers riding on motorcycles on either side. Governor Connally and his wife both later said they heard Jackie saying: "They have killed my husband – I have his brains in my hand."

After hearing the first shot, Secret Service agent Clint Hill, who had been standing on the left front running board of the car immediately behind the president's Lincoln, jumped off into the road. As he began to run towards the limo he heard a second and then a third shot. After the second shot, Jackie began to climb onto the back of the car, although later she said she had no memory of doing so and had no idea what would prompt her to do it. Hill jumped onto the back at the same time as Jackie slumped back into her seat. He held on as Greer gunned the Lincoln's 300bhp V8 engine and accelerated out of Dealey Plaza towards nearby Parkland Memorial Hospital.

After the shooting, bystander Howard Brennan, who had been across the street from the Texas School Book Depository as the motorcade was passing, told police that he had looked up after the first shot and seen a man with rifle take a second shot from a corner window of the building. He also said he'd seen the same man watching from the window minutes earlier but had thought nothing of it. Two further witnesses, James Jarman Jr and Harold Norman, who both worked at the book depository, then came over and told the officers who were speaking to Brennan that they had been watching the motorcade from the fifth floor of their building and had heard shots being fired directly above them. Norman even said he had heard the sound of a rifle's bolt action being worked and the sound of spent cartridges hitting the floor. Brennan's description of the shooter was broadcast to all Dallas police units three times – at 12.45pm, 16 minutes after the shots were fired, at 12.48pm and again at 12.55pm. At the same time, officers sealed off all entrances to the book depository. Lee Harvey Oswald, who was supposed to be at work with his colleagues, was reported missing by his supervisor.

Dallas police officer J. D. Tippit – a Second World War combat veteran whose father had named him 'J. D.' after a character called J. D. of the Mountains he had read about in a book – was in his 1963 Ford Galaxie squad car patrolling his usual Oak Cliff area beat when he received a radio order to move towards the city centre 15 minutes after the shooting. He radioed control at 12.54pm to say that he was in position. At about 1.11pm, he was driving slowly down East 10th Street when he spotted a man matching the description of Oswald as broadcast earlier. He pulled up alongside the man, who walked over to the police car, and the two of them had a conversation. Tippit then got out of the car. Oswald drew his .38 Smith & Wesson revolver and shot Tippit three times in the chest. When the police officer collapsed, Oswald walked over and shot him in the head. A witness who was crouched down hiding in a taxi cab as Oswald fled the scene later reported that he heard him muttering "poor dumb cop" or "poor damn cop".

At 1.40pm the ticket clerk at the Texas Theater cinema rang police to say that a man acting suspiciously had been seen slipping into the premises without paying while she was distracted. Officers arrived and arrested Oswald, who was sitting watching a screening of War Is Hell, a black and white film about the Korean War. It was later reported that he had resisted arrest shouting "well, it's all over now," and attempted to draw his pistol, resulting in the arresting officer giving him a blow to the head. Oswald was charged with the murders of both Kennedy and Tippit but denied both.

Police officer J. D. Tippit had the misfortune to spot and stop Lee Harvey Oswald as he fled. Tippit was shot four times at close range.

Jackie Kennedy holds her children's hands at her husband's funeral in Washington DC. Representatives of 92 countries were there.

Death of a president

Kennedy reached Parklands Memorial Hospital but although attempts were made to restart his heart it was clear from his massive head wound that the president was dead. This was officially pronounced at 1pm. A priest, Father Oscar Huber, administered last rites and acting White House press secretary Malcolm Kilduff made a statement confirming Kennedy's death at 1.33pm to a nurses' classroom packed with representatives of the press. He said: "President John F Kennedy died at approximately 1pm today, here in Dallas. He died of a gunshot wound to the brain. I have no other details regarding the assassination of the president." Meanwhile, Governor Connally was undergoing emergency surgery for his wounds.

Shortly after 2pm Kennedy's special assistant Ken O'Donnell, who had been in the car behind Kennedy's during the shooting, backed up by Secret Service agents, forced medical staff to hand over the president's body which was technically under the jurisdiction of the Dallas coroner. Kennedy was put into a casket and driven to Air Force One but Vice President Lyndon B Johnson, who had also been in a car in the motorcade behind the president's during the shooting, refused to allow the aircraft to leave for Washington, D. C. without Jackie Kennedy. When she arrived, he took his oath of office to become the 36th president of the United States and Air Force One departed. An autopsy was carried out on Kennedy's body at the Bethesda Naval Hospital in Bethesda, Maryland, between 8pm and midnight, by three naval pathologists with three Secret Service agents and two FBI special agents present. A further 18 other medical personnel and six other military personnel were present at various times during the procedure.

In the early hours of Saturday morning, embalmers from Gawler's Funeral Home in Washington arrived at the hospital to perform cosmetic restoration and embalming work on the body before it was placed in a new coffin. At 4.30am, Kennedy was taken to the White House and put in the East Room on the spot where Abraham Lincoln's body had lain nearly 100 years earlier on April 19, 1865. Jackie Kennedy decided that the coffin would be kept closed during all viewings and during the funeral itself. The casket lay there for 24 hours in private, during which time a mass was said and other family members, friends and government officials came to pay their last respects. These included former presidents Harry S Truman and Dwight D Eisenhower.

On the Sunday, Kennedy's flag-covered coffin was taken down the White House drive and along Pennsylvania Avenue to the Capitol Rotunda where he was to lie in state for the public to pay their respects. An estimated 250,000 people saw the coffin over a period of 18 hours up to 9.05am on the Monday morning. At 10.50am, the coffin was put onto a caisson, a horse-drawn artillery cart, and a procession back to the White House began at 11am. From there, the procession continued on to St Matthew's Cathedral led by Kennedy's widow and his two brothers, Robert and Edward. Representatives of 92 countries including 19 heads of state and government attended the funeral and afterwards Kennedy was laid to rest at Arlington National Cemetery in Virginia. The Russians were represented by deputy premier Anastas Mikoyan.

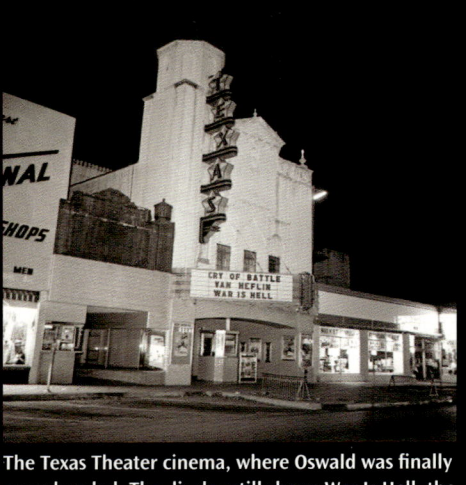

The Texas Theater cinema, where Oswald was finally apprehended. The display still shows War Is Hell, the film Oswald had been watching.

Oswald is led down a police station corridor prior to another round of questioning on the day after the shooting.

The strange saga of Kennedy's caskets

John F Kennedy's original casket was ordered from O'Neal's Funeral Home in Dallas shortly after his death on November 22, 1963. It was a solid bronze Handley Britannia coffin built by the Elgin Metal Casket Company with white satin lining, weighed 400lb and cost $3995. It was driven to Parklands Memorial Hospital by the funeral home proprietor Vernon B O'Neal and taken to Trauma Room One minutes after the president had been pronounced dead. Nurses wrapped his head in white sheets to prevent blood seeping out onto the coffin and he was placed inside. When the casket was later opened in Bethesda Naval Hospital's morgue it was found that the wrapping had become saturated with blood and the coffin's lining had been damaged. Another funeral home, Gawler's, was contacted and it supplied a second casket – a top of the line Marsellus 710 made from hand rubbed 500-year-old African mahogany with a $3140 price tag. Having transferred the president's body, Gawler's took possession of the Handley Britannia and stored it in a warehouse in Washington, D. C. In January the following year, O'Neal billed the US government for the coffin at full retail price.

The government refused to pay the full amount since none of the funeral homes other services had been required and eventually forked over $3160. O'Neal, however, had really wanted the bloodstained Handley Britannia returned to him rather than the cash. He had reportedly received offers of up to $100,000 from people who wanted to display it as a morbid curiosity. The casket was eventually taken into the custody of the General Services Administration in 1965. It was determined that the coffin had no value as evidence in the investigation into Kennedy's death and on February 18, 1966, it was taken to Andrews Air Force Base in Maryland. USAF personnel drilled 40 holes into it, filled it with three 80lb sandbags and put it inside a wooden crate with parachutes attached. This was loaded onto a C-130 Hercules transport aircraft and flown out over the ocean. At 10am, at about 100 miles out, the plane descended until it was 500ft from the water, the rear hatch was opened and the crate was pushed out. The chutes opened and the crate hit the water. The aircraft circled for 20 minutes to make sure the crate and the casket inside had sunk before returning to base. It is believed to have settled on the ocean floor 9000ft down.

ABOVE: Kennedy is brought home on November 22 in his first coffin – a solid bronze Handley Britannia. This was later drilled full of holes, stuffed with sandbags and dropped out of a plane.

The shooter is shot

The investigation that followed the assassination of John F Kennedy began with Dallas homicide and robbery bureau officer Captain Will Fritz and FBI Special Agent James Hosty questioning Oswald on and off for around 12 hours between 2.30pm on November 22 and 11am on November 24 at the Dallas Police Department headquarters. There were no tape recording of these interviews and Fritz kept only brief notes. These show that Oswald repeatedly denied any involvement in Kennedy's assassination or in officer Tippit's murder. He denied owning a rifle but told Fritz all about his three years in Russia and his support for Castro in Cuba. He recognised Hosty's name and took the opportunity to tell him he didn't appreciate him coming over to his home and questioning his wife, and he complained about being hit by the officer who arrested him.

At 3.54pm, it was announced on NBC news that "Lee Oswald seems to be the prime suspect in the assassination of John F Kennedy. At 4.45pm Oswald was put into a line up for Tippit murder witness Helen Markham and during the process of getting him into line he complained: "It isn't right to put me in line with these teenagers. You know what you are doing, and you are trying to railroad me. I want my lawyer. I am out there – the only one with a bruise on his head."

Dallas nightclub owner Jack Ruby shoots Lee Harvey Oswald after walking unchallenged into the police headquarters where he was held.

Conspiracy theories

During the 10 months that it took the Warren Commission to compile its report, numerous alternative theories to the 'official version' of events began to surface. Most of these centre on allegations that Kennedy was fired on by two or more shooters and that there was a government conspiracy to cover this up. It is suggested that the most likely position of a second gunman was on a 'grassy knoll' beside the route of the presidential motorcade. Seven out of the 500 or so witnesses interviewed by the Warren Commission claimed to have seen gunsmoke in the area of the stockade fence behind the knoll.

Supporters of the 'grassy knoll' theory point to inconsistencies in Kennedy's autopsy report which they claim leave the origin of the bullet which killed him in doubt.

If there was a 'second shooter', there are many suggestions as to his identity and motives. Up to 26 alternative assassins' names have been put forward including Cuban exile and career terrorist Orlando Bosch, CIA deputy director Desmond FitzGerald, actor Woody Harrelson's estranged father Charles Harrelson, former US marine and mercenary Gerry Hemming, a 'tramp' photographed on the grassy knoll at the time of the shooting Chauncey Holt and Chicago mobster John 'Handsome Johnny' Roselli.

Other conspiracy theorists question Oswald's motives. It has been suggested that when he went to Mexico he travelled on the bus with a man called Albert Osborne, aka John Howard Bowen, a First World War veteran born in Lincolnshire who had dual British and US citizenship. Osborne is alleged to have left the Army with excellent marksmanship skills and then moved to the US before running a school for assassins in Oaxaca, Mexico under the cover of doing missionary work. He had extreme right wing views and had connections to the FBI. Did Osborne set Oswald up on behalf of a faction of the FBI or even J Edgar Hoover himself?

The Russians are implicated in several conspiracy theories while the governments of Cuba and South Vietnam, mob boss Sam Giancana and Lyndon Johnson are all put forward as being suspected of supporting the unknown extra assassins.

It has even been suggested that the driver of Kennedy's car, Bill Greer actually turned round with a gun in his hand and shot the president in the head at close range. Some suggest that J. D. Tippit was really a CIA operative sent to silence Oswald, while others claim that Oswald had a mysterious accomplice in Tippit's murder. Few if any of these theories have even the remotest chance of being accurate.

Carousel Burlesque, the Dallas nightclub owned by Jack Ruby.

Police tested Oswald's hands and cheek for gunshot residue and the results came back positive for his hands but negative for his cheek. At 11.20pm Oswald was put forward for a press conference at which Jack Ruby, the owner of local strip club was present. He publicly denied shooting either Kennedy or Tippit before being taken back to his jail cell. His wife Marina and his mother Marguerite Oswald came to visit him at 1.10pm on November 23. He told his mother that everything was fine and not to worry about a thing. He told his wife that it was all a mistake and as she burst into tears he comforted her and told her that there was nothing to cry about. He said: "You mustn't worry about me. Kiss Junie and Rachel for me. I love you."

His brother Robert came to see him at 3.30pm and Oswald told him that he'd not been hit since the theatre and "I don't know what is going on. I just don't know what they are talking about. Don't believe all the so-called evidence." Robert later told investigators that his brother's answers to his questions were "mechanical" and that he had not been speaking to the Lee that he knew. After his brother left, Oswald faced further questioning.

At 11.10am on the Sunday morning preparations were made to transfer him by armoured car from the police department basement to the county jail while Fritz continued his questioning. The transfer began at around 11.20am. Meanwhile, Jack Ruby walked into the police headquarters off the street and made his way down to the basement. Amid the confusion that surrounded Oswald's move he walked right up to him through a crowd of press reporters and shot him in the abdomen at close range with his snub-nosed .38 Colt Cobra revolver. The transfer was being televised so millions of TV viewers saw the murder as it happened. Ruby was immediately arrested. Ruby claimed that he had acted to help Dallas "redeem" itself and that Oswald's death would mean Jackie Kennedy would not have to sit through a lengthy trial.

Oswald survived the shooting but quickly lost consciousness and was taken to Parklands Memorial Hospital where John F Kennedy had been pronounced dead two days earlier. He died at 1.07pm.

This left the men investigating Kennedy's shooting without their prime suspect and the process of determining exactly who had killed the president came to depend on witness statements and the gathering and assessment of forensic evidence.

President Lyndon Johnson established the President's Commission on the Assassination of President Kennedy, commonly known as the Warren Commission, on November 29. It received reports from numerous sources – including the FBI report which was completed within 17 days of the shooting – before eventually producing its verdict on September 24, 1964. Its 888 page report concluded that Lee Harvey Oswald had acted alone in murdering Kennedy and wounding Governor Connally and that Jack Ruby had acted alone in murdering Oswald.

What happened next?
The Cold War after 1963

Britain's role in the Cold War diminished after 1963 but it still had one eye on a return to greatness and a seat at the top table of world politics when the circumstances demanded it.

1964

- The leader of the military coup that replaced South Vietnamese President Ngo Dinh Diem, General Duong Van Minh, is himself deposed by General Nguyen Khanh. A sea battle in the Gulf of Tonkin off the coast of North Vietnam provides the US with the justification it needs to escalate American involvement in the conflict and the first major student protests against the Vietnam War are held in the US.
- The Warren Commission Report on the assassination of President John F Kennedy rules out any Soviet involvement.
- Leonid Brezhnev and Alexei Kosygin replace Nikita Khrushchev as leaders of the USSR.
- The Labour Party's Harold Wilson becomes Britain's prime minister after defeating Sir Alec Douglas-Home at the polls.
- China explodes its first atomic bomb, known as 596.
- Greville Wynne, a British businessman who had been imprisoned in Moscow for spying, is exchanged for Soviet spy Gordon Lonsdale, the mastermind of the Portland spy ring.

Soviet leader Leonid Brezhnev.

1965

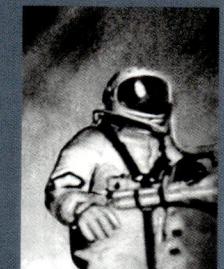

- Front line American combat troops arrive in Vietnam. An American jet fighter is shot down over the war torn country for the first time. President Johnson increases the number of US troops in South Vietnam from 75,000 to 125,000 and doubles the number of men being drafted each month from 17,000 to 35,000. Australia sends troops to aid the American military effort in Vietnam. The USSR announces that it has shipped rockets to the Vietcong.
- India and Pakistan fight a five week war over Kashmir.
- Vickers Valiant bombers are retired from RAF service.
- SNAP-10A becomes the first and only American nuclear reactor in space. It shuts down after 43 days but is still in orbit today. American spacecraft Mariner 4 sends back the first images of the surface of Mars.
- Cosmonaut Alexei Leonov becomes the first person to walk in space after leaving his spaceship, Voskhod 2, for 12 minutes.

Cosmonaut Alexei Leonov outside his spaceship Voskhod 2.

CHAPTER 15

An estimated 30,000 women formed a human chain around Greenham Common in December 1982 during an 'embrace the base' protest against the stationing of American nuclear missiles in Britain.

With Prime Minister Harold Macmillan out of the picture, caretaker PM Sir Alec Douglas-Home took over until his defeat by Labour's Harold Wilson at the 1964 general election. Wilson was a fiery character but he was no cold warrior – he couldn't afford to be. He'd inherited the leadership of a financially challenged country in the early stages of a dramatic cultural shift and wanted to concentrate on industrial and social matters at home such as state intervention in industry through wage and price controls, the nationalisation of the steel industry, the abolition of capital punishment, decriminalisation of gay sex, legalisation of abortion and the abolition of censorship in British theatres.

Kennedy's replacement in the US, Lyndon B Johnson, also faced an election in 1964 but having been JFK's vice-president, he won by a landslide. Like Wilson, he wanted to concentrate on domestic affairs such as civil rights, protecting the environment, fighting poverty, improving standards in education and setting up Medicare – America's Government administered system of medical insurance. Unlike Wilson though, he inherited a nation tied into an unpleasant and ongoing overseas war.

At first Johnson, still stunned by Kennedy's death – he had been a few cars back in the presidential motorcade when the shots rang out – and paranoid that he might be next, tried to ignore Vietnam. He focused on his social reforms until it became apparent that the situation in South Vietnam was going from bad to worse. A second coup saw the military revolutionary council that had overthrown President Diem replaced by another set of military leaders – at a time when the military was supposed to be concentrating on defeating the Vietcong rather than ruling the country.

Two incidents in the Gulf of Tonkin, the body of water immediately adjacent to North Vietnam, on August 2, 1964, saw US vessels engaged in confused encounters with Vietcong torpedo boats and radar returns which may or may not have been Vietcong torpedo boats. How these began is still unclear even today but it was enough for the US Congress to pass the Gulf of Tonkin resolution on August 7 which gave Johnson the power to fight the Vietcong without having to declare war on them. This was the final nail in the coffin of the Geneva Accord of 10 years earlier and effectively allowed the US to put as many troops as it liked in Vietnam.

The number of American soldiers in Vietnam rose accordingly, to 16,500. Realising that they were about to be on the receiving end of an assault from one of the world's most powerful and technologically advanced military forces, the Vietcong began a massive recruitment drive which saw their numbers rise from about 5000 in 1959 to 100,000 by the end of 1964. On December 6, 1964, less than two months after becoming prime minister, Harold Wilson met President Johnson at a summit meeting in Washington.

Wilson was keen to renew the friendship Macmillan had enjoyed with the Americans but Johnson had other ideas. He dropped strong hints to Wilson about Britain's economic situation and asked whether he wanted Britain to remain a world power before asking whether he would be willing to send troops to bolster the American military effort in Vietnam.

Wilson said no but the president thought he might be able to wear Wilson down and eventually persuade him to expand Britain's 'commitment' which at that time amounted to some training of the South Vietnamese police force and British counterinsurgency specialist Sir Robert Thompson's efforts to win over 'hearts

1966

- US troops in Vietnam total more than 250,000 by the end of the year. Republic of Korea soldiers supporting the US war effort round up and slaughter 1200 civilians in the Tay Vinh Massacre, then kill 380 at Go Dai, 280 at Tinh Son and 430 at Binh Hoa. Soviet premier Leonid Brezhnev demands that US forces leave Vietnam and pledges to support North Vietnam. US aircraft begin bombing Hanoi.
- British spy George Blake, a double agent working for the Soviet Union, escapes from Wormwood Scrubs prison and makes his way to Moscow.
- An unmanned Soviet spacecraft, Luna 9, makes the first controlled landing on the moon and sends back photographs from the surface which are intercepted by a receiver at Jodrell Bank Observatory in Britain and published in the Daily Express.

Soviet spy George Blake.

1967

- Huge public demonstrations are held against the Vietnam War. China agrees to give aid to North Vietnam. President Johnson gathers together America's foremost military leaders, known as the Wise Old Men or 'WOMs', to try and find a way to succeed in Vietnam.
- Britain's first Polaris nuclear submarine, HMS Resolution, enters service with the Royal Navy. Two more Resolution class vessels, HMS Repulse and HMS Renown, are launched.
- The Six Day War between US and British-backed Israel and a combined Soviet-backed force from Egypt, Syria and Jordan sees the Israelis victorious after inflicting massive casualties.
- China tests its first hydrogen bomb.
- Tension between the USSR and China results in a Soviet troop build-up on the Chinese border.
- Svetlana Alliluyeva, the daughter of Joseph Stalin, defects to America adopting the name Lana Peters.

Israeli tank crews in training ahead of the Six Day War.

The aristocratic Sir Alec Douglas-Home, who served as British prime minister for less than a year following the retirement of Harold Macmillan.

Charismatic and passionate, Harold Wilson ensured that Britain did not enter the disastrous Vietnam War after his election as prime minister in 1964.

US President Lyndon B Johnson was deeply shaken by John F Kennedy's sudden death and struggled to deal with the difficult situation in Vietnam.

US ambassador Adlai Stevenson was involved in efforts to ensure all sides agreed that orbital nuclear weapons platforms were a really bad idea.

and minds'. The Americans even considered that Wilson might allow some British Army officers to quietly take part in front line operations.

As much as he wanted to foster a close relationship with Johnson though, Wilson knew that his Labour Party would never support British involvement in Vietnam. The prime minister was forced to refuse Johnson's requests on a number of occasions during the early years of his premiership and it drove a wedge not just between the two men but also between the two governments. This became increasingly apparent as the war continued to escalate and American casualties continued to mount and lingered even after American involvement in the conflict ended in 1973.

Nuclear bans for outer space and down on the ocean floor

As the space race escalated throughout the 1950s and into the 1960s, there was serious discussion on both sides of the Iron Curtain about alternative ways of positioning nuclear weapons. Britain at this time was still nominally part of the space race since its Blue Streak missile and later Black Arrow rocket were being developed as satellite launch systems.

The United States was the first to see the terrifying possibilities of an orbital platform equipped with nuclear missiles pointed downwards at targets below and suggested in 1957 that all objects intended for launch into the atmosphere should be examined by a team of international inspectors. The USSR was in the midst of developing its space programme and testing its first intercontinental ballistic missile at the time and turned down the American proposal.

Undeterred, the Western powers including Britain brought a succession of proposals forward between 1959 and 1962 to ban the use of outer space for military purposes. The Soviets agreed to this in principle but since the Western proposals were linked to suggestions for a more general disarmament programme they continued to decline. The Soviet position changed in 1963 however and Minister of Foreign Affairs Andrei Gromyko told the United Nations General

The *USS Maddox* was attacked by small North Vietnamese torpedo boats in the Gulf of Tonkin. This allowed the US to launch all-out war on North Vietnam.

1968

- Vietcong forces attack targets across South Vietnam including the US embassy in Saigon during the Tet Offensive. South Korean soldiers in Vietnam massacre 70 unarmed civilians at Phong Nhi and Phong Nhat and 135 more at Ha My. US Army soldiers slaughter between 347 and 504 civilians at My Lai in South Vietnam, most of them women, children and elderly people. Bombing of Laos is commenced. President Johnson announces that he will not seek re-election.
- The Soviet Union leads Warsaw Pact troops in an invasion of Czechoslovakia to end a reformist political movement.
- North Korean forces seize the American research ship USS Pueblo, claiming that its crew was spying in their territorial waters.
- France detonates its first hydrogen bomb.
- Two Russian tortoises aboard the Soviet Zond-5 spacecraft become the first living creatures to fly around the moon and land safely back on earth.

A Vietcong officer is executed during the Tet Offensive.

1969

- Richard M Nixon succeeds Lyndon B Johnson to become the 37th president of the United States of America. Nixon announces the first American troop withdrawals from South Vietnam. He declares that America's Asian allies will have to start taking care of their own defence requirements.
- Representatives of the US and USSR meet at Helsinki for the first round of talks which will result in Strategic Arms Limitation Treaty I or SALT I to limit the number of nuclear weapons possessed by both sides.
- Chinese troops ambush and kill 59 Soviet soldiers on the Chinese-Soviet border. A further 94 Soviets are wounded.
- Neil Armstrong becomes the first man to walk on the moon as part of the Apollo 11 mission.
- Teacher Gerald Brooke is returned to Britain in exchange for Portland spies Peter and Helen Kroger. Brooke was accused of smuggling anti-Soviet leaflets into the USSR.

Buzz Aldrin, the second man to walk on the moon.

Assembly that the USSR wanted to ban orbiting objects carrying nuclear weapons. US ambassador Adlai Stevenson reciprocated and the UN adopted a resolution on October 17, 1963, welcoming the American and Soviet positions and calling on all states to keep outer space free of nuclear weapons.

Draft treaties for a ban on nuclear weapons in space were submitted by both sides on June 16, 1966, but while the US version only dealt with 'celestial bodies' the Soviet one went further and covered the whole of outer space in every respect. The US went with the Soviet version and a treaty was formally opened for signing in Washington, Moscow and London in 1967. It came into force later that year.

A similar issue arose over the depths of the ocean in the 1960s. Technological advances made it easier to reach previously unreachable depths and once again concerns arose that the seabed might become a new place to conceal fixed military positions capable of maintaining and launching nuclear weapons. The UN General Assembly set up a committee to look into ways of preserving the seabed for peaceful purposes on December 18, 1967. Less than two years later, in March 1969, President Richard Nixon suggested that a treaty similar to that already established for outer space, and another drawn up for the arctic, should be drafted for the ocean floor to "prevent an arms race before it has a chance to start".

The Soviet Union presented a draft treaty for the demilitarisation of the seabed beyond a 12 mile limit but this time the US countered with a draft treaty prohibiting the emplacement of nuclear weapons on the ocean floor outside of a three mile limit. Careful wording left the way open for American undersea submarine surveillance installations fixed to the seabed. After some confusion about how to define territorial waters and whether undersea equipment and installations within the limits of territorial waters should be made available for inspections, a final draft was approved by the UN on December 7, 1970. The vote was 104 to two in favour with only El Salvador and Peru voting against. There were two abstentions – Ecuador and France.

On February 11, 1971, the Seabed Arms Control Treaty – more properly known as the Treaty on the Prohibition of the Emplacement of Nuclear Weapons and other Weapons of Mass Destruction on the Sea-Bed and the Ocean Floor and in the Subsoil Thereof – was opened for signatures in Washington, Moscow and London. It came into force on May 18, 1972.

Carriers and troops of B Company of the 7th Royal Australian Regiment in Phuoc My Province, southeast of Saigon. The Australian public's support for their country's involvement in Vietnam was strong at first.

1970

- American troops invade Cambodia, neighbouring Vietnam, in a bid to destroy Viet Cong forces there. More than 100,000 people join a demonstration against the Vietnam War held in Washington DC. President Nixon pledges the withdrawal of 40,000 more US troops before Christmas.
- Conservative Ted Heath defeats Labour's Harold Wilson during a general election to become the next British prime minister.
- The Treaty on the Non Proliferation of Nuclear Weapons comes into force, having been signed by 56 nations. Nations refusing to sign it include North Korea, Israel, Pakistan and India.
- China launches its first satellite, Dong Fang Hong 1. It continually broadcasts a Chinese song of the same name, meaning 'the east is red', for 26 days.
- President Nixon is authorised to sell arms to Israel.

British Prime Minister Ted Heath.

1971

- Britain, the US and the Soviet Union, along with 84 other countries, sign the Seabed Arms Control Treaty banning the establishment of fixed undersea nuclear weapons platforms.
- South Vietnamese troops invade Laos. Half a million Americans march in protest against the Vietnam War. Australia and New Zealand decide to withdraw troops from Vietnam.
- A Soviet lander from the vehicle Mars 2 becomes the first man-made object to arrive on Mars. The three crewmen of Russian spacecraft Soyuz 11 are killed when their capsule depressurises in space.
- Russian space scientist Anatoli Fedoseyev is granted asylum in Britain after defecting to the West.
- The British government cancels the Black Arrow rocket programme, ending its efforts to keep up in the space race. Just months after the official cancellation, a Black Arrow rocket is used to put a British satellite, Prospero, into orbit. It was deactivated in 1996 but contact with it is still made periodically.

Russian Soyuz spacecraft.

1972

- President Nixon agrees the start of the American space shuttle programme.

President Richard Nixon meets Mao Zedong.

He also spends eight days in China and meets Mao Zedong, announces that no more conscripts will be sent to Vietnam, defeats Democratic rival George McGovern during the presidential election and is taped talking about using CIA operatives to obstruct an FBI investigation into a break-in at the Watergate Hotel.
- Britain, the US and the Soviet Union, along with dozens of other nations, sign the Biological Weapons Convention, banning the stockpiling of biological weaponry.
- President Nixon and Soviet premier Brezhnev sign up to the first round of SALT I which limits the number of areas that can be protected by anti-ballistic missile systems to two each.
- Unemployment in Britain reaches one million for the first time since the Second World War as fears for the economy grow.
- The De Havilland Sea Vixen is retired from Royal Navy service.

1973

- American involvement in the Vietnam War ends as a ceasefire is declared between the US and North Vietnam and the Paris Peace Accord is signed. The first American prisoners of war are released from North Vietnam. Top White House aides resign as the Watergate Scandal rumbles on. Nixon insists: "I am not a crook."
- The Yom Kippur War between US-backed Israel and Soviet-backed Egypt and Syria results in huge Egyptian losses and a tactical victory for Israel. The Arab nations backing Egypt begin oil embargoes against the countries that backed Israel – the US, Portugal, South Africa and Rhodesia – resulting in soaring fuel prices.
- Britain enters the European Economic Community, which later becomes the European Union. Strikes cause electricity shortages and the government establishes a three-day week to save power.
- The first American space station, Skylab, is established in orbit.
- General Augusto Pinochet, with support from the US, overthrows Chile's democratically elected government.
- The SEPECAT Jaguar ground attack aircraft enters RAF service.

An RAF SEPECAT Jaguar.

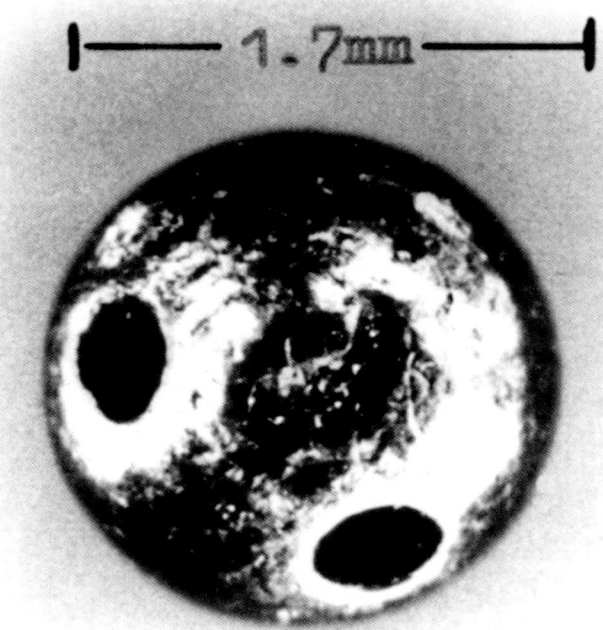

The tiny pellet removed from the body of assassinated Bulgarian journalist Georgi Markov. Traces of ricin were found inside.

English Electric Mustard and losing the space race

While cash was drying up for military projects in 1963, the British space programme continued to receive significant funds. The Government's thoughts had turned to putting British vehicles into space as early as 1950 but the first real steps towards achieving this took place in 1957 with the completion of the Blue Streak nuclear missile design by De Havilland.

When it became apparent that Blue Streak was too expensive and too vulnerable to enemy attack as a weapon, it was turned over for use as a spacecraft launch vehicle. It was to be combined with another missile developed by Saunders-Roe, Black Knight, to form a two stage rocket known as Black Prince. Work was begun on designing Black Prince but as the cost soared to more than £35 million it was cancelled in late 1960.

A new project was begun, this time with NASA, to create a satellite that could perform experiments in space. The result, Ariel 1, was intended to study cosmic rays, solar emissions and the ionosphere. It was launched on an American Thor Delta rocket on April 26, 1962. It transmitted data until it was switched off in November 1964.

Meanwhile Britain, as part of the European Launcher Development Organisation developed a launcher named Europa by combining Blue Streak with a French Coralie rocket for the second stage and a German vehicle for the third. Italy worked on a satellite, the Netherlands and Belgium the launcher's electronic systems and Australia hosted the launcher and its team during testing.

Ten Europas were tested at Woomera in Australia before testing was moved to a French site in South America. The ultimate development of Europa, the F11, was launched from there in November 1971 but its autopilot

1974

- After an indecisive general election result, Conservative British Prime Minister Ted Heath resigns and is replaced by Labour's Harold Wilson.
- The Arab oil embargo against the US and other nations that supported Israel during the Yom Kippur War is ended.
- India detonates its first nuclear weapon during Project Smiling Buddha.
- President Nixon resigns in the wake of the Watergate Scandal and is succeeded by Gerald Ford as the 38th US president.

President Nixon gives his farewell speech.

1975

- Hostilities recommence in Vietnam and without US backing the South Vietnamese military is swiftly defeated by North Vietnam's forces. The American embassy is evacuated.
- The Soviet Union deploys SS-20 Saber mobile nuclear missile launchers at 14 sites in Eastern Europe causing deep concern in NATO countries fearful of an attack on Western Europe.

South Vietnamese scramble to reach the last American helicopters out of Saigon.

Rocket scientist Ray Wheeler with a full scale model of the Prospero Satellite that his team developed at Saunders-Roe on the Isle of Wight. The satellite is still in orbit but was switched off in 1996.

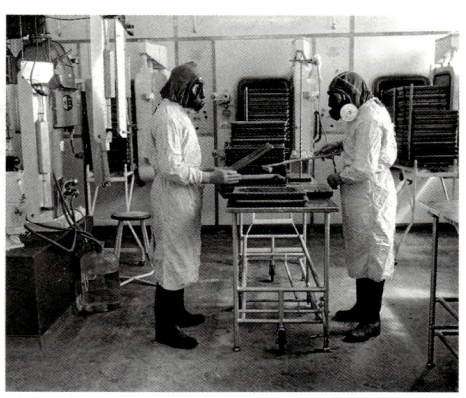

The Porton Down facility in Wiltshire was at the centre of British efforts to develop weaponised versions of diseases such as tularemia or 'rabbit fever', anthrax, brucellosis and botulism.

The Black Arrow vehicle was used to put Britain's Prospero satellite into orbit. artq55

failed and it broke up. The project was then abandoned. More British-made satellites, Ariels 2-6 were launched between 1967 and 1979.

Long before the American space shuttle, a British team came up with the idea of a 'space plane' or Multi-Unit Space Transport And Recovery Device (MUSTARD). Designs completed in 1965 under a Government contract consisted of a three-stage spacecraft which would consist of three similar looking delta winged vehicles stacked on top of each other and launched together. Two of these would boost the third into space before flying back down to earth.

Once its payload of up to 5000lb had been delivered into orbit, the third vehicle would then also return home. MUSTARD was cancelled in 1966 due to lack of Government interest and three years later the Americans came up with their space shuttle idea.

Britain finally succeeded in putting its own satellite into space in 1971 with the fourth and final launch of the Black Arrow project.

This used existing technology from Black Knight and shortly after it was cancelled Black Arrow put a satellite called Prospero into orbit. It is still there today, although it was finally switched off in 1996.

Anthrax and the Biological Weapons Convention

Whereas the outer space and ocean floor weapons treaties had been primarily established by the US and USSR, Britain was the prime mover behind a third important ban on weapons of mass destruction in 1972 – the Biological Weapons Convention. This was ironic, since Britain was responsible for the development of some of the world's most deadly biological weapons during the 1940s and 1950s.

A programme to develop weaponised versions of diseases such as tularemia or 'rabbit fever', anthrax, brucellosis 'Crimean fever' and botulism was launched in Britain, the US and Canada in 1941 as a response to developments in Japan and developments that were suspected to be taking place in Nazi Germany. Much of this work was carried out at the Porton Down facility in Wiltshire. In 1942, a British bio-weapon was tested on animals on the Scottish island of Gruinard. It was a highly virulent strain of anthrax known as Vollum 14578. Scientists from Porton Down transported 80 sheep to the island and exploded bombs containing spores of the disease on top of poles above them. The sheep became infected and began to die within days of exposure. The bodies of the sheep were later incinerated and efforts made to decontaminate the island but it was found that the anthrax spores were extremely tough to kill and the island was placed under indefinite quarantine.

Research and development of biological weapons continued after the war but by 1956 Britain abandoned moves to establish any offensive biological capabilities. Britain was no slouch when it came to chemical weapons either. A chemist working at the US-based Plant Protection Laboratories of British firm Imperial Chemical Industries, Ranajit Ghosh, discovered

1976

- British Prime Minister Harold Wilson resigns from office aged 60 claiming physical and mental exhaustion. He was also suffering from early-onset Alzheimer's disease. He is succeeded by James Callaghan. Britain, still struggling to keep its economy afloat, takes out a £2.3 billion loan from the International Monetary Fund.
- Democrat Jimmy Carter defeats Republican Gerald Ford to become the United States' 39th president.
- General Jorge Videla overthrows President Isabel Martinez de Peron of Argentina to become the country's military dictator. His rule is notorious for the 'disappearances' of his political opponents, torture and murder of political activists and secret concentration camps.
- Chairman Mao Zedong of China dies. He is succeeded by Hua Guofeng.
- A Soviet MiG-25 jet fighter lands at Hakodate in Japan. The pilot, Lieutenant Viktor Belenko, requests political asylum in the US. His aircraft, for which he brought the instruction manuals, is dismantled and examined by US engineers before being shipped back to the USSR in bits.

Prime Minister James Callaghan.

1977

- President Carter proposes a nuclear non-proliferation act to Congress. The US signs Protocol I of the Treaty of Tlatelolco prohibiting nuclear weapons in Latin America.
- The first US Space Shuttle, Enterprise, undergoes unpowered atmospheric flight tests for the first time.
- Anwar Sadat, the Egyptian president, makes an official visit to Israel to establish peace talks with Prime Minister Menachem Begin.

Space Shuttle Enterprise during its first flight test.

1978

- Soviet nuclear spy satellite Cosmos 954 burns up in the Earth's atmosphere and radioactive debris is scattered over the Northwest Territories of Canada. The Soviet Union eventually pays three million Canadian dollars in compensation.
- President Carter signs the Nuclear Non-Proliferation Act in the US and decides to postpone production of a neutron bomb – a weapon which kills enemy soldiers through radiation but leaves their structures and equipment intact.
- Two CH-47 Chinook helicopters of the Imperial Iranian Air Force are shot down by a MiG-23 after they stray into Soviet airspace.
- Bulgarian defector Georgi Markov is killed in London by a Bulgarian secret police agent using a poison-pellet injector hidden in an umbrella.

1979

- Conservative Margaret Thatcher defeats Labour's James Callaghan in a general election and becomes Britain's first female prime minister.
- Iran undergoes an Islamic revolution following the return of Ayatollah Ruhollah Khomeini after nearly 15 years in exile.
- The first fully functional space shuttle, Columbia, arrives at the Kennedy Space Centre and preparations are made for its first lift-off.
- Deadly airborne anthrax spores are accidentally released from a Soviet bioweapons facility at Sverdlovsk, killing 66 people and hundreds of animals.
- The SALT II agreement is signed by Jimmy Carter and Leonid Brezhnev in Vienna limiting the number of nuclear warheads on either side to a maximum of 2250.

Prime Minister Margaret Thatcher.

- Jimmy Carter approves secret aid to anti-Soviet forces in Afghanistan.
- Saddam Hussein becomes the president of Iraq.
- America's nuclear strike forces are put on high alert after an American defence computer detects a massive Soviet nuclear strike. This is quickly determined to be the result of a realistic training tape being accidentally inserted into the machine.
- The first Panavia Tornado multirole jet fighters enter RAF service.

Argentine prisoners of war massed in Port Stanley, capital of the Falkland Islands, after their surrender to the British Falkland Islands task force.

in the early 1950s that a certain class of organophosphate compounds made extremely effective pesticides. One of these was actually marketed as Amiton in 1954 but had to be withdrawn because it was so toxic. Its deadly nature attracted the attention of the scientists at Porton Down and samples were sent there for evaluation. This resulted in the compounds being reclassified as nerve agents – the V agents. One of the most lethal of these was VX, codenamed Purple Possum, which was tasteless, odourless and had a gloopy oil-like texture which enabled it to linger in the environment for far longer than runny water-like toxins.

If you came into physical contact with Purple Possum you would suffer muscle twitching and sweating, followed by nausea, vomiting and death. Breathing it in as a gas would give you a runny nose and shortness of breath before vomiting and death.

Murder by umbrella – the Georgi Markov scandal

As September 1978 started, BBC World Service presenter Georgi Markov, 49, was doing well in life. It had been nine years since his defection to the West from the People's Republic of Bulgaria and he was having a fine time criticising the autocratic communist regime running his native land on air. He was living in London where he'd learned to speak English and had married London-born author Annabel Dilke, with whom he'd had a baby daughter. He would probably not have been too surprised to learn that the Bulgarian Durzhavna Sigornost or secret police had opened a file on him, under the codename Wanderer, and increasingly regarded him as a dissident. He had been classified as a 'non person', which meant he had no rights, and this was a dangerous position

to be in. Markov was not afraid and continued his broadcasts to Bulgaria. He might have been surprised to learn, however, just how badly the Bulgarian secret police wanted him dead.

On September 7, he was on his way to work at the BBC and walked over Waterloo Bridge on the Thames to wait at a bus stop for his ride in. He suddenly felt a sharp pain in his leg and looked down to see a man nearby had dropped his umbrella. The man quickly picked up the umbrella and hurried off. Thinking no more of it, Markov went into work as usual but the pain continued and rolling up his trouser leg he saw a reddish spot developing on his skin as though he had been bitten by an insect. That evening he developed a high fever and was taken to hospital. Markov admitted to doctors that he thought he'd been poisoned. Three days later he was dead.

Given Markov's background, police launched an investigation into his death and a thorough

1980

- President Carter announces a grain embargo against the USSR and says the US will not attend the Olympic Games in Moscow. The Soviet invasion of Afghanistan prompts him to require that 18-25 year-old men register for a military draft. He is then defeated by Ronald Reagan during the presidential election.
- Youth riots in Estonia, a Soviet state, are rapidly suppressed.
- A strike at the Gdansk shipyard in Poland is led by Lech Walesa.
- The Iran-Iraq War begins.
- A Vostok-2M rocket explodes during fuelling at the Plesetsk Cosmodrome in Russia killing 50 people.

1981

- Shuttle Columbia successfully makes its first return journey into space.
- Israeli forces destroy Iraq's Osirak nuclear reactor and kill 300 civilians during bombing raids in Beirut.
- Two Libyan Sukhoi Su-22 Fitter jet fighters are destroyed by two American F-14 Tomcat jets over the Gulf of Sidra.
- Egyptian President Anwar Sadat is assassinated.
- Talks begin in Geneva between the US and the USSR on the reduction of intermediate range nuclear missile stockpiles.

Egyptian President Anwar Sadat.

1982

- Britain defeats Argentine forces after they attempt to seize the Falkland Islands. Argentina's last military dictator Leopoldo Galtieri resigns as a result and democratic elections follow.
- More than 750,000 people attend a demonstration against nuclear weapons in New York City.
- Unemployment in Britain hits a new postwar record of 3,070,621.
- Soviet premier Leonid Brezhnev dies in office and is replaced by Yuri Andropov.
- British Prime Minister Margaret Thatcher writes to President Reagan requesting that Britain be allowed to buy advanced Trident II missiles to replace its ageing Polaris weapons. The request is granted.

Argentine dictator Leopoldo Galtieri.

Royal Marines line up for a weapons check in the hangar of *HMS Hermes* in the South Atlantic on April 20, 1982. Two days later the British task force arrived at the Falkland Islands.

1983

- Conservative Margaret Thatcher is re-elected by a landslide majority.
- President Reagan unveils plans to develop a laser missile defence system dubbed 'Star Wars' by the media.
- Korean Airlines Flight 007 is shot down by a Soviet Su-15 jet fighter with the loss of all 269 on board after it strays into Soviet airspace.
- Peace campaigners gather outside RAF Greenham Common after 96 American ground-launched Gryphon nuclear cruise missiles are stationed there.
- Stanislav Petrov averts nuclear war by identifying a missile warning as a false alarm. A second scare results from NATO exercise Able Archer 83 which some Soviet officials mistake for a nuclear attack.

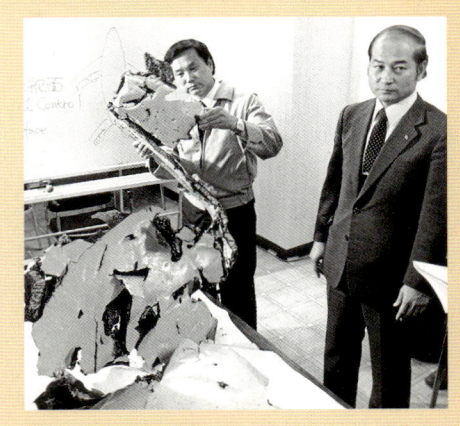

Investigators examine pieces of Korean Airlines Flight 007.

autopsy was carried out. Pathologists were shocked to discover a metal pellet the size of a pin head – 1.7mm in diameter – stuck in the muscle of his calf. This was found to be made of platinum and iridium. Two minute shafts had been drilled right through it to form an X-shaped cavity inside. Scientists at Porton Down found that this cavity contained traces of deadly ricin poison. A sugary substance designed to melt at precisely 37°C – normal human body temperature – had been used to hold the ricin in place. Markov's body had melted the sealant, allowing the ricin to enter his bloodstream.

Markov's account of the circumstances at the bus stop where he had been shot with the pellet led investigators to believe that the dropped umbrella had actually contained a concealed firing mechanism. Attempts have been made to work out how such an 'umbrella gun' might work and it seems likely that a small cylinder of compressed air would have been used to propel the poison pellet out through the tip and into the intended victim. The Scotland Yard investigation into Markov's death has yet to be concluded.

Keep your hands off – fighting the Falklands War

As Britain's overt military role in the Cold War diminished, there were many who came to doubt the nation's will and even its ability to wage war – even in Britain. In particular, there were those in the military dictatorship of Argentina who thought it highly unlikely that Britain would react to losing a very small part of its former empire not too far off the Argentine coast. These people had long regarded the Falkland Islands, or Las Islas Malvinas, as Argentine property since it is claimed that the Spanish first discovered them and that Argentina is Spain's successor in the region.

In 1981 it was deemed that an invasion of the Falklands would rally public support for the Government and divert attention away from public rights abuses at home. A plan to invade was drawn up and put into action in 1982. It began with Argentine scrap dealer Constantino Davidoff arriving in South Georgia to assess the work required to take apart an old whaling station. His crew for this mission included Argentine soldiers posing as scientists. They established a camp, defaced British signs and shot reindeer in contravention of conservation laws. An Argentine special forces unit then landed in March and a full scale invasion began on April 1, rapidly overwhelming a small force of Royal Marines on the islands who were forced to surrender. Around 2000 Argentine soldiers were occupying the islands by April 2.

The British response was a task force of 127 ships including 43 Royal Navy vessels to retake the islands. A number of Vulcan bombers were also flown over from RAF Waddington in Britain to RAF Ascension Island then on to their targets on the Falkland Islands, being refuelled several times along the way. The US was worried that Argentina might seek support from the Soviet Union, turning the crisis into an overt Cold War conflict, and urged a peaceful solution but the Argentine government refused to withdraw its forces. It also refused to comply with a UN Security Council resolution demanding that it withdraw. America therefore sided with Britain and imposed sanctions on Argentina. A plan was even drawn up to loan the British an aircraft carrier, USS Iwo Jima, if either of the Royal Navy's task force carriers – HMS Hermes and HMS Invincible – were destroyed.

The British task force arrived on April 22 and by April 25 the nearby South Georgia Islands were in British hands and the Argentine Navy submarine Santa Fe, a Second World War vessel formerly known as USS Catfish bought from the Americans in 1971, had been damaged by anti-ship missiles fired from a Westland Wasp helicopter and abandoned by its crew.

If an alert had been sounded, the BGM-109G Gryphon launchers based at RAF Greenham Common would have dispersed via local roads into the surrounding countryside, making it more difficult to knock them out all in one go.

The Falkland Islands' three airfields were unsuitable for Argentina's fighter and attack aircraft so the Argentine air force had to launch its attacks from the mainland. The extreme distance meant pilots had very little time to conduct their attacks before being forced to head for home due to lack of fuel. A strike force of 36 aircraft was sent to attack British ground forces on May 1 but British Sea Harriers succeeded in shooting down three of them and a fourth was damaged and finished off by friendly fire from the ground at Stanley, the Falklands' capital.

On May 2, an Argentine Navy cruiser, the General Belgrano, formerly the USS Phoenix, was sunk by the British nuclear submarine HMS Conqueror with the loss of 323 lives. Two days later, HMS Sheffield was destroyed by an Exocet missile fired from a Super Etendard which, although it failed to explode, caused a devastating fire. Twenty crew members were killed and another 24 seriously injured. British forces launched an amphibious assault at San Carlos Water on May 21 but naval casualties began rapidly mounting. HMS Ardent was sunk on May 21 and HMS Argonaut was hit by two bombs which both failed to detonate, HMS Antelope was sunk on May 24 and MV Atlantic Conveyor and HMS Coventry on May 25. These attacks cost the Argentines 22 aircraft.

Despite facing difficult conditions, the British ground forces made good progress and captured Goose Green from a numerically superior Argentine force and by June 1 plans were being drawn up for an assault on Stanley. On June 8, RFA Sir Galahad was gutted by an air attack causing 48 deaths and RFA Sir Tristram suffered severe damage. The attack on Stanley went ahead on June 11 and the Argentine commander Brigade General Mario Menendez surrendered three days later after a ceasefire. Hostilities finally came to an end on June 20 when the British retook the South Sandwich Islands.

The British victory had demonstrated to the world that the nation still had a formidable military capability and was prepared to use it. Years after the war's end it was suggested that Argentina may have been given surveillance support by the Soviet Union during the conflict.

1984

- Soviet leader Yuri Andropov dies after just 15 months in office and is replaced by Konstantin Chernenko. It is announced that the Soviet Union will boycott the Olympic Games in Los Angeles, California.
- President Reagan is re-elected. During a sound check for a radio broadcast he tests the microphone by saying: "My fellow Americans, I'm pleased to tell you today that I've signed legislation that will outlaw Russia forever. We begin bombing in five minutes."
- The last Avro Vulcan bomber is retired from RAF service.

1985

- Mikhail Gorbachev becomes the Soviet Union's third new leader in as many years. He meets President Reagan for the first time.
- US Navy communications specialist John Anthony Walker Jr is arrested and is later found to have been working for the Soviet Union since 1967. He has helped the Russians decrypt more than one million classified American military messages.
- Debt ridden aerospace engineer Thomas Patrick Cavanaugh is given a life sentence for trying to sell details of American stealth bomber developments to the USSR.

Soviet leader – Mikhail Gorbachev.

1986

- American Space Shuttle Challenger disintegrates shortly after take-off. The crew survived the blast but were killed when their intact crew compartment plummeted back to earth.
- The Mir space station is launched by the Soviet Union.